Fintech for ESG and the Circular Economy

Scrivener Publishing
100 Cummings Center, Suite 541J
Beverly, MA 01915-6106

Fintech in a Sustainable Digital Society

Series Editors: Ernesto DR Santibanez Gonzalez and Prasenjit Chatterjee

New and disruptive financial strategies and practices based on technology are key to reduce carbon emissions and save the planet. By establishing new sustainable cross-industry ecosystems and business models, the series "Fintech in a Sustainable Digital Society" aims to get a deeper understanding of fintech, insurtech, and blockchain at the intersection of sustainability. It also covers application-focused research in fintech perspectives on AI, cloud computing, machine learning, optimization, and scientific computing. The series disseminates monographs and edited volumes concentrating on all new fintech fields.

Publishers at Scrivener
Martin Scrivener (martin@scrivenerpublishing.com)
Phillip Carmical (pcarmical@scrivenerpublishing.com)

Fintech for ESG and the Circular Economy

Edited by

Ernesto D.R. Santibanez Gonzalez
University of Talca, Chile

Vinay Kandpal
Dept. of Management Studies, Graphic Era University, Dehradun, India

Peterson K. Ozili
Central Bank of Nigeria

and

Prasenjit Chatterjee
Dept. of Mechanical Engineering, MCKV Institute of Engineering, West Bengal, India

Scrivener Publishing

WILEY

This edition first published 2024 by John Wiley & Sons, Inc., 111 River Street, Hoboken, NJ 07030, USA and Scrivener Publishing LLC, 100 Cummings Center, Suite 541J, Beverly, MA 01915, USA

For more information about Scrivener publications please visit www.scrivenerpublishing.com.

Wiley Global Headquarters
111 River Street, Hoboken, NJ 07030, USA

For details of our global editorial offices, customer services, and more information about Wiley products visit us at www.wiley.com.

Library of Congress Cataloging-in-Publication Data

ISBN 978-1-394-23396-0

Cover image: Pixabay.Com
Cover design by Russell Richardson

Set in size of 11pt and Minion Pro by Manila Typesetting Company, Makati, Philippines

Printed in the USA

10 9 8 7 6 5 4 3 2 1

The editors would like to dedicate this book to their parents, life partners, children, students, scholars, friends, and colleagues.

Contents

Preface

In an era where technological advancement and sustainability form the twin pillars supporting the future of finance, this volume presents a timely exploration of the intersection between financial technology (FinTech), Environmental, Social, and Governance (ESG) criteria, and the circular economy. This book originated from a shared recognition of the pressing need for inventive remedies in response to worldwide environmental and societal difficulties. This manuscript represents a compilation of ideas, research, and practical knowledge contributed by a diverse group of experts who share a common goal: to utilize FinTech in the promotion of ESG objectives and to support the principles of the circular economy.

Each chapter delves into the complexities and nuances of its topic, from the granular details of machine learning algorithms in ESG analytics to the broader impacts of blockchain on sustainable finance. Chapter 1 sets the foundation, exploring the role of big data and machine learning in enhancing ESG practices within the framework of a circular economy. This leads to a detailed analysis in Chapter 2 of how blockchain technology is not just a tool but a potential game-changer in fostering sustainable finance and investment strategies. The focus then shifts from the global to the particular, with Chapter 3 examining the specific dynamics within Turkey's financial ecosystem, before scaling back to a broader view in Chapter 4, which explains how to leverage FinTech to advance the circular economy.

The scope of Chapter 5 is on how cyber ecosystems and digital currencies capture the current state of play in sustainable finance, while Chapter 6 navigates the intricate legal landscape of green finance in India, providing a critical analysis of the challenges and opportunities that lie ahead. The seventh chapter discusses how ESG factors and the principles of the Circular economy influence the financial decision-making process. It covers how companies and investors integrate sustainability metrics into their analyses and the financial instruments that support these considerations. In Chapter 8, we explore the role of financial institutions in enabling crowdfunding platforms and their success in African markets, with examples of regulatory environments, technological infrastructure, and case studies that demonstrate the impact of crowdfunding on financial inclusion and entrepreneurship.

Chapter 9 delves into the legal implications of using blockchain and smart contracts within the FinTech sector. It examines the challenges and opportunities of smart contracts in financial services, including compliance, enforcement, and the evolving legal landscape. In Chapter 10, the convergence of digital business models with ESG excellence is highlighted, with an overview of how e-businesses can adopt circular economy principles to enhance sustainability, reduce waste, and create value in the digital age. Chapter 11 presents case studies on how FinTech initiatives have driven social change, with examples of financial products and services that have had a social impact, discussing both successes and lessons learned.

Focusing on India, Chapter 12 analyzes the role of digital currencies in sustainable finance and investment within the country. It discusses the potential of cryptocurrencies and central bank digital currencies (CBDCs) in promoting financial inclusion and supporting sustainable economic growth. Chapter 13 explores *tokenomics*, which involves studying the economic principles governing cryptocurrency tokens, and analyzes its implications for sustainability. This chapter investigates how token-based systems incentivize sustainable behaviors and contribute to the development of green economies. Finally, Chapter 14 examines the specific case of Tanzania and how digital finance innovations are leveraged to improve financial inclusion. It covers mobile money platforms and digital banking and how these technologies overcome barriers to financial services for the unbanked population.

The Editors
June 2024

Acknowledgments

The editors wish to express their warm thanks and deep appreciation to those who provided valuable input, support, constructive suggestions, and assistance in editing and proofreading of this book.

The editors would like to thank all the authors for their valuable contributions in enriching the scholarly content of the book.

Mere words cannot express the editors' deep gratitude to the entire editorial and production teams of Scrivener Publishing, particularly Martin Scrivener for his great support, encouragement, and guidance all through the publication process. This book would not have been possible without his significant contributions.

The editors would like to sincerely thank the reviewers who kindly volunteered their time and expertise to shape such a high-quality book on a very timely topic.

The editors wish to acknowledge the love, understanding, and support of their family members during the book's preparation.

Finally, the editors use this opportunity to thank all the readers and expect that this book will continue to inspire and guide them in their future endeavors.

The Editors

1

Data-Driven Sustainability: Unlocking the Potential of Machine Learning and Big Data for ESG Integration & the Circular Economy

Priya Soni

School of Business & Commerce, Department of Business Administration, Manipal University, Dehmi Kalan, Off Jaipur-Ajmer Expressway, Jaipur, Rajasthan, India

Abstract

The paradigm of sustainable development has assumed a central position in international agendas as the globe faces rising difficulties brought on by climate change, resource depletion, and environmental degradation. Environmental, social, and governance (ESG) principles have become crucial indicators in this environment for evaluating the sustainability and moral implications of corporate practices. Achieving long-term ecological balance also requires the adoption of circular economy techniques, which put a premium on reducing waste and improving resource efficiency.

The revolutionary potential of big data and machine learning (ML) technologies is thoroughly explored in this chapter with a view to promoting ESG objectives and accelerating the shift to a circular economy. These innovative technologies' confluence presents unheard-of prospects for the analysis of huge, complicated information, the extraction of insightful conclusions, and the facilitation of data-driven decision-making for sustainable practices.

Organizations may acquire a thorough insight into their sustainability performance by using extensive data sources that include environmental impacts, social responsibility indexes, and corporate governance frameworks. By recognizing patterns, forecasting future trends, and evaluating risk factors, ML algorithms further improve predictive skills, enabling stakeholders to execute proactive sustainability policies.

Email: priya.soni@jaipur.manipal.edu; drpriyasoni26787@gmail.com; Parineeta2787@gmail.com

Ernesto D.R. Santibanez Gonzalez, Vinay Kandpal, Peterson K. Ozili and Prasenjit Chatterjee (eds.) Fintech for ESG and the Circular Economy, (1–12) © 2024 Scrivener Publishing LLC

Circular economy activities may be optimized to reduce waste creation, enhance recycling procedures, and support circular product design through the intelligent processing of various datasets linked to material lifecycles, supply chain management, and product consumption patterns. ML models allow for dynamic demand forecasting, adaptive resource allocation, and the development of closed-loop systems that promote resource conservation and sustainable growth.

In summary, the application of big data and ML to the circular economy and ESG provides a paradigm-shifting step toward a sustainable future. Businesses, decision-makers, and stakeholders may make wise choices, track development, and collaborate to meet global sustainability targets by leveraging the power of data-driven insights. To guarantee that these breakthroughs function as agents of change in the effort to create a regenerative and socially responsible society, it is necessary to strike a careful balance between technical developments and ethical considerations.

Keywords: Big data, machine learning, ESG (environmental, social, and governance), circular economy, sustainability, ethical business practices

1.1 Introduction to Big Data and Machine Learning

The amount of data produced from many sources has increased tremendously in today's linked society. Big data, a massive collection of data, offers enormous potential for businesses to learn important lessons and make wise decisions. However, the complexity and size of big data cannot be handled by the conventional methods of data analysis and processing. Herein lies the application of machine learning (ML), a branch of artificial intelligence.

The phrase "Big data" refers to extremely large and intricate data sets that are too complex for standard data processing software to handle, store, and analyze efficiently. These datasets are defined by the three Vs: variety (both organized and unstructured), velocity (fast data creation), and volume (huge amounts of data). Big data is information gathered from a wide range of sources, such as sensors, social media, transactional records, and more (Wang, 2020) [1].

Contrarily, the artificial intelligence discipline of ML enables computer systems to learn from data without explicit programming. ML algorithms employ patterns in the data to enhance their performance over time rather than depending on predetermined rules. These algorithms can find hidden patterns, anticipate the future, and change their behavior on the fly in response to input [2].

Numerous industries, including banking, healthcare, marketing, and transportation, have undergone radical change because of the union of big data and ML. Their combined strength enables organizations to analyze enormous volumes of data, resulting quickly and effectively in more accurate decision-making, improved customer experiences, and the identification of profitable possibilities.

As companies and organizations try to strike a balance between economic development, environmental preservation, and social responsibility, sustainability has become a crucial worldwide concern. Big data and ML are crucial to the advancement of sustainability initiatives because they offer strong tools for gathering, analyzing, and drawing conclusions from vast volumes of data (Wang, 2020) [3]. The following are some significant ways that these technologies promote sustainability:

Data-Driven Decision Making: Big data enables businesses to collect and analyze significant amounts of data from a variety of sources, including supply chain records, social media, satellite imaging, and environmental sensors. These data may be processed by ML algorithms, which can then spot trends and produce insightful findings. These revelations make it possible to make decisions based on facts in fields like resource management, energy efficiency, waste minimization, and sustainable product design (Mishra, 2019) [4].

Environmental Monitoring and Management: Real-time monitoring of environmental factors including air quality, water quality, and biodiversity is made possible by big data and IoT (Internet of Things) devices. These data may be processed by ML algorithms to find abnormalities, forecast environmental changes, and maximize resource use. This aids in effective pollution management, early warning systems for natural catastrophes, and ecosystem preservation (Mishra, 2019) [5].

Supply Chain Transparency: Big data may provide businesses with complete insight into their supply chains, allowing them to follow the flow of products and raw materials from their point of origin to their destination. This data may be analyzed by ML to detect possible dangers, evaluate the social and environmental effects of supply chain operations, and assist sustainable sourcing techniques.

Energy efficiency and smart grid management are made possible by big data analytics and ML, which may be used to optimize energy usage patterns, forecast demand changes, and operate smart grids. As a result, there is less energy wasted, more dependence on renewable energy sources, and an energy infrastructure that is more durable (Grattieri, 2020) [6].

Integration of the Circular Economy: Figure 1.1 provides evidence of the integration of techniques such as big data, deep learning, and machine learning, which can help facilitate the shift to a model based on product lifecycles, consumer behavior, and waste streams. These technologies can

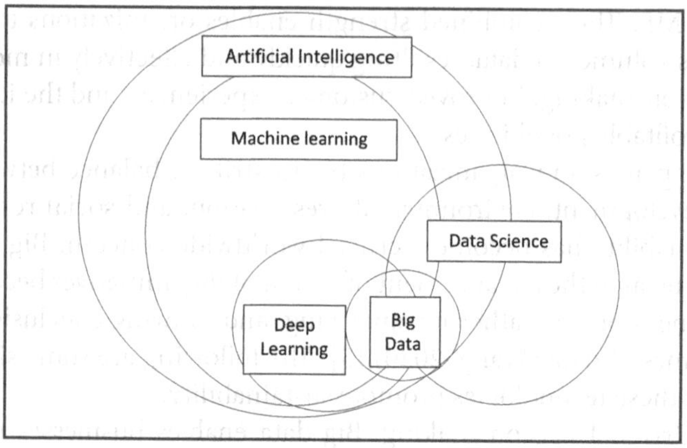

Figure 1.1 The role of big data and machine learning in sustainability.

spot chances for material recovery, recycling, and remanufacturing, reducing waste and fostering environmentally friendly manufacturing methods.

Big data and ML are useful tools for measuring the social effect of corporate operations and activities. Organizations may better understand the mood and perception of their stakeholders and use these insights in their social responsibility practices by analyzing data from social media, consumer reviews, and staff surveys.

Predictive Analytics for Climate Change: The phenomena of climate change are dynamic and complicated. Big data and ML algorithms may examine past weather patterns, climate data, and other pertinent information to anticipate potential future climate scenarios. The creation of adaptable solutions and laws to lessen the effects of climate change benefits greatly from these ideas.

Environmental, Social, and Governance (ESG) and Circular Economy: Circular economy and environmental, social, and governance (ESG) are two interrelated frameworks that direct companies and organizations toward ethical behavior. These frameworks have become increasingly important in recent years as businesses have realized how important it is to take into account not just their financial success but also their effects on society, the environment, and corporate governance.

1.2 Environmental, Social, and Governance (ESG)

Environmental: The "E" in ESG stands for environmental impact and management of a company's interaction with the environment. This includes initiatives to control waste and pollution, lower carbon emissions, conserve resources, encourage the use of renewable energy sources, and more. Companies are rated according to how committed they are to sustainability and how eco-friendly they are.

Social: The "S" in ESG stands for a company's social effect and its interactions with different stakeholders, such as its workers, clients, suppliers, and neighbors. Fair labor practices, employee well-being, diversity and inclusion, community involvement, and contributions to society's welfare are all examples of social elements.

Corporate governance and the framework that monitors a company's activities are the "G" and "G" in ESG. This covers things like board impartiality, openness, accountability, executive pay, anti-corruption safeguards, and adherence to moral standards.

Strong ESG performers seek to maximize long-term value while minimizing harm to society and the environment. Investors and stakeholders are increasingly using ESG criteria to evaluate the sustainability and ethical standards of the firms they invest in or work with.

1.3 Circular Economy

An economic strategy known as the "circular economy" aims to separate economic expansion from the depletion of limited resources. Through recycling, reusing, and remanufacturing, it seeks to eliminate waste and prolong the useful life of goods, materials, and resources. The notion of imitating natural systems, where waste from one process becomes a resource for another, is what gave rise to the concept (Ma and Dai, 2020) [7].

The following are important circular economy tenets:

- Creating things with extended life and repairability
- Encouraging goods rental and sharing above ownership
- Facilitating material recovery and recycling
- Promoting the use of sustainable resources
- Reducing waste production over the whole value chain

The circular economy stimulates innovation, generates new business possibilities, and boosts economic resilience in addition to reducing the environmental effect of production and consumption.

1.4 ESG and Circular Economy Integration

ESG and circular economy are intertwined in sustainability initiatives. As it encourages resource efficiency, waste reduction, and sustainable product design, adopting circular economy concepts can have a beneficial influence on a company's environmental performance (E). Since circular economy practices can strengthen social fairness and working conditions, they also have an impact on social aspects (S). By making thoughtful decisions and planning, governance (G) is strengthened in accordance with ethical and sustainable governance principles.

1.4.1 Machine Learning Applications for Sustainable Practices

Applications of ML may significantly advance and promote sustainable practices in a variety of industries. Here are some ways that ML might support sustainability:

Energy Optimization: ML algorithms can analyze data from sensors and devices to reduce the amount of energy used in manufacturing processes, transportation networks, and buildings. ML can recommend energy-efficient practices and lower carbon footprints by spotting patterns and trends.
Predictive Maintenance: ML can be used in industries to forecast equipment breakdowns and maintenance requirements. This proactive strategy minimizes resource waste, downtime, and unexpected malfunctions.
Management of Smart Grids: By anticipating energy demands and balancing renewable and conventional energy sources, ML may assist manage power distribution in smart grids. This optimization promotes energy efficiency and lessens reliance on non-renewable resources.
Climate Prediction and Adaption: ML models can analyze climate data, forecast extreme weather, assist adaption plans, and provide early warning systems.
Precision Agriculture: agricultural practices may be improved by analyzing data from sensors, satellites, and weather stations. Insights regarding crop trends, water use, and soil health are provided by ML, which aids in boosting agricultural output while consuming fewer resources.
Trash Management: ML may be used to streamline the procedures for sorting and recycling trash. Recycling materials may be recognized using image recognition algorithms, improving trash sorting and resource recovery.
Sustainable Supply Chains: To develop SSC, ML may evaluate the environmental and social practices of suppliers. Businesses may choose suppliers

more wisely by researching supplier performance and compliance data (Borade, 2020) [8].

Environmental Monitoring: To monitor and evaluate the state of the environment, ML models may analyze data from sensors, drones, and satellites. Among other things, this information may be used to manage air quality, monitor deforestation, and save animals. Green Building Design: ML can help with green building design by simulating energy performance, optimizing layouts, and suggesting eco-friendly materials.

Circular Economy: By examining customer behavior and supply chain data to promote recycling, product refurbishing, and reuse, ML can aid in the transition to a circular economy.

Businesses, governments, and organizations may use the power of ML to make data-driven choices that support sustainable practices, lessen environmental consequences, and contribute to a future that is more sustainable. To get the best outcomes in sustainability applications, it is vital to make sure that the data used to train ML models is accurate, representative, and devoid of bias.

1.4.2 Circular Economy Implementation with Big Data and Machine Learning

Big data and ML use in a circular economy may greatly improve the efficacy and efficiency of circular practices. These are a few applications for these technologies like managing waste and recycling in which big data may be used to monitor and analyze the rates of garbage creation, collection, and recycling across various geographic areas. To cut down on transportation emissions, ML systems can anticipate garbage amounts, use image recognition to find recyclable products in the waste stream, and optimize waste collection routes. In addition, big data may be used to collect information on a product's complete lifespan, including its raw ingredients, manufacturing processes, usage trends, and end-of-life care. ML may examine this data to find areas where product design might be enhanced, durability could be increased, and recycling could be made easier.

Moreover, reverse logistics and remanufacturing facilitate the effective return, refurbishing, and remanufacturing of goods and components, big data and ML may help manage reverse logistics (Durand, 2019) [9]. ML algorithms can streamline the process of choosing whether to recycle, remanufacture, or fix a piece of equipment. In terms of predictive maintenance, ML algorithms can analyze data from embedded sensors and linked devices in things like equipment and appliances. Businesses may increase product lifespans by anticipating maintenance requirements, lowering the need for premature replacements, and preserving resources.

Big data and ML may be used to analyze consumption trends, customer preferences, and consumer behavior (Mishra, 2019) [10]. This data can help firms make decisions regarding possible product return policies, incentives for circular behavior, and promotion of product-sharing or leasing models. In general, the use of big data and ML in the circular economy can allow more precise, timely, and data-driven processes, resulting in a more resource-effective and sustainable future. Addressing data privacy and security issues is crucial, as well as ensuring that the insights generated from these technologies are applied responsibly and morally.

1.4.3 Risk Management and ESG Compliance through Data-Driven Approaches

Tracking and Reporting of Carbon Emissions:

Many businesses use data-driven strategies to correctly measure and report their carbon emissions. To measure emissions from its supply chain, for instance, the international retail firm Walmart built a data-driven approach. Walmart can identify high-emission suppliers and work with them to lower their carbon footprint by gathering data from thousands of suppliers and using ML algorithms to analyze the information (Wang, 2020). The proof of appropriate algorithmic management in any organisation is displayed in Figure 1.2. This data-driven approach enables the organization to manage environmental risks and achieve ESG goals related to climate change. One of the biggest food and beverage corporations in the world, Nestlé, employs

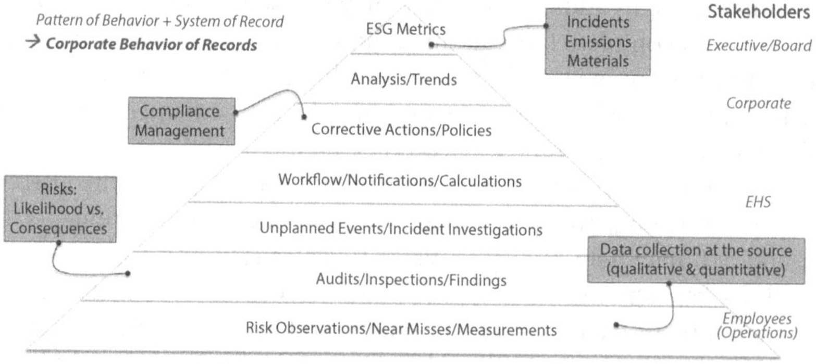

Figure 1.2 ESG reporting frameworks.

data-driven strategies to manage its supply chain responsibly. Nestlé collects information on supplier performance, environmental effects, and compliance with regulations using a digital supply chain platform.

Financial institutions are increasingly incorporating climate risk assessments into their risk management procedures: Climate Risk Assessment for Financial Institutions. For instance, the biggest asset manager in the world, BlackRock, has created data-driven algorithms to evaluate climate-related risks in its investment portfolios. BlackRock can identify assets vulnerable to climate risks and make wise investment decisions to limit these risks by analyzing climate data, legislative changes, and other ESG variables.

Investment businesses are using ESG data analytics for decision-making investment and businesses are using ESG data analytics for their decision-making processes. For instance, JPMorgan Asset Management assesses the ESG performance and possible risks of corporations using data-driven methods. The business acquires a greater knowledge of ESG-related risks and opportunities by combining alternative data sources, such as satellite imagery and social media sentiment research, which results in more sustainable investing strategies.

Sustainable Finance Solutions Powered by AI:

Several startups and businesses are utilizing AI-powered platforms to make sustainable finance solutions possible. For instance, True Value Labs analyzes unstructured data from diverse sources using AI algorithms to evaluate organizations' ESG performance in real time. This data-driven strategy enables businesses and investors to make data-supported choices, improving risk management and ESG compliance.

Leading CRM providers like Salesforce use data-driven technologies to keep track of their social impact projects. Salesforce can monitor and assess the results of its social programs using data analytics, ensuring that the funds allotted to them are successful in accomplishing their intended objectives.

These instances show how data-driven methods are becoming increasingly important for risk management and maintaining ESG compliance across a range of sectors. Organizations are better equipped to understand their environmental and social implications, make wise decisions, and deepen their commitment to sustainability and ethical business practices by utilizing data and sophisticated analytics.

Ethical consideration:

To guarantee that the use of data is consistent with ethical and just practices, ethical concerns in data-driven sustainability are of the highest significance. To inform their sustainability initiatives, organizations are relying more and more on massive information, making it critical to address possible ethical issues. Data security and privacy are of particular significance since it may be possible to gather and analyze private information about people, groups, and ecosystems. To uphold people's rights and avert potential damage, it is crucial to get informed permission and safeguard data from unauthorized access. In addition, data biases need to be recognized and eliminated to prevent perpetuating injustices or miscalculating the sustainability implications.

Building trust with stakeholders requires transparency in data gathering, analytical techniques, and decision-making procedures. Additionally, to guarantee that data-driven sustainability projects prioritize human well-being, social justice, and environmental preservation in a fair and ethical way, partnership with impacted communities and responsible data governance are crucial.

1.5 Future Trends and Challenges in ESG and Circular Economy

Initiatives related to the circular economy and ESG will face both opportunities and problems in the future. Increased investor understanding of sustainability risks and possibilities has led to a strong trend toward the inclusion of ESG factors into investment choices. Technology breakthroughs like artificial intelligence and blockchain are anticipated to be crucial in improving resource efficiency, supply chain transparency, and data analytics. As more and more governments throughout the world see how urgent it is to solve environmental and social challenges, regulatory moves toward sustainable practices are expected to pick up steam.

With more businesses adopting product-as-a-service models and recycling initiatives, circular business models are also growing in popularity. However, problems still exist. Accurate ESG reporting and comparison are hampered by problems with data quality and standardization. Greenwashing is still a problem; hence accountable and open practices are required. Complex supply chains make it difficult to apply the concepts of the circular economy, necessitating efficient material tracing and management on the part of businesses. Careful thought must be given to achieving social and economic justice while pursuing sustainability objectives. Collaboration, creativity, and long-term thinking are essential for building a sustainable and circular future that can effectively navigate current obstacles and embrace future trends.

References

1. Wang, H., Big Data: A Crucial Asset in Today's Interconnected Society. *J. Data Anal. Manage.*, 15, 3, 45–58, 2020.
2. Smith, J., Harnessing the Power of Machine Learning in Various Industries: A Review of Applications and Implications. *J. Artif. Intell. Data Anal.*, 8, 2, 112–125, 2023.
3. Wang, Q., Harnessing Big Data and Machine Learning for Sustainability Initiatives: A Review. *J. Sustain. Dev.*, 15, 3, 78–92, 2020.
4. Mishra, S.K., Leveraging Big Data for Data-Driven Decision Making in Sustainability Initiatives: A Comprehensive Overview. *J. Sustain. Bus. Manage.*, 12, 4, 213–230, 2019.
5. Mishra, S.K., Integrating Big Data and Machine Learning for Environmental Monitoring and Management: A Review. *J. Environ. Sci. Manage.*, 14, 2, 87–102, 2019.
6. Grattieri, M., Leveraging Big Data Analytics and Machine Learning for Energy Efficiency and Smart Grid Management: A Comprehensive Review. *J. Energy Manage. Sustain.*, 8, 3, 45–60, 2020.
7. Ma, Z. and Dai, Y., Advancing Towards a Circular Economy: Principles and Strategies for Sustainable Resource Management. *J. Sustain. Dev. Strategies*, 17, 2, 35–50, 2020.
8. Borade, A., Leveraging Machine Learning for Sustainable Supply Chain Management: A Review of Strategies and Applications. *J. Sustain. Bus. Pract.*, 14, 3, 78–92, 2020.
9. Durand, M., Leveraging Big Data and Machine Learning for Reverse Logistics, Remanufacturing, and Predictive Maintenance: A Comprehensive Review. *J. Sustain. Supply Chain Manage.*, 16, 4, 112–128, 2019.
10. Mishra, S.K., Leveraging Big Data and Machine Learning for Consumer Behavior Analysis and Circular Economy Initiatives: Opportunities and Challenges. *J. Sustain. Bus. Strategies*, 15, 2, 65–80, 2019.

2

Blockchain Technology and Its Potential in Sustainable Finance and Investment

Neeti Misra[1]*, Abhilasha Chauhan[2] and Nikita Siddhu[1]

[1]*UIM, Uttaranchal University, Dehradun, Uttarakhand, India*
[2]*FMS, Shoolini University, Solan, Himachal Pradesh, India*

Abstract

Blockchain has recently become a widely used information technology due to its efficiency as an intermediary platform. The widespread adoption of blockchain technology is revolutionizing various industries by leveraging its efficiency as an intermediary platform. This study systematically explores the multifaceted applications of blockchain in pivotal sectors such as finance, supply chain, healthcare, education, and energy consumption, thereby catalyzing the development of decentralized databases on the Internet. This research investigates the challenges and opportunities in the realm of blockchain technology, emphasizing its pivotal role in sustainable finance and investment. The current study scrutinizes the intricate relationship between blockchain and sustainable financing, illustrating how this innovative technology can reshape traditional financial models and contribute to environmentally and socially responsible investment practices. Furthermore, the study delves into the dynamic landscape of technology adoption, shedding light on the challenges encountered by diverse sectors in successfully integrating blockchain solutions. By offering a detailed elucidation of these hurdles, the research provides valuable insights into the evolving nature of blockchain implementation and lays the groundwork for formulating effective strategies to overcome obstacles. In summary, the study provides comprehensive information on the current state of blockchain technology, its applications across vital sectors, and its indispensable role in driving sustainable finance and investment. Through a meticulous examination of challenges in adoption, the research significantly contributes

**Corresponding author*: neeti.cm@gmail.com; ORCID: https://orcid.org/0000-0003-1797-080
Abhilasha Chauhan: ORCID: https://orcid.org/0000-0002-5457-3539
Nikita Siddhu: ORCID: https://orcid.org/0009-0009-0892-3751

Ernesto D.R. Santibanez Gonzalez, Vinay Kandpal, Peterson K. Ozili and Prasenjit Chatterjee (eds.)
Fintech for ESG and the Circular Economy, (13–30) © 2024 Scrivener Publishing LLC

to the ongoing discourse surrounding the transformative potential of blockchain, which plays a key role in shaping a more resilient and sustainable future.

Keywords: Blockchain, sustainable development, sustainable finance, investment

2.1 Introduction

Innovation in various services such as transport, electricity, and water, sectors that account for the bulk of global emissions, can have a significant impact on reducing emissions. But this will require a game-changing approach, rethinking how low-carbon transitions can be achieved cost-effectively and fairly. The key features of blockchain and other distributed ledger technologies enable deep technological integration, standardization, and the possibility of new business models. Their ability to integrate with other key technologies such as IoT and artificial intelligence can have a significant impact on traditional services. Blockchain technology (BCT) can open up new areas of financing and support the promise of lowering costs for existing businesses by creating new sources. The stated goal is to increase revenue, transparency, and access to finance while reducing the cost of capital for infrastructure projects.

The integration of BCT in various fields has attracted much attention due to its transformative potential, especially in the field of finance and sustainable investment. The purpose of this work is to investigate the multifaceted aspects of blockchain's impact on sustainable financial practices using various academic partnerships.

Blockchain's role in sustainable finance is underscored by its ability to address longstanding challenges in traditional financial systems. Naderi and Tian (2022) [1] emphasize the potential of blockchain in tokenizing green assets, offering a mechanism to fill critical gaps in green finance. The study conducted by Parmentola *et al.* (2022) [2] systematically reviews the environmental sustainability implications of blockchain, providing a foundational perspective within the context of sustainable development goals (SDGs). This examination of blockchain's influence extends beyond environmental considerations to encompass broader implications for financial inclusion (Mhlanga, 2023) [3] and supply chain sustainability (Ayan *et al.*, 2022) [4].

The motivation behind this study is a recognition of the urgency to address global environmental challenges, as highlighted by influential bodies such as the United Nations Environment Programme (UNEP, 2020) [5] and the Intergovernmental Panel on Climate Change (IPCC, 2021) [6]. The need for innovative solutions in sustainable finance is underscored by the World Bank Group (2021) [7] and the Organization for Economic

Co-operation and Development (OECD, 2023) [8], as evidenced in their strategies to leverage blockchain technologies.

Moreover, the burgeoning interest and strategic considerations in various regions, as exemplified by the comprehensive "Blockchain: The India Strategy" document released by Niti Aayog (2020) [9], reflect a broader global commitment to exploring the potential of blockchain in advancing sustainable finance.

Against this background, the research aims to help understand how BCT can play a revolutionary role in sustainable finance and investment. By combining the results of several studies, this article focuses on key points in the existing literature and provides the basis for future research and practice in this field.

2.2 Literature Review

BCT has emerged as a transformative force, capturing considerable attention for its potential to reshape industries and, notably, foster environmental sustainability. In a seminal contribution, Parmentola *et al.* (2022) [2] conducted a systematic review that provided a comprehensive understanding of how blockchain aligns with the SDGs. Their work elucidates the intricate ways in which blockchain contributes to addressing contemporary ecological challenges, positioning it as a pivotal tool for sustainable solutions.

Expanding the discourse across industries, Ayan *et al.* (2022) [4] adopted a mixed-method approach to delve into the practical applications of blockchain. Their research underscores the adaptive versatility of blockchain, showcasing its role in instilling sustainability practices and optimizing supply chain management across diverse sectors. This exploration resonates with the broader theme of blockchain's applicability across industries.

Shifting the focus to financial inclusion, Mhlanga's study (2023) [3] adds differentiation by investigating how blockchain bridges financial gaps in Industry 4.0 era. The study positions blockchain as a catalyst for sustainable economic growth, emphasizing its potential to democratize access to financial services and foster inclusive development.

Addressing the green finance gap, Naderi and Tian's work (2022) [1] proposes innovative solutions through the tokenization of green assets. This not only aligns financial systems with sustainable practices but also underscores blockchain's transformative potential in shaping the future of green finance. The industry-specific lens adopted by Ata *et al.* (2023) [10] strengthens the argument. By investigating the impact of blockchain on the income of investment projects, this research provides tangible insights into how blockchain influences specific domains, offering a nuanced understanding of its real-world implications.

On a broader strategic level, national and global bodies have recognized blockchain's potential for sustainable development. The India Strategy on Blockchain (Niti Aayog, 2020) [9] has an immense scope as a digital enabler for sustainable infrastructure, underscoring the imperative of integrating blockchain into sustainability strategies at both domestic and worldwide levels.

Also, the environmental conservation is amplified by the United Nations Environment Programme (UNEP, 2020) [5]. Their report emphasizes blockchain's potential contributions as a catalyst for sustainable practices, shedding light on its role in environmental conservation efforts.

Lastly, this review underscores the transformative potential of blockchain in propelling sustainability across diverse domains. The next section will investigate deeper into the specific role of blockchain in sustainable finance and investment, unraveling its details and broader implications for the financial landscape.

2.2.1 Blockchain Technology

Blockchain, the basis of Bitcoin, has started to attract attention recently. Blockchain acts as an immutable ledger that allows transactions to occur in a distributed manner. Blockchain-based applications continue to emerge, including financial services, reputation, Internet of Things (IoT), and more. Blockchain is a tamper-proof system used to record transactions on a public or private network. Once distributed to all participants in the network, the list is permanently locked in the block. In blockchain, many functions (anonymity functions, cryptographic information, legal contracts, smart contracts, and reputation) are integrated into a distributed system. The system can manage many types of services for end users - agentless, open, consistent, traceable, and secure services at low cost but without unnecessary interference. Blockchain provides strong support for business: decentralization, security and behavior, immutability, and functions such as ideas and even actions work and good reasoning (Chen *et al.*, 2022) [11].

Each confirmed and validated block is called a blockchain because it is linked from the beginning to the end of the chain. Instead of depending on a third party, such as a financial institution, to settle transactions, blockchain network participants use a consensus process to agree on recorded data, cryptographic hashes, and digital signatures to secure transactions.

This method is recommended to allow enough time to write to the digital file so that the metadata is not retrieved or altered. It can be defined as a software protocol that cannot work without the Internet. Peer-to-peer blockchain networks prevent a single participant or group of participants from controlling the underlying processes or systems. All network participants are equal and follow the same rules.

2.2.2 Sustainable Finance and Investment

Sustainable finance refers to the process of long-term investing in businesses and projects, including environmental, social, and governance (ESG) and the decisions to invest in financial markets. Thinking about the environment covers many areas, not only climate change and adaptation but also biodiversity conservation, pollution prevention, and circular economy. Leadership, labor relations, skills, expertise, social investment, human rights issues, etc., we can examine these in sustainable finance and investment issues. Public and private management (management standards, employee relations, salaries, etc.) play an important role in taking into account society's energy and environmental views (Gonzalez, 2021) [12].

Sustainable finance refers to the financing of things that are environmentally friendly today (green money) and things that turn into environmentally friendly performance over time (financial change). Climate change refers to the use of private financing to reduce existing carbon emissions or other environmental impacts and for climate change transition and economic sustainability. For example, these could be investments in green manufacturing or reducing the environmental footprint of non-green technologies. Economic reforms are urgently needed to reduce greenhouse gas emissions and environmental impacts by 55% by 2030. Companies that want to be sustainable but will need to increase often need bridge financing, in other words, companies with different starting points are looking for financing for their operations next trip (Levy and Kolk, 2002) [13].

Sustainable finance means taking into account the ESG aspects of the project when choosing an investment. It aims to determine the economic value of SDGs such as reducing carbon monoxide emissions, promoting sustainability, and protecting natural resources.

This financial perspective considers the long-term impact of investment decisions on returns and the wider impact on society and the environment. It allows companies to invest in projects that improve livelihoods, protect ecosystems, and preserve natural resources for future generations. A positive environmental impact can improve personal health and increase personal investment (Thompson, 2023) [14].

Sustainable finance is financial policies, procedures, standards, and products aimed at protecting the environment. Connect financial systems to your business and people by supporting your agents as they achieve growth goals. In addition, a sustainable financial framework provides a pathway for these financial activities to ensure that investment and finance operate effectively in line with development goals (Strandberg, 2005) [15].

Environmental, social, and corporate governance is an important aspect of financial sustainability (ESG). Environmental considerations often include climate change, mitigation, and environmental issues. The word "thinking" can refer to issues such as human rights, investment in human capital, labor relations, inequality, and participation. Governance includes public and private administration. Therefore, it plays an important role in ensuring that social and environmental factors are taken into account in the decision-making process.

Therefore, financial stability management of financial disclosure has become important because investors and stakeholders want more transparency and accountability from companies and financial institutions. These regulations help investors make investment decisions regarding the safety of their investments (Chandler, 2014) [16].

These business decisions benefit customers and consumers. Sustainable financial development covers many activities. Examples of these activities include ownership, sustainable lending, green finance, impact investing, microfinance, and sustainable finance.

In addition, this approach can support and improve the competitiveness, efficiency, and success of your business now and in the future. It also helps protect and restore ecosystems and promote culture and health. Additionally, sustainable financial principles minimize environmental and social impacts by promoting good financial practices (Gann *et al.*, 2019) [17]. These investment principles are:

- It is good for growth.
- Transparency and disclosure
- Stakeholder engagement
- Responsible investment and lending
- Corporate responsibility

Building a more secure future requires a multidisciplinary approach that includes finance.

The financial sector has great power in financing and raising awareness of sustainability issues, supporting alternative energy research and development, and supporting companies that work with the principles of justice and common sense. Sustainable finance is defined as investment decisions that take into account the ESG aspects of a business or project.

Environmental factors such as reducing pollution and using sustainable resources. Community topics include human and animal rights, as well as consumer protection and various forms of employment.

Management process refers to the management, employee relations, and compensation of public and private organizations. Sustainable finance involves investment decisions that consider ESG issues as well as financial returns, also known as "green finance" (Boffo and Patalano, 2020) [18].

Sustainable finance involves investment decisions that consider the ESG aspects of a business or project. Sustainability is here, and over time investors have become increasingly interested in ESG solutions. ESG also includes human rights. Environmental pollution, health, and social problems. End poverty has equal rights in the workplace. Strictly comply with local, state, federal, and international regulations. Many countries are implementing new sustainable finance strategies and sustainable finance development projects (Krambia-Kapardis *et al.*, 2023) [19]. Environmental considerations include mitigating climate impacts and using sustainable resources. Community topics include human and animal rights, as well as consumer protection and various forms of employment. The management process refers to management, employee relations, and rewards in public and private organizations (Dhaliwal and Malik, 2021) [20].

Community development is investing in people, eliminating problems, and ensuring justice, security, dignity, and respect for all citizens. Education, care, job creation, health and livelihoods, and safe communities contribute to health. Today, companies are more aware of the importance of investing in society and the indirect benefits of their actions for its employees and for the public itself. From an organizational perspective, companies not only view ESG as "a decision" but also make such decisions in a broader context (El Khoury *et al.*, 2023) [21].

A sustainable business definition depends on business leaders making decisions that benefit people, the environment, and the economy. Business leaders must have business knowledge, first, responsibility for profit, second, responsibility for success, and third, environmental responsibility. Business leaders must be ethical leaders whose results support our sustainable business bottom line. Virtue honesty gives business leaders integrity and helps them make good decisions about factories, people, and profits. Leaders must apply ethical rules in their daily lives that will help them make decisions not only for the benefit of the business organization but also for current and future pressing needs (Lenka and Kar, 2021) [22].

Value investing includes a variety of activities, from investing in green projects to investing in companies with proven value, such as quality of social inclusion and good governance with women on boards.

Sustainable finance has become an important concept in cross-cutting areas: financial goals and sustainability. Sustainability financing should include all activities and activities that contribute to financial stability and growth (Kumar *et al.*, 2022) [23].

The focus points in the green investment process of the development of the international economy are defined as follows: 1) increased demand from government and commercial enterprises, commercial enterprises, and families to attract stable capital to increase the levels of local and international competitiveness markets; 2) national economy. Significant changes in ecology lead to the diversification of financial instruments; 3) The differentiation of the business model of the world financial market and the emergence of new organizations; 4) Geographical and instrumental asymmetries and depth (Ilnytskyy and Stoliarchuk, 2023) [24].

There are many different types of fixed income depending on the definition of fixed income and fixed investment (Cunha *et al.*, 2021) [25]. It includes:

2.2.2.1 Sustainable Foreign Direct Investment (SFDI)

SFDI generally refers to cross-border investment from developed to developing countries for sustainability purposes. SFDI is seen as a way to achieve the goals set by the United Nations 2030 Agenda for Sustainable Development. Sustainable development is important in the development of foreign direct investment, which will support job creation, increase productivity, and improve people's living standards. Lawmakers will concentrate on sustainable development to attract foreign direct investment (Sheikh *et al.*, 2022) [26].

2.2.2.2 Impact Investing

Impact investing is designed to generate good returns and have a healthy impact on society or the environment. Impact investors consider a company's ESG performance and sustainability information when making investment decisions. Impact investing helps people and the environment without creating financial impact. It seeks to solve global problems in energy, water, sanitation, food, health, and education by exploring new solutions (Barber *et al.*, 2021) [27].

2.2.2.3 *Socially Responsible Investment (SRI)*

SRIs make investment choices based on social or ethical principles. Being socially responsible may include avoiding investments that are harmful to society, such as the manufacture of weapons or cigarettes, and seeking companies committed to social justice. Socially responsible investing (SRI) is defined as a strategy that selects investors based on growth capital with ESG responsibility and financing. Companies and financial institutions can expand the investor base of responsible products by promoting financial products that increase the personal value of investors while generating satisfying income (Bollazzi and Risalvato, 2018) [28].

2.2.2.4 *Green Finance*

Green finance refers to any financial activity applied to an ESG environment. Narrower in scope than sustainable development, green money allows investors to concentrate on environmental financial issues such as decarbonization and impact negatively biodiversity: green bonds, cash loans, green cash, etc. Continuous renewal of new green products can help improve green cash flow and promote green business (Berrou *et al.*, 2019) [29].

2.2.3 Five Pillars of Sustainable Finance Projects (Greenfield, 2022) [30]

1. Definition: use of proceeds
2. Selection: Project evaluation process
3. Traceability: revenue management
4. Transparency: monitoring and reporting
5. Verification: assurance through external review

A sustainable finance approach focuses on ensuring that environmental, societal, and governmental (ESG) considerations are taken into account when making investment decisions. Capital finance has determined that the investment business is stable. The impact of financial crimes, especially cybercrime, on sustainability is missing from this list of decisions (Levin, 2023) [31]. In the fight against cybercrime and technology that facilitates cybercrime, it has the effect of reducing the impact of cybercrime by making financial targets sustainable, leading to the success of the business copy and thus improving financial stability.

2.3 Role of Blockchain Technology in Sustainable Finance and Investment

Promoting green investment and developing the green economy are a necessity for the transition from traditional business models to efficient and effective business models. It has a long-term goal to achieve sustainable development, also known as green investment, environmental investment, environmental investment, social and economic management, social or sustainable business, or responsible investment. Green capital generation will narrow the regional gap in green innovation, thereby affecting the regional level of green development (Zheng *et al.*, 2017) [32]. Tokenizing physical assets or debt/assets will reduce transaction costs, increase transparency, and reduce scale and revenue by eliminating intermediaries and automation as done by European Green Bond Standard, International Sustainable Finance Platform, etc. Many financial instruments and measures to promote green investment, such as Therefore, there is potential for further consideration of green investment at the global, national, and organizational levels (Gernego *et al.*, 2022) [33]. The advantages of blockchain extend not only to the economy but also to politics, people, social, and scientific fields, and blockchain resources are already being used by groups specifically to solve real-world problems. Blockchain can act as a public repository for the entire community, including the record of all information, events, identities, and assets. In this system, any device can become a smart device, which is the idea of understanding each asset on the blockchain with a unique identifier so that assets can be tracked, controlled, and exchanged (buy or sell) on the blockchain. This means that all types of physical assets (houses, cars) and digital assets can be recorded and traded on the blockchain.

However, according to a study (Mudaliar *et al.*, 2018) [34], the following barriers continue to prevent impact investing from progressing to meet the financing needs of the SDGs:

- Possible termination options
- Complexity of impact measurement applications
- High-quality investment opportunities.

BCT enables new investments and transactions by seamlessly transferring value, providing trust as immutability, and converting assets into tokens that can be produced through smart contracts. Blockchain-enabled solutions hold particular promise for solving critical problems in disruptive business transactions.

BCT can revolutionize the banking industry by making daily processes more transparent, secure, and efficient. This list acts as a distribution list that can track trade between two parties (Kaur *et al.*, 2022) [35].

Blockchain-based systems do not require intermediaries, reduce transaction costs, and eliminate human error, risk, and time loss. For example, Kotak Mahindra Bank is using BCT to reduce the time required to open a letter of credit with JPMorgan Chase from 20 to 30 days to a few hours.

Blockchain is distribution-based and every update on the network requires consensus. Miners are user-friendly; they provide computer hardware to analyze updates and reach consensus (Chiu and Koeppl, 2019) [36], which is the goal of sustainable development (Banga, J. 2019) [37].

The integration of blockchain platforms and the integration of the Oracle network not only shows that the payment process is automated and transaction costs are reduced but also has many changes in the process that can be paid for profit using smart contracts. Financial models using technology can reduce transaction costs and create new opportunities (Chung, 2022) [38].

2.3.1 Benefits of Sustainability in Finance

1. Starting a sustainable business can be very profitable and profitable. For example, using scarce resources such as carbon or water has a direct impact on costs.
2. Environmental and social risks can also be financial risks. In this complex and interconnected world, an effective approach to risk management is essential. This is due to the increase in insurance claims due to weather damage.
3. Long-term thinking enables financial groups to innovate by adapting business models, technologies, and processes.
4. Focusing on social and human capital and investing in talent will make your business more flexible and give you a competitive advantage. The advantages are:
   - Strengthen relationships with stakeholders
   - Increase efficiency and reduce costs throughout the company.
   - Improve reputation
   - Improve employee access and retention

Business modeling estimates that CIF's Clean Technology Fund (CTF) portfolio will create at least 5 million jobs and more than US$40 billion in economic activity each year. Such job creation and increased entrepreneurship help the economy (Karambia-Kapardis *et al.*, 2023) [19].

Investment in renewable energy can improve energy security and strengthen local services. Promoting clean energy (e.g., solar power in India) and renewable energy markets (e.g., Turkey) can also help poor businesses and households benefit from the economy by improving energy efficiency and reducing costs.

It also supports rural communities and small farmers to withstand the impacts of shocks such as the COVID-19 pandemic by expanding access to trade, increasing agricultural production, and strengthening food.

CIF's experience shows that large-scale financial investments combined with political and regulatory support can create incentives and capacity to tackle cloud change. Kazakhstan is a good example of how CIF provides support for the metered use of renewable energy. These efforts helped attract more than US$1 billion in new investment, along with loans to solve business problems.

Both the Covid-19 pandemic and the climate crisis have revealed and deepened inequality. Without sacrifice, these two things can turn into chaos and hit the world's most vulnerable people hard. Short-term weather-related livelihood programs and cash transfers can provide immediate relief. For example, in Honduras, CIF funds are supporting solar mobile neighborhood clinics to improve access to basic health services in response to new demand related to COVID-19.

ESG investments have become more accessible to investors due to the need for financing and related resources, such as investment funds focused on ESG investments. That's why many companies pay for ESG investments because of business rules or regulations or the specific needs of stakeholders. Companies rely on ESG information coming directly from companies and sustainability rating agencies (SRAs) to "hold themselves accountable for their ESG performance."

BCT has the potential to make business development more efficient, cheaper, or completely automated. The development of BCT has been achieved by making all transactions on the blockchain immutable and providing immutable records of all transactions. Blockchains create irreversible blocks that can be used to settle financial transactions. When cryptographic hashes are concatenated to form a data file, they make the data immutable. This is good for quality assurance because no one can go back and edit or change existing information.

2.4 Challenges of Blockchain Technology

In organizational fields, there is a lack of appropriate skills, financial barriers, and a lack of participation and management support. In the field of environment, there are also legal issues, non-compliance with regulations, market and ecosystem readiness, and sustainability concerns (Tamayo-Orbegozo, 2017) [39].

Awareness will increase of the importance of ESG data quality and the potential problems of relevance, accuracy, and reliability that can occur when collecting and disclosing business information. Lack of comparability of ESG information is a concern for companies, as they make investment decisions while analyzing the processes behind the data and decide to follow the process, they find most appropriate (Jonsdottir *et al.*, 2022) [40].

Performance and efficiency issues such as transaction processing are slow and power-intensive, so they must be optimized for real-time data access. Establishing a governance framework and building trust among participants are essential and require strong consensus mechanisms and effective governance structures (Javaid *et al.*, 2022) [41].

One of the major challenges is the lack of digital infrastructure in the region, as many regions lack internet access and reliable mobile networks (Mohd and Kaushal, 2018) [42], which can limit the effectiveness and hinder the adoption of blockchain-based solutions. Additionally, there are concerns about privacy and data security, especially in countries with limited regulatory oversight. Major changes can be made to local government finances in line with green business standards. Central government debt positions or partial guarantee pools can support local governments to support fiscal models and achieve green development goals. Financing enhancement of municipal green bonds, municipal revenues, and PPP financing projects can also come as insurance. Facilitate the discovery and trading of green bonds through the exchange of trade data. In addition to environmental investments, significant investments must be made to increase the efficiency of public investments by attracting more private capital countries in general home savings (Kidney *et al.*, 2015) [43].

2.4.1 Challenges of Adoption of Blockchain Technology in Sustainable Finance and Investment

Scalability and storage capacity are currently the main challenges for blockchain. In BCT, blockchain continues to grow. For example, for Bitcoin, each block grows by one megabyte every 10 minutes, and a copy of the chain is stored only in each node, that is, each node in the network that validates and purchases blocks. As the chain grows, the nodes need more storage, so the physical capacity decreases. Also, large chains can affect system performance and increase connection time for new users (Dhaliwal and Malik, 2021) [20].

In a predatory attack, the fraudster deals directly with the seller, who quickly accepts the deal. Fraudsters then exploit authentication delays to create conflicts and exchange the same tokens across the network. In that case, the second transaction is likely to be fraudulent, defrauding the merchant. Therefore, faster detection times are needed to prevent these attacks.

The growth of IoT devices is staggering and there is a constant need to create advanced and efficient systems to meet data privacy and security in IoT networks. Limitations such as scalability, latency, and packet loss are major challenges for IoT security systems (Satamraju, 2020) [44].

Investment professionals can benefit from this action. Business owners should develop strategies for using BCT in digital financial services that are compatible with users' businesses. Reputation/value users can benefit from this research focusing on the use of blockchain to improve digital banking services (Kumari and Devi, 2022) [45].

Therefore, it is necessary to be careful about security or privacy issues, as these can cause users to lose. Although the technology itself is constantly evolving, new technologies are still emerging and applications are becoming more familiar and stable.

2.5 Conclusion

This article highlights the potential of BCT to improve financial management and sustainable financial management. The theoretical framework developed in this article provides a basis for understanding how BCT can increase budget efficiency and transparency. BCT has the potential to create collaborative platforms and network systems that can help achieve national investment goals, including lower costs. However, some policies must be implemented to facilitate the secure and fair development of blockchain-based solutions. Proper configuration is important for solving network issues and speed challenges, as well as reducing security risks. This leads to awareness of the facts and the education of decision makers has a significant impact on knowledge of the potential of technology.

Its introduction allows digital financial instruments to be customized based on investors' wishes, thus expanding the market for investors, reducing issuers' costs, and reducing counterparty risk.

Provide accurate information to Internet users using consistent standards, procedures, and practices. Business partners can now more easily collaborate, manage information, and agree on technology (Javaid *et al.*, 2022) [41].

It is necessary to be aware and careful about security issues or privacy issues because these problems can cause users to lose. While the technology itself continues to evolve, new technologies continue to emerge, applications become more complex and stable, and solutions against various threats are coming from the industry. Finance is embracing BCT and investments, including cryptography, consensus algorithm development, key management, multiple validations, and process analysis.

2.6 Implications

This paper illuminates that BCT has the potential to revolutionize financial management and promote sustainability. The theoretical framework establishes a basis for understanding how blockchain enhances budget efficiency and transparency, fostering the creation of collaborative platforms for national investment goals. However, effective policy implementation is crucial for secure and equitable blockchain development. Configuration, addressing security, and educating decision-makers are vital for harnessing blockchain's potential. The technology's introduction customizes digital financial instruments, expanding the investor market, reducing issuer costs, and mitigating counterparty risk through shared standards. Yet, cautious navigation of security and privacy concerns remains imperative. Constant attention to emerging threats and ongoing adaptation is necessary for blockchain's seamless integration into the financial and investment landscape, emphasizing a dynamic and balanced approach to technological advancement and policy implementation.

2.7 Suggestion and Recommendations

The limitations of this study are based on the need to understand the use and impact of BCT in financial and capital markets. Therefore, further research focusing on developing standards and guidelines for the efficient and effective use of the US dollar is needed to examine potential applications where BCT can impact business and influence the management process.

References

1. Naderi, N., and Tian, Y., Leveraging blockchain technology and tokenizing green assets to fill the green finance gap. *Energy Res. Lett.*, 3, 3, 2022.
2. Parmentola, A., Petrillo, A., Tutore, I., Defi Leith , F., Can Blockchain Improve Environmental Security? Analysis and research methods from the perspective of the Sustainable Development Goals (SDGs). *Bus. Strategy Environ.*, 31, 1, 194–217, 2022.
3. Mhlanga, D., Is blockchain technology helping the 4.0 digital economy, including finance, move towards sustainable development? *Blockchain Front.*, 6, 1035405, 2023.
4. Ayan, B., Güner, E., Son-Turan, S., Blockchain technology and connected devices enable sustainability and a closer look at a different business: integration. *Logistics*, 6, 4, 85, 2022.
5. Environment Agency, Blockchain technology and environmental sustainability, 2020, Retrieved from https://wedocs.unep.org/bitstream/handle/20.500.11822/34226/FB019.pdf?seq uence=1&isAllowed=y.
6. IPCC Sixth Assessment Report, Climate Change, 2021, Retrieved from https://www.statista.com/study/83335/ipcc-climate-change-sixth-assessment-report-2021/.
7. World Bank Group, Accelerating green growth: The role of business and investment climate policies in the private sector's construction environment, 2021, Retrieved from https://openknowledge.Worldbank. org/server/api/core/bitstreams/bac51860-0356-51e7-b026-9c11a80072fe/content.
8. OECD, Job creation and local economic development in 2023: Closing the green gap, 2023, Retrieved from https://www.oecd.org/greengrowth/job-creation-and-local-economic-development-26174979.htm.
9. Aayog, N., Blockchain: A Strategy for India, 2020, Retrieved from https://www.niti.gov.in/sites/default/files/2020-01/Blockchain_The_India_Strategy_ Part_I.pdf.
10. Ata, S.N., Hassan, A.K., Selim, H.S., Hammad, B.E., Abdelhalim, H.M., Abdelhalim, A.J., Application of blockchain technology and perspective on the financial functioning of Ministry of Sports resources. *Economy*, 11, 5, 140, 2023.
11. Chen, Y., Lu, Y., Bulysheva, L., Kataev, M. Y., Applications of blockchain in industry 4.0: A review. *Inf. Syst. Front.*, 1–15, 2022.
12. Gonzalez, C., II, Overview of international and European financial security institutions. *Bank Spain Papers*, 30, 21, 2021.
13. Levy, D.L. and Kolk, A., Effective responses to global climate change: The debate on oil diversification. *Bus. Econ.*, 4, 3, 275–300, 2002.
14. Thompson, B.S., Impacts of consensual biodiversity investments: Analysis of financial and environmental risks. *Bus. Strategy Environ.*, 32, 1, 353–368, 2023.

15. Strandberg, C., Best practices in sustainable finance, in: *Strandberg Debate*, 2005.
16. Chandler, C.S., Investor Relations from the CEO's Perspective. *Int. J. Strateg. Commun.*, 8, 3, 160–176, 2014.
17. Gann, G.D., McDonald, T., Walder, B., Aronson, J., Nelson, C.R., Jonson, J., Dixon, K., International guidelines and standards for ecological restoration practices. *Restor. Ecol.*, 27, S1, S1–S46, 2019.
18. Boffo, R. and Patalano, R., *ESG Investing: Implementation, Progress, and Challenges*, OECD, Paris, 2020.
19. Krambia-Kapardis, M., Stylianou, I., Savva, C. S., Ethical leadership as a prerequisite for sustainable development, sustainable finance, and ESG reporting, in: *Sustainable Finance and Financial Crime*, pp. 107–126, Cham: Springer International Publishing.
20. Dhaliwal, A. and Malik, S., Blockchain technology and adoption: Assessing security and privacy issues, in: *Blockchain for Business: How It Works and Creates Value*, pp. 231–249, 2021.
21. El Khoury, R., Nasrallah, N., Alareeni, B., ESG determinants in MENA banking: good or necessary? Competitiveness Review. *J. Int. Bus.*, 33, 1, 7–29, 2023.
22. Lenka, P. and Kar, S., The role of ethical leaders in corporate governance: An Aristotelian perspective on ethics. *Probl. Ekorozwoju*, 16, 1, 201–207, 2021, DOI: 10.35784/pe.2021.1.22.
23. Kumar, S., Sharma, D., Rao, S., Lim, W.M., Mangla, S.K., Past, present and future of financial sustainability: Insights from big data analytics through machine learning research. *Ann. Oper. Res.*, 1–44, 2022.
24. Ilnytskyy, D. and Stoliarchuk, Y., Greening the energy sector and the new characteristics of globalization. *Int. Econ. Policy*, 38, 7–38, 2023.
25. Cunha, F.A.F.D.S., Meira, E., Orsato, R.J., Sustainable Finance and Investment: Analysis and Research Methods. *Bus. Strategy Environ.*, 30, 8, 3821–3838, 2021.
26. Sheikh, M.R., Ali, M., Ahmad, R., Bashir, F., Does foreign direct investment in Pakistan promote sustainable development? ARDL Analysis. *iRASD J. Econ.*, 4, 4, 647–657, 2022.
27. Barber, B.M., Morse, A., Yasuda, A., Impact investing. *J. Financ. Econ.*, 139, 1, 162–185, 2021.
28. Bollazzi, F. and Risalvato, G., Social responsibility and ROA: Evidence from Borsa Italiana. *Asian Econ. Financ. Rev.*, 8, 4, 565–570, 2018.
29. Berrou, R., Dessertine, P., Migliorelli, M., Overview of green finance, in: *The rise of green finance in Europe: Opportunities and challenges for investors, traders and businesses*, pp. 3–29, 2019.
30. Greenfield, E., Sustainable financial markets, 2022, Retrieved from https://sigmaearth.com/sustainable-finance-market/.

31. Levin, A., How the Battle Against Cybercrime Strengthens Sustainable Finance, in: *Sustainable Finance and Financial Crime*, pp. 329–352, Cham: Springer International Publishing, 2023.
32. Zheng, Z., Xie, S., Dai, H., Chen, X., Wang, H., Blockchain technology overview: architecture, consensus and future generations, in: *2017 IEEE International Big Data conference*, pp. 557–564, IEEE, June 2017.
33. Gernego, I., Urvantseva, S., Sandulskyi, R., Green investment in permaculture. *Manage. Theory Stud. Rural Bus. Infrastruct. Dev.*, 44, 2, 185–194, 2022.
34. Mudaliar, A., Bass, R., Dithrich, H., 2018 Annual Investor Impact Survey, 2018, Retrieved from https://thegiin.org/research/publication/annualsurvey2018/.
35. Kaur, J., Kumar, S., Narkhede, B.E., Dabić, M., Rathore, A.P.S., Joshi, R., Challenges in Blockchain adoption in financial chain: The case of Indian SMEs. *Electron. Commer. Res.*, 1–38, 2022.
36. Chiu, J. and Koeppl, T., Incentive compatibility on the blockchain, pp. 323–335, Springer International Publishing, 2019.
37. Banga, J., Green Bond Markets: A source of financial security for developing countries. *J. Sustain. Financ. Inv.*, 9, 1, 17–32, 2019.
38. Chung, K., Data fusion, hedonic pricing and blockchain: reducing barriers to investment in sustainable business (Doctoral thesis), 2022, https://deepblue.lib.umich.edu/handle/2027.42/174388.
39. Tamayo-Orbegozo, U., Vicente-Molina, M.A., Villarreal-Larrinaga, O., A conceptual model of ecological innovation. Many studies from eco-innovative regions of Europe. *J. Clean. Prod.*, 142, 1347–1367, 2017.
40. Jonsdottir, B., Sigurjonsson, T.O., Johannsdottir, L., Wendt, S., Limiting the use of ESG data in investment decisions. *Sustainability*, 14, 9, 5157, 2022.
41. Javaid, M., Haleem, A., Singh, R.P., Suman, R., Khan, S., Review of blockchain technology in financial services, in: *Measurement, Standards and Evaluation Business Committee*, p. 100073, 2022.
42. Mohd, S. and Kaushal, V.K., Green finance: a step towards sustainable development. *MUDRA: J. Financ. Account.*, 5, 1, 59–74, 2018.
43. Kidney, S., Oliver, P., Sonerud, B., Climate Bonds Initiative. Chapter 10: Greening China's bond market, in: *Greening China's financial system*, M. Halle (Ed.), pp. 249–253, International Institute for Sustainable Development, 2015.
44. Satamraju, K.P., Proof of concept for integration of IoT and blockchain in healthcare. *Sensors*, 20, 5, 1389, 2020.
45. Kumari, A. and Devi, N.C., Investment Professionals Using Blockchain Technology: A Discrete TPB Model. *J. Financ. Rep. Acc.*, 21, 1, 45–59, 2023.

3

The Relationship Between FinTech and Financial Sustainability: Turkey Case

Seda Yıldırım[1]*, Tuğba Kantarcı[2], Durmuş Çağrı Yıldırım[1] and Kenan Aydın[2]

[1]*Tekirdag Namik Kemal University, Tekirdag, Turkey*
[2]*Istanbul Gelisim University, Istanbul, Turkey*

Abstract
The 21st century has proven that innovation and technology will change the world forever. Through the expansion of the usage areas of ICT (information and communication technologies), important developments have occurred in basic business areas such as finance, banking, marketing, and production. At this point, the financial technology (FinTech) phenomenon has come to the fore in terms of financial sustainability. FinTech is a phenomenon that emerged as a result of the application of technology in the field of finance. In other words, financial services and activities are offered together with technology. FinTech is vital for the digital age. The use of technology and innovation in the financial field has confronted countries with new competition. FinTech applications, especially for developing countries, will provide a significant advantage in the global market. This study aims to examine the FinTech applications in Turkey, a developing country, and to explore its relationship with financial sustainability. In the study, the case of Turkey will be discussed and it is planned to give a profile of the FinTech market in Turkey in the context of financial sustainability.

***Keywords*:** FinTech, financial sustainability, finance market

**Corresponding author*: sedayil1@gmail.com; ORCID: https://orcid.org/0000-0003-4367-6652
Tuğba Kantarcı: ORCID: https://orcid.org/0000-0002-2257-430X
Durmuş Çağrı Yıldırım: ORCID: https://orcid.org/ORCID: 0000-0003-4168-2792
Kenan Aydın: ORCID: https://orcid.org/0000-0002-0496-5665

Ernesto D.R. Santibanez Gonzalez, Vinay Kandpal, Peterson K. Ozili and Prasenjit Chatterjee (eds.) Fintech for ESG and the Circular Economy, (31–48) © 2024 Scrivener Publishing LLC

3.1 Introduction

The financial service sector can be seen as a rising sector in the past decades. However, it can be said that the financial services sector is an industry whose existence has always been needed when looking at the history of civilization. In the early days of civilization, the barter mechanism, which means exchanging goods in return for services provided, was widely used [1]. Because people have entered into a commercial life from the moment they started producing. As we approach today, the financial sector has grown significantly, and digital commerce has replaced physical commerce. The leading technological financial products create more efficient commercial relationships between sellers and buyers through digital payment tools such as credit cards or e-payments [2].

Financial markets around the world have been deeply affected by the Internet-Digital Revolution in the 90s. One of the most important effects is related to reducing the costs of financial transactions [3]. Recently, many new challenges have emerged in the traditional banking method. Therefore, the financial sector has undergone some significant changes in addition to the traditional methods used to provide financial activities and services. These changes have emerged as a direct result of the financial crisis and advances in technological innovations [4]. At this point, technological developments driven by the Internet revolution have significantly changed the framework of the financial services industry. It can be said that "e-finance" was introduced to the marketplace when considering all digital banking, insurance, and finance services [3].

The term financial technology (FinTech) essentially is based on a project initiated by Citigroup in the 90s. However, the sector got attention in 2014 with the rapid development of Internet and mobile technology. FinTech has recently been seen as a close collaboration between financial services and information technologies [5]. In 2008, major financial institutions defaulted on the demands of their funds due to insufficient capital and high leverage. This was soon followed by a chain of defaults from multiple entities that were part of the investment chain. This situation has led to the bankruptcy of many banks, central banks, and the financial services sector. The developments have brought about many financial initiatives that will change the ways of conducting financial business. In this context, it can be said that the term "FinTech" emerged to represent all of these companies as a group [1].

When considering the term FinTech, derived from the combination of the words "financial" and "technology", it is more clear that FinTech is the new financial world of the Digital Age. In recent years, the number of newly established FinTech companies and the number of consumers and businesses using the products of these companies has been increasing rapidly. During COVID-19, both consumers and businesses have significantly increased their usage of FinTech products [6]. Initiatives for the FinTech market in the world are the power of FinTech startups that will become more prominent in the future. For example; According to the numbers recorded in May 2023, 11,651 are in the Americas; there are 9,681 FinTech startups in the EMEA region and 5,061 in the Asia Pacific region. The force with the most integrated FinTech startups operating in the United States in 2023 [7].

With the increasing importance of financial sustainability, the FinTech phenomenon has also been on the rise. In the digital age, the financial sector is also integrated with technology. Therefore, in this study, FinTech indicators for Turkey will be examined based on the relationship between FinTech and financial sustainability. Using current reports, Internet sources, and statistics, a general profile will be drawn for FinTech in Turkey. It is thought that the study will benefit the literature by providing updated data. In the study, firstly, the FinTech and financial sustainability phenomena were examined in order to better understand the subject. Afterward, current indicators specific to the FinTech sector in Turkey are given. Thirdly, in line with the purpose of the study, comments were made for FinTech development and financial sustainability in Turkey.

3.2 The Framework for FinTech and Financial Sustainability

In this part, the framework for FinTech and financial sustainability is given below:

3.2.1 The FinTech

As seen in Figure 3.1, the FinTech concept can be expressed as an interdisciplinary subject combining "Finance, Technology Management, and Innovation Management". In particular, FinTech is known to propose technology solutions according to different business models. Therefore, FinTech covers all kinds of innovative ideas that improve financial service processes and can lead to new business models and new jobs [8]. The purpose of financial technology, called FinTech, is to provide new financial

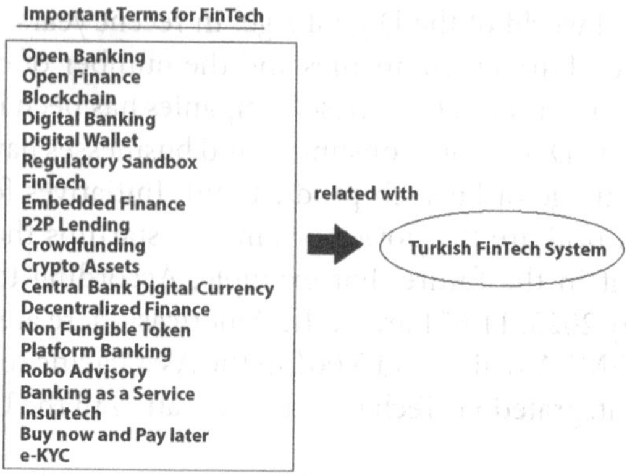

Figure 3.1 Important terms in FinTech. Source: Created by the authors based on data from the Presidency of the Republic of Türkiye Finance Office [25].

support or increase the value of existing services. In this way, transparency is achieved in the market and the best financial solutions can be offered to customers [9].

When the concept of FinTech is considered, most people only think of financial technologies. There is much more underlying the term in question. FinTech companies attract significant attention today, especially from companies that want to offer attractive offers to customers. This situation paves the way for creating a serious investment area [10]. FinTech as a sector refers to technological startups that offer a range of services, from mobile payment solutions to crowdfunding platforms, from online portfolio management to international money transfers. On the other hand, while doing these, it competes with traditional banking and financial market players. For this reason, FinTech companies attract the attention of financial service users, on the one hand, and investment firms, which see them as the future of the financial sector, on the other hand [5]. FinTech as a discipline is based on three basic concepts as given below [2]:

- **Data capture:** It refers to the process of collecting and storing data and information.
- **Data analysis**: It refers to developing methodologies.
- **Information collection and application:** It is expressed as the process that includes the use and application of data-based information.

FinTech can deepen financial inclusion by offering better and more qualified products and services [11]. FinTech is considered one of the most critical innovations in the financial industry. FinTech is developing rapidly under the influence of the sharing economy, favorable regulation, and information technology [12]. All these include messaging, transactions, order processing, and payment systems. It is integrated with [13]. FinTech products have minimal tangible components because they are developed on digital platforms. Therefore, FinTech products are based on technological advances in the management of information, telecommunications, and large data sets. For example, smartphones, which emerged with the special development of applications that enable payment tools and money transfers for mobile phones, have become an important element of the FinTech ecosystem. Mobile phones have helped significantly reduce the cost of financial services [14].

The most basic feature of FinTech companies is serving digital and mobile products and services related to the finance market. This is achieved through applications or digital, electronic platforms that facilitate communication with customers and meet their needs instantly with instant access services. The first distinguishing feature of FinTech development is shown as "digital predisposition". Digital aptitude radically changes the structure of the company-customer relationship. In general, technology allows for breaking down geographical boundaries and conducting cross-border business. It contributes to the faster and cheaper circulation and updating of information. On the other hand, it plays a role in changing relationships with customers and implementing financial transactions through technological applications and digital channels [15].

An important area of the digital transformation process accelerated by the COVID-19 pandemic is seen in the finance sector. E-finance has also left its mark on emerging fields such as e-government, e-health, and e-education. Digital transformation makes significant contributions to reshaping the market outcomes of the financial services sector. FinTech strengthens financial development, inclusion, and efficiency. In addition, FinTech contributes significantly to growth and poverty reduction by providing the financial services necessary for the development of the digital economy [16].

The development of FinTech is closely related to the development of enabling technologies. The development of FinTech consists of four periods: FinTech 1.0, FinTech 2.0, FinTech 3.0, and FinTech 3.5. In the FinTech 1.0 era, enabling technologies include the Trans-Atlantic transmission cable and mainframes. These technologies have made significant contributions to producing related financial technology products such as SWIFT and ATMs. In the FinTech 2.0 era, the Internet and the Internet of Things stand out among the relevant technologies. In the FinTech 3.0 era, more and more data technologies have been developed [8].

3.2.2 What is Financial Sustainability?

The phenomenon of sustainable development, the effort to achieve a sustainable society, especially the 2030 Sustainable Development Goals (2030 SDGs) and the Paris Agreement, is the priority agenda of this century [17]. The 2030 Sustainable Development Goals (2030 SDGs) are the main guide for countries in building a sustainable future by the United Nations (UN) in 2015. By determining 17 basic goals, the sustainable policies and strategies necessary to achieve these goals by 2030 have come to the agenda of the countries. Sustainable policies and strategies that consider the balance between economy, environment, and social welfare are important for societies in business, education, health, employment, energy, etc. (Yıldırım *et al.* [18]; Yildirim, [19]; Yıldırım and Yıldırım, [20]; Yıldırım and Kantarcı, [21]). At this point, financial sustainability has become mandatory for businesses to maintain this balance. Today, sustainable finance is thought of more as "finance for sustainability". However, this represents a significant deviation from its original meaning. In this regard, it is important to define possible sustainability dimensions. Protecting the environment and ecosystems, preserving biodiversity, combating climate change, and eliminating poverty and hunger constitute the first part of the sustainability dimension. The second dimension is based on the assessment of each economic sector or activity's achievement of at least one of the relevant sustainability dimensions or its contribution to the improvement of these dimensions [17]. Financial sustainability ensures that the financial system can sustainably finance long-term growth. Therefore, it is to contribute to the creation of an economy with low CO2 emissions and resistance to climate change. All of this requires reforms that support investments in clean technologies and their use [22]. The importance of financial sustainability is most evident in situations of financial instability. Financial instability results in many negative events, from bank liquidations to hyperinflation or stock market crashes. In this context, financial stability plays an important role in assessing risks to the healthy functioning of the financial system [23].

Financial sustainability means "better development" and "better financing", which must be sustainable in each of its economic, social, and environmental elements. Sustainable finance is a comprehensive approach that brings together various perspectives to improve the social, economic, and environmental performance of the financial system. Broadly speaking, sustainable finance refers to a financial system that supports sustainable economic development rather than growth. Achieving these goals requires a clear perspective that can be understood, applied, and measured in practice [22].

Banks, which are one of the important actors in the financial sector, examine which sectors and projects are suitable for lending and whether they are suitable for lending in line with their lending strategies. Similarly, investment funds can determine which assets to invest in or not by determining their investment strategies [24].

3.3 The Profile of FinTech in Turkey

Turkey has taken important steps toward financial sustainability in recent years. The first of these steps is the establishment of the Turkish Presidency Finance Office. The Turkish Presidency Finance Office has created a guide for FinTech management, defined important concepts, and continues to develop the necessary legal regulations. At this point, it can be said that versatile infrastructure support and information support are provided for FinTech development in Turkey.

According to the Finance Office of Presidency, important concepts that need to be defined and known within the scope of the FinTech Presidency of the Republic of Türkiye Finance Office [25] are shown in Figure 3.1.

The FinTech sector in Turkey has its own ecosystem. Over the past 3 years, the FinTech sector has made great progress in Turkey. For this progress to support financial sustainability, government and official organizations have prepared guides for the FinTech sector as seen in Figure 3.2. It is thought that this guide will be a guide for the parties in the FinTech sector in Turkey [26]. According to the "Turkey FinTech Outlook Study", the share of global investments in the FinTech sector exceeded US$91 billion with an increase of 82% in 2021. FinTech companies, which operate in a total of 12 areas, including payments, blockchain, banking, insurance, and corporate finance, have accelerated their development as a result of the quality analytical data service trend in the markets [27].

According to a report prepared by T.C. Cumhurbaşkanlığı Finans Ofisi [28], the below statements can be said for FinTech in Turkey:

- While there were 6 acceleration programs in Turkey in 2010; in 2020, the number reached 65 acceleration programs, and in the first half of 2021, the number of acceleration programs increased to 69.

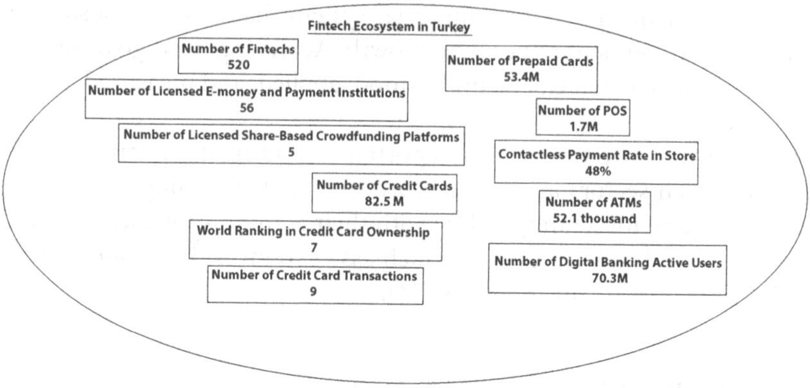

Figure 3.2 The FinTech ecosystem in Turkey. Source: The figure is created by the authors based on data from Türkiye Cumhuriyeti Cumhurbaşkanlığı Finans Ofisi [28].

- With the growth in the entrepreneurial ecosystem and the resulting demand, the number of incubation centers in Turkey has reached 82 in the past 10 years.
- In June 2021, the number of co-working spaces is 38.
- While the number of active technoparks was 27 in 2010 and this number increased to 68 in 2021, there are currently 16 technoparks under construction.
- The state-supported angel investor accreditation program, which started in 2013, reached 674 by September 2021, providing tax advantages to active angel investors.
- Angel investor networks have become very popular in Turkey recently. Accredited angel investor networks, the number of which has reached nine as of November 2021, are ARYA, EGİAD, Erban, Galata Business Angels, GAP BAN, Keiretsu Forum, Mavi Ocean, Company Partnership, and TR Angels.

With the help of updated legislation and increasing investors, it is envisaged that a new era will begin in Turkey where many players will enter this field. Players in Turkey who are likely to apply for this license and turn their routes in this direction can be examined under five groups [6]:

- FinTech founded by independent entrepreneurs,
- FinTech units of traditional banks,
- FinTech units of telecom operators,
- FinTech initiatives of e-commerce and retail players,
- Existing foreign new generation digital banks.

A company in the FinTech industry is a technology company that focuses on providing financial services using digital technologies. Companies operate in many areas such as payment processing, investment, credit evaluation, asset management, insurance, and other financial services. They use digital technologies to enable faster, safer, and more cost-effective delivery of financial services. They undertake to reflect the power of modern technology to institutions or organizations that carry out their operations with traditional technologies. FinTech Companies in Turkey include organizations that design applications that will improve payment methods such as Papara and MenaPay. The ease of payment methods in Turkey is a system that is very popular among users [29].

In the digital transformation process in the financial sector, the primary function is payment services that serve as fund transfers between economic units. Payment services play a supporting role in increasing economic activities. On the other hand, it makes significant contributions to the growth of the economy, the stabilization of the financial system, the smooth continuation of trade, and the effective functioning of goods and services markets. In this context, this transformation, which is described as financial technologies and manifests itself in the financial sector in general and payment services in particular, requires policymakers and regulatory authorities of the sector to take various measures. It also emphasizes that competition authorities take various initiatives [30]. Accordingly, it is important to which activity businesses in the Fintech sector serve. So, it can help in better analysis of businesses growing in the Fintech market. As shown in Table 3.1, some important Fintech companies from Turkey can be summarized below:

The following developments are seen in the 2022 Turkey Fintech Ecosystem Status Report prepared by the Presidency of the Republic of Turkey Finance Office: [31] "digital banking regulation, open banking, The development of FAST system and Istanbul Financial Center Law was launched and also Digital Turkish Lira was used in a first time."

The pandemic period has led to a trend parallel to the global trend for the FinTech sector in Turkey. The FinTech ecosystem in Turkey continues to grow with the strong support of the banking system. The "contactless transaction" trend, which strengthened during the pandemic period, supported the need to quickly implement new technologies. At this point, a unique market infrastructure has emerged for FinTech start-ups to grow. In 2020, Turkey reached 139 million funds and ranked by third among Middle Eastern countries [32].

Table 3.1 Some important FinTech companies in Turkey.

Company's name*	Function
PayCore	Payment service (Paycore website, n.d.)
Papara	Payment service; it operates as an "Electronic Money Institution" (Papara website, n.d.).
Tarfin	Financial services for farmers (Tarfin website, n.d.)
Parasut	Payment services and financial services for small and medium-sized businesses (Parasut website, n.d.).
Figopara	Provides a digital platform to resolve cash flow mismatch (Figopara website, n.d.).
Ininal	Payment services both for individuals and corporations (Ininal website, n.d.).
Paym.es	Online payment services via social media (Paymes website, n.d.).
KolayBi	Financial services to small and medium-sized businesses (KolayBi website, n.d.).
DigiliraPay	Transactions are made on crypto money. (DigiliraPPay website, n.d.).
manibux	Mobile app and prepaid card for kidsEdu-Fintech (Manibu website, n.d.).
Kassa	Joint with QNB Finansbank, financial transactions, mobile application (Kassa website, n.d.). https://www.kassa.co/
Payfull	Online collection via virtual POS you obtain from banks and payment institutions (Payfull website, n.d.).
Tekkredi	Collects credits in one place (Tekkredi website, n.d.).
Moneymo	Mobile shopping platform via all bank applications and e-wallets (Moneymo website, n.d.).
StockGround	Financial analysis software solutions (StockGround website, n.d.).

(*Continued*)

Table 3.1 Some important FinTech companies in Turkey. (*Continued*)

Company's name*	Function
Pospratik	Online collection service, (Pospratik website, n.d.).
Finmaks	Smart Finance App (Finmaks website, n.d.).
Resardis	Cryptocurrency management and trading (Resardis website, n.d.).
Arya	Finance management service (Arya website, n.d.).
Kobakus	Produces open banking projects, (Kobakus website, n.d.).
Manim	Management of transactions in different banks (Manim website, n.d.).
DGI Works	Digital banking products (DGI Works website, n.d.).
ComPay	Payment service (ComPay website, n.d.).
Bitlo	Cryptocurrency exchange (Bitlo website, n.d.).
Moka	POS Service and products (Moka website, n.d.)
Param	Payment service (Param website, n.d).
United Payment	Payment service United (Payment website, n.d.).
HASO	Payment service (Haso website, n.d.).
Masraff	Expense management services, mobile applications, (Masraff website, n.d.).
CryptoIndexSeries	Crypto market analysis, information, and data service (CryptoIndexSeries website, n.d.).
Architecht	Kuveyt Turk Participation Bank's 100% subsidiary information and payment services (Architecht website, n.d.).
weepay	Payment service, (Weepay website, n.d.).
Sigortam.net	Provides the best insurance offers to its customers when needed (Sigortam.net website, n.d.).
Startsub.com	Software company https://www.startsub.com/hakkimizda

(*Continued*)

Table 3.1 Some important FinTech companies in Turkey. (*Continued*)

Company's name*	Function
Bigpara	Provides information about investment instruments markets (Bipara website, n.d.).
PayPoint	Payment service 7/24 (PayPoint website, n.d.).

*The company's name is based on FinTech.Coffee, (n.d.).
Source: The table is created by the authors.

3.4 Conclusion

The emerging literature in the field of FinTech and sustainable finance consists of studies that examined the advancement of sustainable finance through FinTech [33]. For example, Cen and He [34] argued that Fintech supports sustainable development in many aspects. In particular, the focus is on the benefits of Fintech, such as providing green financing, reducing cost and information asymmetry, increasing efficiency, valuing nature's assets, and enabling practical sustainable lifestyles. In other words, it has been suggested that FinTech provides an important solution for sustainable finance. Arner *et al.* [35] argued that FinTech has a significant potential to transform not only finance but also economies through financial inclusion and sustainable balanced development. Puschmann *et al.* [36] the review on "green FinTech" was discussed within the scope of Switzerland and they concluded that a special focus should be made on the aspects of green FinTech that were mostly not mentioned. Macchiavello and Siri [37] drew attention to the issue of rethinking traditionally applied models in the relationship between sustainability, finance, and technology. Especially during the COVID-19 pandemic crisis, steps that lead to greater reliance on technology and sustainability have been shown to be important. On the other hand, the study emphasized the importance of relevant legal issues that need to be addressed in order for FinTech to fulfill its promises and potential in the sustainable finance sector. In the study conducted by Vergara and Agudo [38], it was determined that sustainable finance and Fintech have many common aspects. Bayram *et al.* [33] emphasized that Turkey plays an important role in promoting sustainable finance through FinTech solutions for emerging market economies.

The necessity of digital transformation for financial sustainability is indisputable. At this point, developments in the use of digital technology and digital tools and equipment have also changed the form of financial transactions and services. Applications and platforms that can perform digital financial transactions have created the FinTech sector, as physical mobility decreases or is not preferred and faster financial transactions are carried out. The cryptocurrency market, which has gained momentum during the COVID-19 pandemic, has become a trend with contactless payment opportunities, virtual shopping, etc. Digital financial and banking activities have encouraged individuals and institutions to conduct transactions through more mobile applications and digital platforms. The rising FinTech market attracts many innovative entrepreneurs. Turkey's FinTech market seems to have a bright future and is conducive to positive growth. Turkey is taking the necessary initiatives to have a global say in the FinTech field. The Finance Office of the President of the Republic of Turkey proves the importance Turkey attaches to FinTech and financial sustainability. It can be said that the FinTech market in Turkey is a developing market. Especially in the past 6 years, there has been an increase in the number of entrepreneurs entering the FinTech market. For example, 90 FinTech startups were established in 2018 and 24 FinTech startups were established in 2022. It was observed that a total of 739 FinTech startups were established in Turkey by February 2023 [39]. As a result, the development of the FinTech market also enables the development of new enterprises and digital goods and services, encouraging financial development and creating a new area for economic growth.

References

1. Arjunwadkar, P.Y., FinTech: The technology driving disruption in the financial services industry, CRC press, New York, 2018, https://doi.org/10.1201/9781351036504.
2. Gupta, P. and Tham, M., *Fintech: the new DNA of financial services*, DeG Press, London, 2019.
3. Lee, I. and Shin, Y.J., Fintech: Ecosystem, business models, investment decisions, and challenges. *Bus. Horiz.*, *61*, 1, 35–46, 2018, https://doi.org/10.1016/j.bushor.2017.09.003.
4. Temelkov, Z., Fintech firms opportunity or threat for banks? *Int. J. Inf. Bus. Manage.*, *10*, 1, 137–143, 2018.
5. Anyfantaki, S., The evolution of financial technology (Fintech), in: *SSRN Bank of Greece Economic Bulletin*, pp. 47–62, 2016.
6. EY, *Dünyada ve Türkiye'de FinTech*, 2022, https://www.ey.com/tr_tr/ey-turkiye-yayinlar-raporlar/dunya-ve-turkiye-fin-tech-pazari-yeni-nesil-dijitalbankalar-in-gelecegi.

7. Statista Research Department, Number of fintech startups worldwide 2018-2023, by region, 2023, https://www.statista.com/statistics/893954/numberfintech-startups-by-region/.
8. Leong, K. and Sung, A., FinTech (Financial Technology): What is it and how to use technologies to create business value in fintech way? *Int. J. Innov. Manage. Technol.* 9, 2, 74–78, 2018, http://www.ijimt.org/index.php?m=content&c=index&a=show&catid=93&id=1138.
9. Arume, C. and Gregorio, M., Fintech and Entrepreneurial Finance: what's coming next?, 2017. Universitat Jaume l, Degree in Finance and Accounting, Academic year 2016/17, Supervised by Amparo Soler Dominguez, 1-34. https://repositori.uji.es/xmlui/bitstream/handle/10234/170463/TFG__2017_MariscalGregorio_CristinaArume.pdf?sequence=1&isAllowed=y.
10. Fintech İstanbul, *Dünyada ve Türkiye"de Açık Bankacılık: Bankacılığın Geleceği*, 2019, https://bkm.com.tr/wpcontent/uploads/2015/06/Dunyadaveturkiyedeacikbankacilik.pdf.
11. Zeidy, I.A., *The Role of Financial Technology (FINTECH) in Changing Financial Industry and Increasing Efficiency in the Economy*, 2021, https://www.comesa.int/wp-content/uploads/2022/05/The-Role-of-Financial-Technology.pdf.
12. Moro-Visconti, R., *MicroFinTech: expanding financial inclusion with cost-cutting innovation*, Springer Nature, Switzerland, 2021.
13. Freedman, R.S., *Introduction to financial technology*, Academic Press, New York, 2006.
14. Reyes-Mercado, P., *FinTech Strategy: Linking Entrepreneurship, Finance, and Technology*, Springer Nature, Switzerland, 2021.
15. Tanda, A. and Schena, C.M., *FinTech, BigTech and banks: Digitalisation and its impact on banking business models*, Springer, Switzerland, 2019.
16. Feyen, E., Natarajan, H., Saal, M., *Fintech and the Future of Finance : Market and Policy Implications (English).* Washington, D.C. : World Bank Group, Washington DC. http://documents.worldbank.org/curated/en/099450005162250110/P17300600228b70070914b0b5edf26e2f9f.
17. Migliorelli, M., What do we mean by sustainable finance? Assessing existing frameworks and policy risks. *Sustainability, 13*, 2, 975, 2021, https://doi.org/10.3390/su13020975.
18. Yıldırım, S., Yıldırım, D.Ç., Gedikli, A., Sustainable Consumption Trends in the World in the Context of Green Economy and Sustainability, in: *Handbook of Research on Green Economic Development Initiatives and Strategies*, M.M. Erdoğdu, T. Arun, I.H. Ahmad (Eds.), pp. 66-84, IGI Global, Hershey, PA, 2016.
19. Yildirim, S., The consumer role for sustainable development: how consumers contribute sustainable development goals, in: *Anthropological Approaches to Understanding Consumption Patterns and Consumer Behavior*, V. Chkoniya, A.O. Madsen, P. Bukhrashvili, (Eds.), pp. 325–341, IGI Global, Hershey, PA, 2020.

20. Yıldırım, S. and Yıldırım, D.Ç., Achieving Sustainable Development Through a Green Economy Approach, in: *Advanced Integrated Approaches to Environmental Economics and Policy: Emerging Research and Opportunities*, S. Patti and G. Trizzino (Eds.), pp. 1–22, IGI Global, Hershey, PA, 2020.
21. Yıldırım, S. and Kantarcı, T., A Review on Sustainability Policies of Businesses: Recycling and Waste Reduction. *J. Recycl. Econ. Sustain. Policy*, 1, 1, 1–9, 2022.
22. Ţîrcă, Apetri, A.N., Aceleanu, M.I., Sustainability in Finance and Economics, in: *Financing Sustainable Development: Key Challenges and Prospects*, Ziolo, M. and Sergi, B.S. (Eds.), pp. 9–52, 2019.
23. Flejterski, S., Sustainable Financial Systems, in: *Financing Sustainable Development: Key Challenges and Prospects*, Ziolo, M. and Sergi, B.S. (Eds.), pp. 267–297, 2019.
24. Schoenmaker, D. and Schramade, W., Financing environmental and energy transitions for regions and cities: creating local solutions for global challenges, in: *Paper for an OECD/EC Workshop on financing environmental and energy transitions*, 2019.
25. Presidency of the Republic of Türkiye Finance Office, Finance Glossary, https://www.cbfo.gov.tr/en/finance-glossary.
26. Aşan, G., *Türkiye Fintek Rehberi*, https://www.cbfo.gov.tr/turkiye-fintekrehberi-web.
27. NTV, *Fintech şirketleri büyüme trendini sürdürüyor*, 2022, https://www.ntv.com.tr/ekonomi/fintech-sirketleribuyume-trendini-surduruyor,ByPkuCO-Qtki1Gk6yn0pZIg.
28. T.C. Cumhurbaşkanlığı Finans Ofisi, *Türkiye Fintek Ekosistem Durum Raporu* 2021, https://www.cbfo.gov.tr/sites/default/files/docs/2023-03/turkiye-fintek-ekosistemi-durum-raporu-2021-compressed.pdf.
29. Oniki, *FinTech Nedir? – Türkiye'deki FinTech Şirketleri*, 20232023, https://oniki.net/fintech-nedir/.
30. Kurulu, R., *Ödeme Hizmetlerindeki Finansal Teknolojilere Yönelik İnceleme Raporu*, 2021, https://www.rekabet.gov.tr/Dosya/sektor-raporlari/odeme-hizmetlerindeki-finansal-teknolojilere-yonelik-inceleme-raporu-20211209145616284-pdf.
31. Türkiye Cumhuriyeti Cumhurbaşkanlığı Finans Ofisi, *Türkiye Fintek Ekosistemi Durum Raporu*, 2023, https://www.cbfo.gov.tr/sites/default/files/docs/2023-03/fintek-durum-raporu-2022_v0.9_digital_lowsize_ayri-sayfalar-compressed.pdf.
32. Cantürk, S., 2021 *Fintech Sektörü Genel Görünümü*, 2021, https://fintech-time.com/2021/09/2021-fintech-sektoru-genel-gorunumu/.
33. Bayram, O., Talay, I., Feridun, M., Can FinTech promote sustainable finance? Policy lessons from the case of Turkey. *Sustainability*, 14, 19, 12414, 2022, https://doi.org/10.3390/su141912414.
34. Cen, T. and He, R., Fintech, green finance and sustainable development, in: *2018 International Conference on Management, Economics, Education, Arts and Humanities (MEEAH 2018)*, Atlantis Press, pp. 222–225, 2018.

35. Arner, D.W., Buckley, R.P., Zetzsche, D.A., Veidt, R., Sustainability, FinTech and financial inclusion. *Eur. Bus. Organ. Law Rev.*, 21, 7–35, 2020, https://doi.org/10.1007/s40804-020-00183-y.
36. Puschmann, T., Hoffmann, C.H., Khmarskyi, V., How green FinTech can alleviate the impact of climate change—the case of Switzerland. *Sustainability*, *12*, 24, 10691, 2020.
37. Macchiavello, E. and Siri, M., Sustainable finance and Fintech: Can technology contribute to achieving environmental goals, A Preliminary Assessment of 'Green FinTech' Sustainable Digital Finance. *SSRN Electron. J.*, 10, 1–36, 2020, https://doi.org/10.1515/ecfr-2022-0005.
38. Vergara, C. and Agudo, F.L., Fintech and sustainability: do they affect each other?,. *Sustainability*, 13, 13, 7012, 2021, https://doi.org/10.3390/su13137012.
39. Presidency of the Republic of Türkiye Finance Office, *Türkiye FinTech Guide*, 2023, https://www.cbfo.gov.tr/sites/default/files/docs/2023-03/turkiye-fintech-guide.pdf.

Websites

Architecht website, (n.d.). https://www.architecht.com/hakkimizda/
Arya website, (n.d.). https://aryafinance.com/about.php
Bipara website, (n.d.). https://www.google.com/search?q=bigpara&oq=bigpara&aqs=chrome.69i57j0i131i433i512j0i512j0i131i433i512l2j0i512j0i3j5.2044j0j4&sourceid=chrome&ie=UTF-8
Bitlo website, (n.d.). https://www.bitlo.com/biz-kimiz
ComPay website, (n.d.). https://www.compay.com.tr/
CryptoIndexSeries website, (n.d.). https://cryptoindexseries.com/en/about/
DigiliraPPay website, (n.d.). https://www.digilirapay.com/about-us
DGI Works website, (n.d.). https://www.dgiworks.com/hakkimizda/
Figopara website, (n.d.). https://figopara.com/hakkimizda
Finmaks website, (n.d.). https://www.finmaks.com/
FinTech.Coffee, (n.d.). *61 Turkey Based Fintech Companies, The Most Innovative Fintech Companies*, https://www.fintech.coffee/research/61-turkey.
Haso website, (n.d.). https://www.haso.com.tr/
Ininal website, (n.d.). https://www.ininal.com/hakkimizda
Kassa website, (n.d.). https://www.kassa.co/
Kobakus website, (n.d.). https://kobakus.com/hakkimizda/
KolayBi website, (n.d.). https://www.kolaybi.com/hakkimizda
Manibux website, (n.d.). https://manibux.com/hakkimizda/
Manim website, (n.d.). https://manim.me/
Masraff website, (n.d.). https://www.masraff.co/?utm_term=masraff&utm_campaign=%2ABranding%20-%20Masraff&utm_source=adwords&utm_medium=ppc&hsa_acc=5010362138&hsa_cam=12618680298&hsa_grp=118731010694&hsa_ad=509564654296&hsa_src=g&hsa_tgt=k

wd-306068341177&hsa_kw=masraff&hsa_mt=e&hsa_net=adwords&hsa_ver=3&gclid=Cj0KCQjw06-oBhC6ARIsAGuzdw0eDAxEmFC0K_mhmwk0PXsAja8K_oefar8S2CHmoUu2XN2Vg1eEhSkaAhcqEALw_wcB
Moka website, (n.d.). https://mokapos.moka.com/?gad=1&gclid=Cj0KCQjw06-oBhC6ARIsAGuzdw05Te2TdrNGh_fGiT0eT6KuMh2hv-tOhMnPlUzbqUM8QANz7c5iuzQaAlkaEALw_wcB
Moneymo website, (n.d.). https://www.moneymo.com/
Papara website, (n.d.). https://www.papara.com/about-us
Param website, (n.d.). https://param.com.tr/hakkimizda
Parasut website, (n.d.). https://www.parasut.com/hakkimizda
Paycore website, (n.d.) https://paycore.com/tr/
Payfull website, (n.d.). https://www.payfull.com/
Payment website, (n.d.). https://unitedpayment.com/tr
Paymes website, (n.d.). https://paymes.com/tr/?campaignid=20116540288&adgroupid=149339917895&adid=658054617519&utm_term=paym.es&utm_campaign=&utm_source=adwords&utm_medium=ppc&hsa_acc=6586644805&hsa_cam=20116540288&hsa_grp=149339917895&hsa_ad=658054617519&hsa_src=g&hsa_tgt=kwd-1231280017665&hsa_kw=paym.es&hsa_mt=p&hsa_net=adwords&hsa_ver=3&gclid=Cj0KCQjw06-oBhC6ARIsAGuzdw3l9oNaehOYNa-l8CM1YZ16JGnop5g8pblz83f8y9Wr4AQVdVtNsrUaAte4EALw_wcB#about
PayPoint website, (n.d.). https://www.paypoint.com.tr/
Pospratik website, (n.d.). https://www.pospratik.com/e-tahsilat/online-tahsilat-sistemi-hakkinda/
Resardis website, (n.d.). https://resardis.com/
Sigortam.net website, (n.d.). https://www.sigortam.net/hakkimizda
StockGround website, (n.d.). https://www.stockground.com/
Tarfin website, (n.d.) https://tarfin.com/hakkimizda
Tekkredi website, (n.d.). http://www.tekkredi.com/
Weepay website, (n.d.). https://weepay.co/

4

Leveraging FinTech for the Advancement of Circular Economy

Radha Agarwal, Mariam Fatima and Amit Malhotra*

School of Commerce, Finance and Accountancy, CHRIST (Deemed to be University), Ghaziabad, Uttar Pradesh, India

Abstract

During the past six decades, there has been a lot of emphasis on increasing production and fulfilling the demands of the fast-growing population. As a result, there has been unprecedented utilization and depletion of natural resources and harm to the environment. It was rightly realized by government and policymakers that there is an indispensable need to align economic development with the environment. In other words, the world needs to pursue environmentally friendly economic development. In order to achieve sustainable development, the thought leaders devised a new approach called circular economy. The circular economy focuses on reusing and recycling materials to reduce the consumption of natural resources and minimize waste creation. In recent years, financial technology commonly known as FinTech has become a significant part of commercial activities across many industries. FinTech has benefited organizations and users in terms of cost and time saving with a high degree of reliability. This article outlines the ways in which FinTech supports the cause of a circular economy. It also explores the impediments in this path.

***Keywords*:** Sustainable development, circular economy, FinTech, FinTech in circular economy, challenges related to FinTech

**Corresponding author*: amit.malhotra@christuniversity.in

Ernesto D.R. Santibanez Gonzalez, Vinay Kandpal, Peterson K. Ozili and Prasenjit Chatterjee (eds.) Fintech for ESG and the Circular Economy, (49–62) © 2024 Scrivener Publishing LLC

4.1 Introduction

In the current scenario, we manufacture something, advertise it, consume it, dispose of it, and recycle it. However, most raw materials do not return to the economic cycle such as plastic, takeaway coffee cups, disposable nappies, polystyrene (foam), syringes or medical waste, and bubble wrap and can no longer be used after a few recycling cycles. As a consequence, resources are being wasted or are permanently lost.

Nations are trying to secure a sustainable future because of environmental damage and the ill effects they face in the present. Likewise, economies face pressure from environmental legislation, activists, regulators, and consumers to make their operations sustainable through improved resource utilization. Therefore, there is a requirement to move from a linear to a circular economy. To facilitate the growth of circular business models is required to bring about structural and technological changes. This includes introducing innovative methods for designing and manufacturing products and services, reducing agricultural inputs, minimizing food waste, and implementing digital technologies to increase the transparency and sustainability of supply chains [1].

Economies are adopting the technology to curb the negative impacts of business activities on the environment and also derive advantages for the organizations and customers. In today's 21st century, technology is a necessary part of human life to make an easy and smooth lifestyle [2]. Technology helps businesses gather data, process, and organize business performance and economic development indicators and does not return to the economic cycle.

In the area of technology, FinTech is an emerging idea. Projections suggest that by 2030, sustainable business models could generate economic opportunities worth US$12 trillion per year and create roughly 400 million jobs. These employment prospects are expected to benefit developing nations the most [3].

4.1.1 Knowing FinTech

The term FinTech is an abbreviation of financial technology. Broadly, it refers to technology-enabled financial services. FinTech combines financial services and information technology to make transactions faster, easier, and more secure. FinTech blends financial services with information technology with a motive to facilitate faster, easier, and more secure transactions. It comprises specialized software and algorithms that are used on computers and smartphones, and it is used by companies, business owners, and consumers to manage their financial operations.

The term "FinTech" originated from the technology used in the backend systems of financial organizations, especially banks. Its usage has been on the rise since early 2015 [4]. Although as a concept and practice, FinTech has evolved over a long period of time. FinTech 1.0 was about infrastructure. It started with technologies like telegraphs, railroads, and steamships that allowed for the first quick transmission of financial information across borders. A significant event occurred when Diner's Club introduced the world's first credit card in 1950, this was taken further with the launching of credit cards by American Express.

FinTech 2.0 brought technology into banking in a major way. In this era, the world's first ATM (automatic teller machine) was installed by Barclays Bank. Another major development was the inauguration of the world's first digital stock exchange—NASDAQ—which later changed how the financial markets operate all over the world. The Society for Worldwide Interbank Financial Telecommunications (SWIFT) was founded in 1973 and remains the primary communication channel for financial institutions to handle cross-border payments. This system is widely used because it manages large transaction volumes.

FinTech 3.0 is primarily centered around startups. This era witnessed the evolution of new technologies and players, especially FinTech startups. The advent of Bitcoin in 2009 also significantly impacted the financial world which was followed by a boom of different cryptocurrencies. The launch of smartphones and easy Internet access also played a vital role in this scenario as by using smartphones, people could use different financial services within the comfort of their homes. In this context, Google Wallet was introduced in 2011, followed by Apple Pay in 2014. FinTech 4.0 involved the application of disruptive technologies. During this phase, Neobanks appeared on the scene, which provided digital, mobile-first financial solutions for payments, money transfers, lending, and more. They allow customers to make deposits and withdraw money. FinTech companies have a crucial role in digitally transferring value to various locations [5]. With the introduction of UPI, Indian FinTechs have taken rapid strides in the payments space in recent years [6] as they have reduced the need to carry physical currency. Countries such as China have demonstrated that progress in FinTech innovation positively impacts green credit, investment, and any sectors that encourage the growth of environmentally friendly practices [7]. FinTechs are quickly reshaping the financial industry by cutting costs, improving the quality of financial services, and creating a financial landscape that is diverse and stable.

4.1.2 Knowing Circular Economy

The current economic model, which is termed the linear economy, works on the principle of "take, make, and dispose of." In a linear economy, the traditional method is followed, where raw materials are accumulated and converted into goods that consumers utilize until disposing of them as waste. The pursuit of profit comes at the expense of sustainability, thereby producing goods designed to be disposed of after use.

In response to the growing concern regarding climate change, deforestation, ozone depletion, overpopulation, and various forms of pollution, including air, water, and land pollution, the circular economy model was conceptualized.

A circular economy can be described as a sustainable model of production and consumption in which the resources are kept in the production cycle for as long as possible and can be used repeatedly to generate much less waste. The life cycle of products is prolonged in this way. The circular economy aims to achieve better management of natural resources with economic development. The approach involves closing cycles with waste and resource reuse, reducing the speed of material cycles, and developing reusable and durable products. It uses a holistic approach to preserve a continual flow of resources by adding, maintaining, and renewing their value, thus contributing to long-term growth.

The idea of a circular economy is based on three fundamental principles:

1. Preserve and enhance natural capital by controlling finite resources and balancing the flow of renewable resources. This approach ensures we do not exhaust non-renewable resources like fossil fuels or rare minerals like gold and silver faster than they can naturally regenerate. It also implies conserving ecosystems, biodiversity, and clean air and water. We can create a more sustainable future by balancing exploitation and renewing resources. This involves appropriate land use, reforestation, and promoting clean energy sources to reduce our ecological footprint on the environment.
2. Optimize the output from resources by circulating products, components, and materials in use at the highest possible levels at all times. This approach minimizes waste, which results in less impact on the environment. The products are designed considering that they are easy to disassemble and durable, which components efficient for reuse and recycling. The materials recovered from these products are utilized in

new products, reducing the requirement for new raw materials. We can minimize waste and environmental damage, conserve energy and raw materials, and ultimately promote sustainability and economic efficiency by optimizing the use of resources.

3. Make the system more effective by minimizing the negative effects of economic activities on the environment, society, and public health. It is important to identify and diminish these adverse impacts to make the circular economy more effective and efficient. Strict regulations, sustainable product design, and responsible consumption practices can help to achieve this. This helps preserve natural resources and reduces the overall environmental and social costs associated with the linear economy, ultimately making the circular economy a more environmentally sound and economically viable model.

The idea of a circular economy has gained wide acceptance as many financial institutions and investors have acknowledged the circular economy as a constructive framework to tackle environmental and economic issues together [8]. There are tangible benefits of adopting a circular economy, for instance, it is reckoned that India may save US$624 billion by 2050 by following the path of circular economy [9]. Surat is a great example of how a circular economy model can thrive in a town where water is sold for revenue [10]. The city has generated funds of INR 140 Cr. by selling 115 MLD of water that has been recycled from wastewater. Indian government uses plastic waste for road construction, and around 703 km of highways have been constructed using plastic waste [11]. Indian companies have attracted investments totaling US$1.8 billion in various sectors in the circular economy ecosystem over the past 5 years. Individuals who follow a circular system will pay less for services than those who have adhered to the standard use-and-discard approach.

4.2 The Circular Economy - FinTech Linkage

FinTech and the circular economy are two distinct but increasingly interconnected areas that have the potential to drive positive change in the way we manage resources and finances. FinTech can be integrated into various aspects of the circular economy, from financing and supply chain management to incentivizing sustainable behaviors and ensuring transparency and traceability. The combination of financial technology and circular economy principles can potentially drive positive environmental and economic change. The relationship is highlighted below:

1. FinTech initiatives funding for the circular economy, including crowdfunding and peer-to-peer lending, provide alternative funding sources for circular economy initiatives. Startups and businesses focused on sustainable and circular practices use FinTech platforms to access capital, allowing them to develop and scale their circular economy projects.
2. Sustainable Investment: FinTech has facilitated the rise of sustainable and impact investing. Investors use FinTech tools to identify and invest in companies that align with circular economy principles, encouraging businesses to adopt more sustainable practices.
3. Supply Chain Financing: FinTech solutions improve transparency and efficiency in supply chains, which is crucial for tracking and managing the flow of resources in a circular economy. Digital platforms provide supply chain financing options, ensuring that materials and products are efficiently reused, remanufactured, or recycled.
4. Blockchain Technology: Blockchain, often utilized in FinTech applications, enhances transparency and traceability in supply chains. This is essential in ensuring the authenticity and quality of recycled materials in a circular economy. Blockchain also supports the creation of digital tokens for recyclable materials, making tracking and trading them easier.
5. Digital Payments and Transactions: FinTech has streamlined payment processes and made transactions more efficient. In a circular economy, these digital payment solutions can be used for various purposes, including incentivizing recycling, rewarding sustainable behaviors, and facilitating the exchange of used goods.
6. Data Analytics: FinTech platforms collect vast amounts of data, which can be harnessed to gain insights into consumer behavior, resource usage, and waste generation. Analyzing this data can help businesses and policymakers make more informed decisions to promote circular practices.
7. Insurtech: Insurance technology (Insurtech) plays a vital role in the circular economy by providing innovative insurance

products tailored to the unique risks and challenges of circular business models. For example, Insurtech companies can develop insurance products for products-as-a-service models or circular supply chains.

8. Financial Inclusion: FinTech can offer financial services to underserved populations, giving them the opportunity to participate in the circular economy. By providing financial inclusion, people can be empowered to practice recycling, upcycling, and other sustainable activities.

FinTech aims to help large businesses become more environmentally friendly by developing a new circular market economy for products to be reused and recycled [12]. An elixir of circular economy and FinTech is based on the use of technologies like blockchain, cryptocurrencies, data analytics, and artificial intelligence. Circular economy uses these technologies for tracking materials, waste reduction, and supply chain management. As technology advances to integrate FinTech and circular economy, new opportunities can be grabbed. Critical drivers of evolution in FinTech and the circular economy are the collection and analysis of data. FinTech can leverage big data and analytics to offer customized financial services while also evaluating the environmental impact of investments. Data helps optimize resource usage, recycling, and waste reduction in the circular economy. Emerging startups focus on combining FinTech and circular economy principles, and agile and innovative companies are pushing the boundaries of sustainable finance, supply chain optimization, and resource efficiency.

FinTech plays a critical role in supporting opportunities in the circular economy by providing solutions to extend the lifetime of goods and materials, regenerate natural capital through initiatives such as implementing a circular design that focuses on reducing waste and pollution, adopting production processes that use or rely on recycled resources, promoting resource efficiency throughout the supply chain, facilitating reverse logistics, and managing the collection, separation, and recycling of used materials. Additionally, FinTech also promotes innovative technologies that enable circular business models to thrive.

The interconnectedness between sustainability, finance, and technology can be evidenced by the pandemic, which compelled industries worldwide to rethink value creation models traditionally deployed and rely more on technology and sustainability. Several companies and FinTech have sprung up in recent years looking to combat the use-once-then-discard paradigm [13]. To state it specifically, artificial intelligence can help reduce waste by predicting when products will likely fail which will facilitate their repair or reuse. The development of mobile applications promotes sustainable behaviors, such as recycling and energy conservation. By utilizing certain apps, it is possible to encourage individuals to adopt eco-friendly habits and lessen their carbon footprint. By doing so, individuals can increase their environmental awareness and take conscious steps toward preserving the planet. These apps are specifically designed to optimize resource usage, minimize waste, and improve the efficiency of supply chains. AI algorithms analyze consumer behavior data, which helps companies to develop more sustainable products and services.

4.3 FinTech-Driven Triumphs of Circular Economy

FinTech identifies the origin, purpose, durability, and potential reuse of materials. FinTech yields various tangible outcomes that benefit the environment, businesses, and individuals, including increased resource efficiency, access to sustainable financing, improved supply chain management, circular business models, and more. FinTech facilitates resource optimization and waste reduction through better tracking, analysis, and governing of resource use, which leads to cost reduction and more sustainable practices. FinTech platforms connect circular economy businesses with investors and lenders interested in supporting environmentally responsible initiatives. This enables businesses to secure funding for sustainable projects. FinTech encourages circular business models, such as product-as-a-service or sharing economy platforms. These models promote longer product lifespans and reduce the need for constant consumption.

FinTech platforms create online marketplaces for the buying, selling, or recycling of used products and enable individuals and businesses to participate in the circular economy more efficiently.

FinTech tools provide real-time data and analytics to track circular economy initiatives' environmental and social impact. This data can be utilized for reporting and accountability. FinTech enhances financial inclusion, enabling participation in circular economy activities such as micro-lending for sustainable businesses and inclusive payment systems for circular products. Through digital payment systems and FinTech platforms, consumers can access software and services in the cloud rather than purchasing physical products, reducing electronic waste. FinTech helps individuals and institutions build diversified portfolios of sustainable investments, encouraging the flow of capital into circular economy projects and businesses. Data analytics and consumer insights from FinTech platforms can inform product designers about consumer preferences and behaviors, leading to the creation of more durable and sustainable products. FinTech enables companies to access financing tailored for circular economy supply chains, allowing them to scale their operations sustainably. FinTech platforms provide carbon accounting tools and mechanisms for individuals and companies to measure and offset carbon emissions and encourage carbon-neutral or carbon-positive practices.

The concrete results mentioned above showcase how FinTech can be instrumental in promoting the circular economy, which in turn leads to environmental sustainability, efficient use of resources, and economic development. These developments encourage a more responsible and circular approach toward business and consumption. Sharing economy companies like Airbnb and Uber are fine examples of FinTech supporting the transition whereby a resource can be shared by multiple users in a pocket-friendly manner with a lesser environmental burden. Carbon tracking software linked to consumers' bank accounts has grown substantially recently. It could contribute to individuals changing spending behavior to align with their carbon footprint reduction goals [14]. Manufacturers recycling e-waste from various electronics, including mobile phones, copy machines, monitors, household appliances, and metals such as copper, lithium, and rhodium that can be extracted, could be the starting point for achieving circularity in the electronic sector. Medals given to athletes during the 2021 Summer Olympics in Tokyo were made from metals that were retrieved from electronic waste collected between April 2017 and March 2019 [15].

Globally, 141 million tonnes of plastic packaging is manufactured each year, and its production, use, and disposal generate about 1.8 billion tons of CO2 emissions [16]. The loop system (pilot revolutionary zero waste e-commerce system) promotes the reuse of product packaging rather than recycling, which is used by 200 major consumer product companies, from Procter & Gamble to Nestlé and significant retailers from Carrefour to Walmart. Another method of cost efficiency and circularity is urban mining.

As per the UN Environment Program, around one-third of food is wasted annually. Sustainable lifestyle apps, such as Too Good to Go, have been introduced to prevent wastage. The app offers a "magic bag" of food at a discounted price from local stores. This food consists of items that are about to expire and may not be sold in time or those that are not sold by the end of the day, particularly in bakeries. A study in China discovered that extracting materials through urban mining is nearly 10 times less expensive than mining from natural sources.

FinTech companies are increasingly exploring innovative solutions to support sustainable practices, reduce waste, and promote resource efficiency through circular supply chain finance, circular marketplace platforms, digital sustainability certifications, green bonds, waste management, and recycling apps, consumer engagement and education, environmental impact assessment tools, circular economy, circular economy investment portfolio, reverse logistics, and recycling solutions.

It is pertinent to mention Twig, an e-money start-up that allows users to upload images of unwanted items to its app and receive a valuation and an immediate offer to sell their items immediately. Twig aims to move toward sustainability through its Web 3.0 payment infrastructure. ANT Group, a Chinese FinTech company, has created a system that monitors human actions and provides incentives for environmentally beneficial choices, such as planting trees. This approach increases efficiency in both financial and ecological domains, resulting in meaningful societal impact.

007fenqi is a company in China that utilizes financial technology to provide young people with better access to financial products and services, as they are often excluded from the majority of financial services. The company's services are focused on four areas—spend, loan, earn, and invest—and they provide micro-loans to college students. Additionally, 007fenqi helps students secure part-time jobs or internships to make timely repayments and earn an income. Educating Chinese youth about financial responsibility is one of the company's primary objectives.

Banco Santander, the Spanish arm of Santander Group, pledged to become carbon neutral by 2020 and cover all its internal electricity usage "where possible" with renewable energy sources by 2025 and is committed to raising and mobilizing €120 billion in green finance by 2025, and €220 billion by 2030 [17]. Skrap, a Mumbai-based startup, provides an end-to-end waste management process at events and offices, and they analyze waste generation data based on the type and size of the event, devise a customized plan, and implement it on the premises. The idea is to reduce waste significantly and recycle a vast mass of what has been produced. Timberland has an interesting initiative—they offer discounts to customers who bring in their old shoes. Starling Bank, one of the leading US markets FinTech companies, chooses planet-friendly options to attract customers to their services. The bank is branchless, paperless, and operates on renewable energy. Lastly, financial institutions can use FinTech to assess ESG risks, make informed decisions, reduce exposure to unsustainable assets, and improve financial stability.

In order to achieve sustainability and circular economy objectives, international organizations such as the United Nations and the European

Union often partner with FinTech companies and provide financial support. This collaboration helps drive innovation and evolution toward a more sustainable future.

4.4 FinTech-Related Challenges that Hinder Circular Economy

FinTech, while having the potential to contribute to a circular economy, also faces several challenges and bottlenecks that can hinder its progress. The promotion of sustainability and circularity is a major goal of the FinTech industry. However, it is not without its obstacles that may hinder its ability to be effective. Since consumers have become very accustomed to a linear economy nowadays, it can be challenging to switch to a circular economy.

Not all individuals and businesses, especially those residing in underserved or remote regions, have access to digital devices and the internet, which are necessary for FinTech solutions. This limited access can exclude a significant portion of the population from participating in circular economy initiatives. FinTech relies heavily on the collection and processing of sensitive financial data. Data privacy and security concerns can deter individuals and businesses from adopting FinTech solutions for a circular economy, as they may fear data breaches or misuse of their information. Instances like Volkswagen revealed a data breach in June 2021, where hackers exploited an unsecured third-party vendor to gain access to data about Canadian and US customers. The company collected data mainly for marketing and sales between 2014 and 2019. Unfortunately, Volkswagen failed to secure this database, leaving it exposed from August 2019 to May 2021, which resulted in the leak of personal information of approximately 3.3 million individuals. The data exposed during the breach included driver's licenses, car numbers, and loan and social insurance numbers of a smaller group of customers.

Many individuals and businesses need to be made aware of FinTech solutions designed for the circular economy, and they lack the requisite knowledge to use these tools effectively, this knowledge gap hinders FinTech adoption for sustainable practices. FinTech companies navigate complex and evolving regulatory environments, varying significantly from one region to another. These regulations slow down the adoption of FinTech solutions for circular economy initiatives like sustainable financing or green investment platforms. Scaling up FinTech solutions to a level where they have a significant impact on the circular economy can be difficult.

The rate of adoption and acceptance of new financial technologies may be slower than needed to drive substantial change. Ensuring the long-term viability of circular economy FinTech solutions and holding stakeholders accountable for their environmental and social impact can be challenging.

People's attitudes and behaviors often resist change, especially in the financial sector. Adapting to new economic practices may necessitate alterations in consumer behavior and business operations, which can be met with opposition. FinTech startups and companies focusing on circular economy solutions may struggle to secure the necessary research, development, and scaling funding. Access to sustainable financing options and venture capital specifically targeting circular economy projects is often limited. FinTech solutions for circular consumption involve investments in sustainable projects, which can carry risks. With the aim to attract investors and stakeholders, practical risk assessment and mitigation strategies are necessary.

Tackling these challenges requires collaboration between FinTech companies, regulators, financial institutions, and stakeholders in the circular economy. It also demands innovations in technology, education, and policy to promote FinTech's sustainable and responsible use in achieving circular economy goals.

4.5 Conclusion

The circular economy redefines the approach to value creation. The new technologies have started to solve asymmetry problems creatively, and they can have a powerful impact on fueling and enabling the circular economy. Recent growth in FinTech is promising, but more capital and activity will be needed to fully scale the circular economy to seize its opportunity. FinTech can enable circular production systems by providing financial infrastructure, tools, and services supporting sustainable and resource-efficient practices. Integrating FinTech and circular flow of income principles can help drive positive environmental and economic outcomes. FinTech opens up a range of opportunities. With it, companies can make a significant contribution to achieving climate goals. They also benefit from a positive image and a competitive advantage. FinTech helps the stakeholders mobilize funds into environmentally friendly and environmentally close avenues and applications. That can be expanded to make people more sensitive toward their carbon footprint and what they can do to reduce it.

As the world continues prioritizing environmental sustainability and resource efficiency, the collaboration between FinTech and the circular economy is expected to drive positive change and promote a more responsible approach to resource management and consumption. Innovations in both areas (FinTech and circular economy) are mutually reinforcing, as FinTech enables and accelerates circular economy practices. In contrast, the circular economy provides a context for FinTech to develop products and services with a positive environmental and social impact. This synergy between FinTech and the circular economy will likely lead to ongoing innovation and evolution in the coming years.

It is expected that the convergence of FinTech and circular economy shall have a significant impact in the near future. By 2025, if the economy shifts toward a circular model, it could potentially create 100,000 new job opportunities and generate a value of US$1 trillion, according to estimates made by the World Economic Forum. This will have long-term benefits as it will create an environment where future generations can thrive and contribute to the development of humanity.

References

1. United Nations Environment – Finance Initiative, Driving the shift to circular economies: New report on role of finance industry, Partnership between United Nations Environment and the global financial sector to promote sustainable finance, 2020, October 13, https://www.unepfi.org/news/driving-the-shift-to-circular-economies-new-report-on-role-of-finance-industry/.
2. Kumar, S., FINTECH ROLE IN THE INDIAN MSMES, 2023, April 23, ResearchGate, https://www.researchgate.net/publication/370211639_FINTECH_ROLE_IN_THE_INDIAN_MSMES.
3. BBVA, This is how fintech can help implement a green economy, 2021, October 21, NEWS BBVA, https://www.bbva.com/en/innovation/this-is-how-fintech-can-help-implement-a-green-economy/.
4. Kandpal, V. and Mehrotra, R., Financial Inclusion: The Role of Fintech and Digital Financial Services in India (March 13, 2019). *Indian J. Econ. Business*, 19, 1, 85–93, 2019. Available at SSRN: https://ssrn.com/abstract=3485038
5. How fintech is making the finance ecosystem more sustainable, Best Instant Personal Loan App-Smart Coin-Best Loan App in India, https://blog.smartcoin.co.in/how-fintechs-are-making-the-finance-ecosystem-more-sustainable/.
6. Trehan, S., Pozhath, R., Pratap, M., Bain, *India Fintech Report 2022: Sailing Through Turbulent Tides, October 19, 2022.* https://www.bain.com/insights/india-fintech-report-2022-sailing-through-turbulent-tides/.
7. Nenavath, S. and Mishra, S., Impact of green finance and fintech on sustainable economic growth: Empirical evidence from India. *Heliyon*, 9, 5, e16301, 2023, https://doi.org/10.1016/j.heliyon.2023.e16301.

8. Carney, M., Unlocking the value of the circular economy, in: How to Build a Circular Economy, Ellen MacArthur Foundation, England, 2021, August 13. https://www.ellenmacarthurfoundation.org/articles/unlocking-the-value-of-the-circular-economy.
9. IndBiz, Pramshu, India's circular economy can reach US$ 45 billion by 2030: Report, Economic Diplomacy Division, 2022, April 25, https://indbiz.gov.in/indias-circular-economy-can-reach-us-45-billion-by-2030-report/.
10. Jain, B. and Sharma, K., Circular Economy – The Surat Model, 2021, November 15, Invest India, https://www.investindia.gov.in/siru/circular-economy-surat-model.
11. India constructed 703 km of highways using plastic waste - Times of India, 2021, July 30, The Times of India, https://timesofindia.indiatimes.com/auto/news/india-constructed-703-km-of-highways-using-plastic-waste/articleshow/84883086.cms.
12. Circular economy fintech Fairown expands to Poland, 2022, July 27, Finextra Research, https://www.finextra.com/newsarticle/40708/circular-economy-fintech-fairown-expands-to-poland.
13. Plug, A., Round and round: how circular economy fintechs are aiming to save the planet, FinTech Futures, 2022, https://www.fintechfutures.com/2022/02/round-and-round-how-circular-economy-fintechs-are-aiming-to-save-the-planet/.
14. Margaroli, I.C., ReCommerce: Fintech boosting circular economy, Fintech Nexus, 2023, January 18, https://www.fintechnexus.com/recommerce-fintech-boosting-circular-economy/.
15. www.ETCFO.com, Circular economy is a business imperative in an increasingly ESG-driven world, 2021, September 20, ETCFO.com. https://cfo.economictimes.indiatimes.com/news/circular-economy-is-a-business-imperative-in-an-increasingly-esg-driven-world/86358182.
16. Reuse rather than recycle packaging: TerraCycle CEO Tom Szaky. The World Economic Forum, 2023, October 6, https://www.weforum.org/agenda/2023/10/reuse-packaging-loop-zero-waste-terracycle-tom-szaky/.
17. Hinchliffe, R., Banco Santander commits to carbon neutrality and renewable energy "where possible, 2019, December 17, FinTech Futures, https://www.fintechfutures.com/2019/12/banco-santander-commits-to-carbon-neutrality-and-renewable-energy-where-possible/.

5

Cyber Ecosystem and Digital Currency: Review and Current Status

Nitish Ojha[1]*, Divya Gohil[2] and Abhishek Vaish[3]

[1]*Department of CSE, Amity University, Noida, India*
[2]*Department of Accounting & Finance, University of Stirling, RAK, UAE*
[3]*Indian Institute of Information Technology, Allahabad, India*

Abstract
Taking a big leap toward a better financial future, the Reserve Bank of India has launched its much-awaited digital currency "the digital rupee" as a pilot project. Major banking organizations have been entrusted to make its success while rolling out in its best manner. However, the main stake of fruitful implementation lies in the cybersecurity ecosystem. Risk and benefits both go hand in hand and the boost in the economy can only be assured if the risk can be minimized. It can only be minimized if cybersecurity controls are deployed appropriately. Achieving the long-cherished dream of a cashless economy with the help of digital currency India sees itself in equal order of the top 3 biggest economies of the world, however, challenges of cybersecurity, i.e., weak transaction system, Prevailing poverty, digital divide, lack of technological literacy, the dominance of unorganized sector in the economy, and dependency on old cash-based system remain open weakening the uniform financial growth. In this chapter, a bird's eye view review has been done where finance and IT security are intersecting with each other, related to previous work along with challenges, their reasons, and the future aspects.

***Keywords*:** Digital currency, virtual currency, cybersecurity, cyber ecosystem, e-currency

**Corresponding author*: nitishkumarojha@gmail.com

Ernesto D.R. Santibanez Gonzalez, Vinay Kandpal, Peterson K. Ozili and Prasenjit Chatterjee (eds.) Fintech for ESG and the Circular Economy, (63–92) © 2024 Scrivener Publishing LLC

5.0 Introduction

Indian financial system saw a significant move when the much-awaited digital currency was launched by the Reserve Bank of India (RBI) on 1 November 2022 recognized as Central Bank Digital Currency (CBDC). The economy was moving already at full pace having the throttling speed with cashless drive applications, i.e., Paytm, PhonePe, UPI, debit cards, credit cards, e-payments, and digital wallets. Blockchain distributed-ledger technology has been used by digital rupee [1]. It will be individually recognized as a standalone token of right tender for the transaction and subjected to Central Bank regulation, much like banknotes. Use, accountability, and after-effect of implementation with sole responsibility rest with RBI. Both online and physical accessibility are planned. Given its historical development, it is noteworthy that on 16 December 2020, the RBI announced the establishment of a regulatory sandbox to test next-generation technologies for cross-border payments [2]. This was done in order to collect field test data and evidence of the benefits and cybersecurity threats as these technologies may pose risks for the financial ecosystem. Person-to-person (P2P) and person-to-merchant (P2M) transaction use cases are being tested by RBI. The RBI also intends to expand institutional and private sector set-up for electronic rupees in international trade [3].

5.1 Digital Currency in Other Countries

In April 2020, the People's Bank of China introduced two pilot programs for the lottery-based distribution of e-yuan. Currently, the Bank for International Settlements (BIS) is collaborating with Canada, Japan, Switzerland, the United Kingdom, Sweden, the United States, and the other European Union on digital currencies. 95% of the global GDP is comprised of the 105 nations developing digital money [4]. Even 16 of the G-20 member nations, or 90% of them, are developing their own digital currencies. The "Bahamas" was the first nation in the world to introduce the "sand dollar" as a digital currency [5]. It is a tiny nation situated in the Caribbean part of North America. More than 105 nations throughout the world are now developing digital currency. Out of them, 52 nations have evolved to the point where they can introduce money. A digital currency called "E-Naira" was introduced in Nigeria, while "Jam-Dex" was introduced in Jamaica. A lot of nations have completed their pilot testing of digital money. Among them are prominent nations like Ghana, Canada, the

United Arab Emirates, Saudi Arabia, Sweden, Uruguay, Australia, Hong Kong, Singapore, and Kazakhstan. China has shown significant success with digital money as a major economy [6]. There, the digital currency will be widely accepted by the people by the end of 2023. Many technologically sound countries are using digital currency as a shield to keep out the dollar in their international transactions. Currently, 15 of China's 23 provinces accept e-CNY (digital yuan) payments. The Central Bank of China has also started using it for cross-border payments. China aims to pioneer global trade settlement with digital yuan to counter dollar unipolar dominance [7, 8].

Countries around the world are turning to digital currencies to protect their citizens from volatile cryptocurrency investments, curb the circulation of counterfeit currencies, and reduce the costs associated with physical cash management.

5.2 Types of Digital Currency

It is an intangible type of payment that only exists electronically. With the use of technology like computers, cell phones, and the Internet, it may be moved between entities or people. Digital currency permits fast transactions and borderless ownership transfer yet is identical to real currencies [9]. Digital money and cyber cash are other names for digital currency. It can be classified into categories.

1. **Cryptocurrency:** Cryptography is used by digital currencies, or cryptocurrencies, to secure and verify network transactions. Cryptography is used to govern and regulate the creation of such currencies. Cryptocurrencies like Bitcoin and Ethereum are a few examples [10].
2. **Virtual Currencies:** Virtual currencies are centrally controlled digital currencies that are managed by the creators, or the founding group made up of numerous process participants. By using established network protocols, virtual currencies may be controlled algorithmically. Virtual tokens in PhonePe, Paytm, Flipkart, Amazon Redeem points, etc. are an illustration of a virtual currency, and their usage is managed by the creators [11].
3. **Digital Currency:** CBDCs are digital currencies that are issued by a country's central bank. CBDCs can be used in place of or in addition to traditional fiat currency. In contrast

to fiat currency, which may be accessible in both physical and digital forms, CBDCs are exclusively available digitally. Uruguay, England, and Sweden are among the countries that are considering the introduction of digital versions of their domestic fiat currencies. In India, the e-rupee has been launched as a digital currency by the RBI [12].

4. **E-Rupee:** It is a digital payment system based on prepaid vouchers regulated by any central bank, like here in India, it is regulated by RBI. The e-RUPI vouchers have both person- and purpose-specific restrictions. e-RUPI is quite distinct from other cryptocurrencies like Bitcoin and other Altcoins since it is backed by the Indian Rupee as an underlying asset—a type of virtual currency that is issued by a central bank (RBI), in contrast to private cryptos like Bitcoin and Ethereum. It serves as an alternative to the old traditional physical money which is in use. It appears as though they are steady coins backed by government funds. Since the legislation of the issuing nation itself backs these virtual currencies [13].

Representation

The following Figure 5.1 depicts the different types of crypto-currency and their name based pictorial representation.
The following Figure 5.2 represents the tokenized version of Indian Rupee which has been issued by Reserve Bank of India, Govt. of India [10].

Figure 5.1 Pictorial representation of cryptocurrency [14].

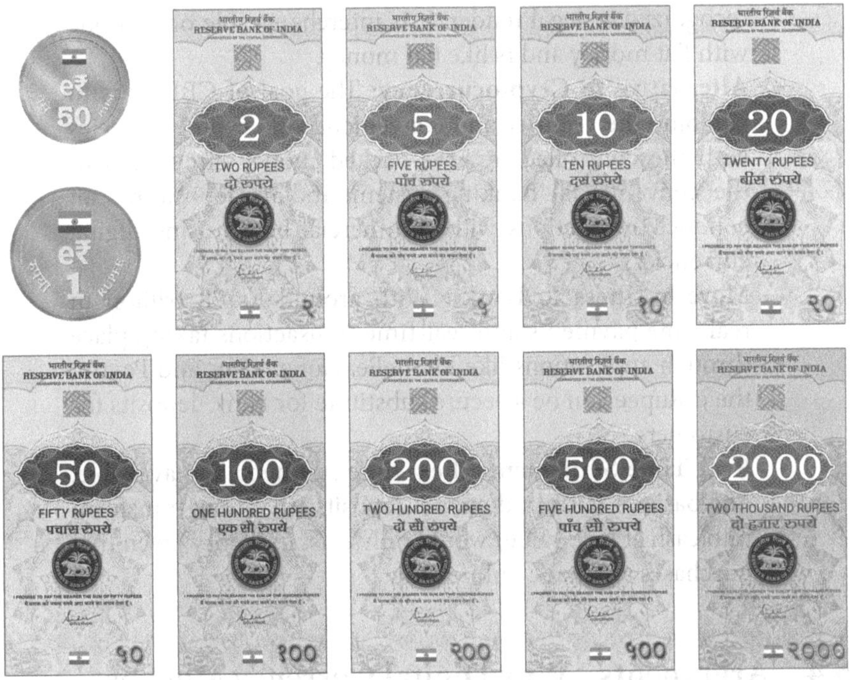

Figure 5.2 Samples of a digital currency issued by the government of India [14, 15].

5.3 Arguments in Favor of Digital Currency

- **Form:** It is an intangible type of payment that only exists electronically.
- **Technology Supported:** With the use of modern technology, including computers, cell phones, and the Internet, it may be shared between people or across organizations.
- **Speedy Transaction:** Digital currency permits fast transactions and borderless ownership transfer yet is identical to real currencies.
- **Transparency:** Digital money and cyber cash are other names for digital currency so best for cyberspace promoting transparency and equivalency and a homogeneous environment of payment without involving a third party.
- **Equivalency:** Contrary to cryptocurrencies, which are unregulated, CBDC is a digital version of fiat money that is issued and guaranteed by a central bank and is therefore

recognized as legal tender. It is interchangeable one-to-one with fiat money and is like fiat money.

- **Alternative to Cryptocurrency:** The goal of CBDCs is to combine the security and convenience of cryptocurrencies with the controlled, reserve-backed money circulation of the conventional banking system. Indian depositors can conduct transactions with commercial banks using digital currencies.
- **More business to Banks:** With around Rs 78 trillion in real-time payments and real-time transactions taking place through applications like PhonePe, Google Pay, and Paytm, the e-Rupee can be a secure substitute for bank deposits for customers.
- **Real-Time Settlements:** Real-time payments are available. The basis of faith in demand deposits (that they transform into cash at face value) would only exist in theory given that purchases are made online [16].

5.4 Arguments - Why Digital Currency Must be Discouraged

5.4.1 Weak Bank Weak Link in the Chain

A bank with a low turnover of cash will be forced to hold low-cash deposits with it if e-cash becomes very popular and the RBI is unable to establish a cap on the amount that may be stored in mobile wallets, strict regulation is needed. To keep it, competition might need to be addressed [17].

5.4.2 Low Bank Penetration

Low bank penetration to the population has been a major issue among less populated countries or developing and poor countries. It has been a phenomenal issue in Africa and in the Asian continent. For example, not only Senegal or Chad but also India is also on the bank of suffering if bank penetration is counted. In contrast to the wealthy nations of the Northern Hemisphere, where mortgages account for the majority of borrowing, the majority of loans in the Southern Hemisphere are used for healthcare and education. In India, 21% of consumers took out loans to pay for medical expenses, 10% for education, 9% for businesses, and only 4% for mortgages. Despite the huge rise in account penetration, the research claims that India is among the nations with the highest percentages of inactive accounts in the world [18].

5.4.3 High Dormancy

The difficulty for policymakers, however, is that creating an account does not guarantee that it will be used. In the world, 15% of individuals with financial institution accounts, or roughly 460 million people, reported not making a deposit or withdrawal in the previous year, rendering their accounts essentially dormant. This indicates that their account has no cash deposits or withdrawals in addition to having no electronic payments or purchases or electronic wage deposits. South Asia has a very high dormancy rate of 42%; the average for all other emerging areas is less than 20%. Of the 460 million adult adults with inactive accounts worldwide, 43% are in India, making up around 195 million people. The dormancy rate in high-income OECD economies is 5% [19].

5.4.4 Poor Quality of Services by Public Sector Banks

It has been observed that people trust employees of public sector banks over private sector banks; however, when it comes to the quality of services which is provided by public sector banks [20], it has been observed in many studies that the quality of service is not up to the mark in Indian Banks, either at Public Sector Bank or Private Bank, and it is a well-established fact. In an independent study [21], the following findings were made. The following Table 5.1 represents the relationship between service quality factor between two type of bank private and public where it is clearly visible that public sector banks are not up-to the mark.

The below table suggests that the services of private-sector banks are better than public-sector banks. The factors that demonstrate a large gap score between public sector banks and private sector banks include the right service the first time, timely service delivery, interest in resolving customer problems, pleasant workers, consideration of client interest, and comprehension of customer concerns. Respondents were happier with public sector banks only in two areas: workers' knowledge of bank personnel and their awareness of clients' specific demands.

5.4.5 Prone to Financial Instability

All economies are aware of the threat it poses to financial stability and even advanced nations are concerned about the declining use of banknotes,

Table 5.1 Empathy chart to describe the quality of service in banks [21].

S. no.	Service quality factor	Public sector bank			Private sector bank		
		Expectation	Delivery	Gap %	Expectation	Delivery	Gap
1	Knowledge of bank staff	1.69	1.33	20	2.0	1.80	10
2	Delivery of services in the first meeting	1.46	1.36	10	2.0	1.68	10
3	Promptness of services	1.86	1.37	10	1.99	1.50	5
4	Interested in solving customers' problem	1.45	1.32	12	1.95	1.60	3
5	Individual employees to each specific issue and service	2.00	1.50	13	1.95	1.80	3
6	Polite employees	1.67	1.20	10	1.50	1.40	2
7	Consideration of your problem and interest	1.00	0.95	5	1.80	1.70	4
8	Follow-up by the bank to solve your problem	1.44	1.20	10	1.60	1.50	5

especially post-COVID. The rural sector economy, which is still reliant on antiquated practices but lacks basic financial services, may run into difficulties when dealing with digital currencies [22]. Additionally, the widespread usage of CBDC will undoubtedly make online transactions more susceptible to cyberattacks. Additionally, technological expertise, operating costs, enhanced cyber protection, training of CBDC operators, and public awareness raising are all necessary for CBDC acceptability. As a result, the RBI may spend significant expenses to successfully execute it across India [23].

5.4.6 Lack of IT Implementation by Banks in their Portals

Most of the banks do not provide multiple services through their online banking services. Only the major banks in India either the public sector or private sector are providing, the rest of the financial organizations are far behind in providing multiple services equipped with Internet banking accounts. While comparing the public sector with the private sector, it has been observed that private sector players are more champions in providing tailored services to their customers than public sector banks [24]. Private banking services include accounts, asset management, investment, specialized credit, and other financial services tailored to the

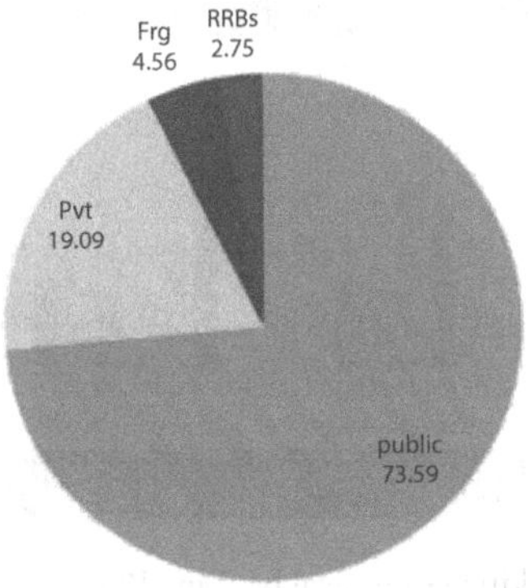

Public Sector Banks	27
Private Sector Banks	23
Foreign Banks	46
RRBs	56
Co-op Banks	
UCBs	55
RuraL credit societies (in 000s)	
Differentiated Banks	Yet to be operational
Payment Banks	11
Small Banks	10

Figure 5.3 Distribution of banking players in Indian systems [25].

specific requirements of the chosen client [25]. The following Figure 5.3 represents the different players operating in Banking sector in India where it is clearly visible that majority of services are being offered by public sector bank which are far behind from Pvt. Bank for implementing technology in their services.

5.4.7 Availability of Bank Services

The next challenge is that private banks are very limited in number considering the large population of India. In remote areas, only public sectors bank is there, and their branches have fixed working time formats so can we say firmly that our banking system is enough mature to handle digital currency-based new endeavors? The following graph represents the status of online banking versus physical branches.

5.4.8 Availability of Diverse Banking Services

Services vary with respect to branch and however, it remains the same in the case of online services. Compared to 73% who visited a physical branch, 79% of online respondents in Asian countries are dependent on online banking for investment transactions directly or through some legal third-party supported executive. Similarly, in North America, 55% of people utilized Internet banking while just 48% went to the bank in person. The following Figure 5.4, represents the graphical comparison of different banking players and their investment ratio in a particular span of time.

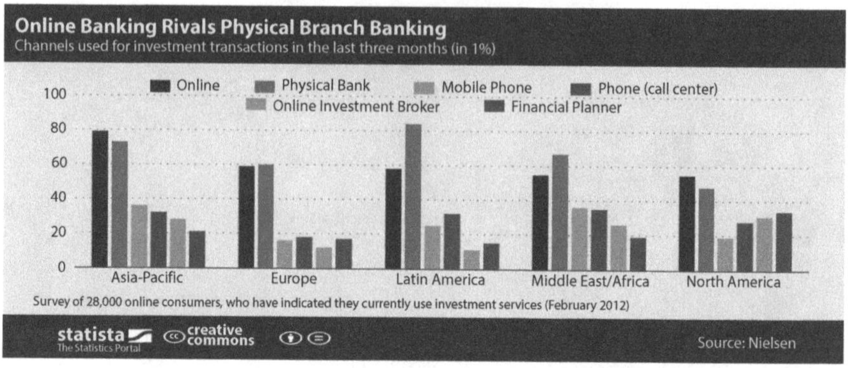

Figure 5.4 Graph depicting the status of online banking vs physical banking [26].

Results from throughout the world demonstrate a tendency toward online investment transaction processing [26].

5.5 Attack on the Banking System

Cyberattacks have been reported in public sector banks at a very high level in comparison to private sector banks as public sector banks do not provide enough security checks and controls [27]. The RBI annual report for 2020–2021 states that public sector banks were responsible for nearly all (94.9%) of the total amount engaged in frauds in that year. Banks in the private sector made up about 8% of the total. PSBs made up about 88% of the total amount engaged in frauds as of 31 March 2021, while private sector banks made up little more than 12% [28].

5.5.1 Vulnerability Vs No. of Online Users

According to the NITI Aayog report, there are around 730 million Internet users in India, with 75% of new users coming from rural regions and using regional languages for data consumption. Nearly a billion people now purchase online, and mobile video content has grown by an astounding 83% in recent years [29]. The following Figure 5.5 represents the categorical attacks and other vulnerabilities in banking system which are very common either at private bank or at public bank.

5.5.2 Technology Supported Attacks

Data volumes and the number of linked devices and sensors are both expected to grow tremendously because of the increased bandwidth provided by 5G technology. India is now one of the top 10 spam-producing nations in the world. Additionally, it is one of the top 5 nations in the world where cybercrime is prevalent. The general lack of response across the board shows a lack of planning and unpreparedness for the very real, continuing, and present cyber threats of today [30].

5.5.3 Rise of Cyber Attacks

As technology is improving, a smaller number of attacks are observed in private sector banks, whereas the public sector banks fail to install the latest software and keep updating the latest security patches along with other security controls that are not followed in the best manner so more and more vulnerability arises leading to more exploitation and attack in the end. The current status can be understood from the following Figure 5.6 where number of fraud cases year-wise and the amount involved has been represented.

In general, there is an increase in banking fraud. The number of fraud cases recorded by banks consistently hovered around 5300 in the previous 10 years increasing to 5935 from 2020 to 2021, according to the Reserve Bank's annual report. The sum engaged in scams rose progressively until rising significantly to Rs 430 billion in 2009–2020. "A large value fraud committed in the gems and jewelry sector was the cause of the quantum jump in the amount involved in frauds during 2019–20", according to the report [32].

Whatever the sort of banking organization is, the attack is always there, according to a different Inventiva study. Customers of ICICI Bank have been the main targets of cybercrime. ICICI Bank alone recorded 34,920 incidents totaling 74.25 crore rupees over the past four years. Despite being one of the largest private commercial banks in India, ICICI Bank, the number of instances is still rather significant. The fact that HDFC Bank has not seen a lot of cyber fraud instances is unexpected. Only 1335 incidents totaling 9.78 crore rupees in value were observed throughout the previous four years. The graph below shows the status of various assaults and the losses incurred as a result of India's various types of banks during the past

Figure 5.5 Cybersecurity Niti Ayog report [31].

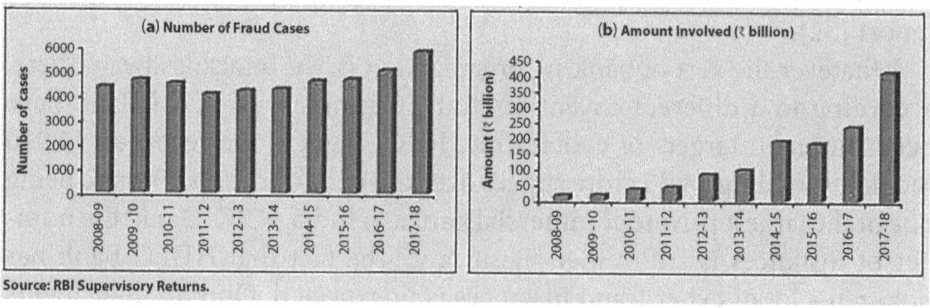

Figure 5.6 Number of fraud cases vs amount involved as per RBI report [32].

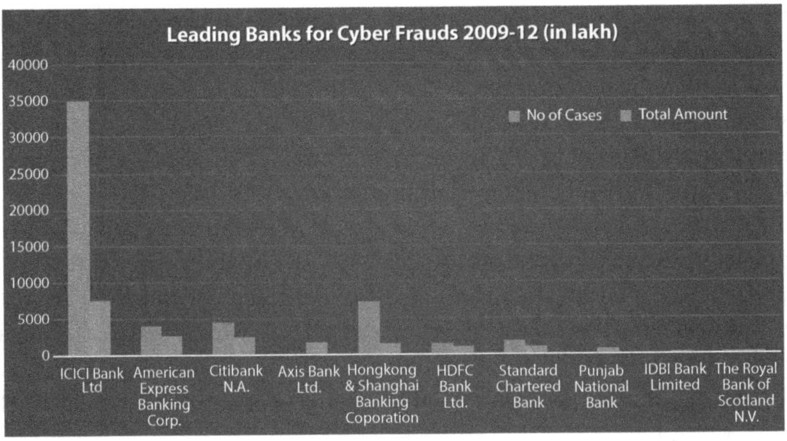

Figure 5.7 Graph showing fraud committed in leading banks in India [34].

10 years [33]. The above Figure 5.7 represents the different types of frauds which has been committed in Indian Baking Industry and status of various amount of rupees over a period of time.

5.6 What are the Biggest Threats to Digital Currency?

The ease and security of conducting financial transactions are the key reason for becoming digital. Carrying cash, using credit cards, or even waiting in line to use an ATM would not be necessary.

In times of emergency, such as in hospitals, it would be very helpful. Because the majority of black money is invested in real estate, a cashless

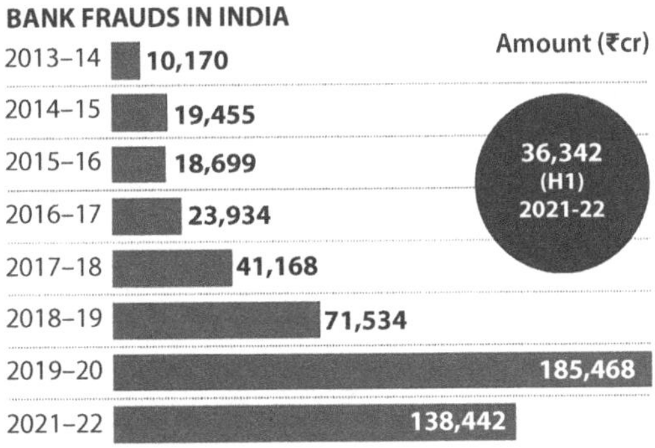

Figure 5.8 Status of different bank frauds in India [39].

economy would lower the likelihood of tax evasion, stop the production of black money, and lower real estate prices. Additionally, being cashless would reduce the cost of money printing from the bank's point of view, but from the customers' side, security is the top priority. The Banking Finance Services and Insurances (BFSI) sector in India is the one that hackers and cybercriminals are most interested in attacking [35].

Researchers from Kaspersky Security Lab, one of the organizations that supplies the Indian cybersecurity agency CERTin with cyber threat intelligence, stated, "Our data suggest that assaults against the BFSI industry have multiplied. The financial year 2021–2022, which saw a significant paradigm change in the most targeted area from North America to Asia, Pacific, and Europe, saw about 10% of all cyber events targeted at this industry" [36].

According to a CNBC article, the research stated that India reported 285 instances in the first half of 2022 and 470 in 2021. Any risks to the banking and financial sector have a ripple impact on a nation's overall economic growth. Not to mention the vast phishing attacks that may be launched if personal identifying information (PII) were to become public. Targeting the weakest links in the chain is done using these advanced Tactics, Techniques, and Procedures (TTPs) and mutating assaults [37].

5.7 Why are Indian Banking Organizations Targeted?

Threats to the banking industry have grown more quickly thanks to digitalization and widely available financial services. Threat actors now have

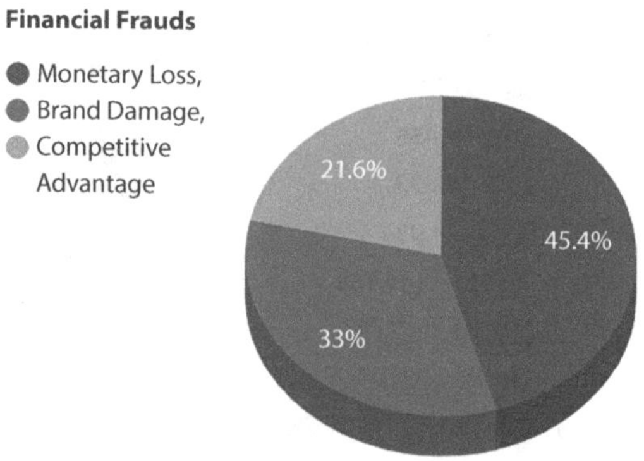

Figure 5.9 Ratio depiction of different security attacks in financial organizations.

unparalleled access to the industry thanks to blockchain, digital money, and cryptocurrency's remarkable rise. This has made it possible to target the banking industry using new and improved PPT (People, Process, and Technology). This is combined with newer and changing phishing tactics. The banking and financial sector is dangerous due to the dispersed structure of players [38].

According to the survey, the rising digitalization and online banking systems that were propelled during the pandemic are to blame for India being the top target for cyberattacks in India [40].

5.7.1 Reasons Behind Cyberattack Against Banks in India

While going into a deep state of analysis of cybercrimes, the concept proposed by famous legal expert H. L. A. Hart in 1961, again proves to be true when finding out the reasons behind the cyberattacks on Indian banking organizations. Hart in his famous research article gave a tremendously significant account of how many forms of norms interact to build the framework of a legal system, arguing that the normativity of law is not always moral. Continue by emphasizing what he called the "rule of recognition"—specifically, the collection of normative premises that guide legal officials' actions in order to confirm the presence of law in their administration. This is also true with the banking sector while analyzing the different types of crimes committed over financial data [41]. In his paper, when Hart talks about the rule of recognition, it is directly related to the compliance issue of cybersecurity where regulatory procedures have to be followed irrespective of size, location, type, way of operation, and category of bank if dealing with digital currency [42].

A significant number of regulatory procedures and cybersecurity technologies have developed over the years as a result of awareness of the growing dangers of cyberinfrastructure in regulated businesses. There are numerous Internet access points, outdated defense technologies, and built-in vulnerabilities in the systems and software used by banks that make them very vulnerable to sophisticated attack methods employed by hackers. The requirement that financial institutions be prepared for cybersecurity, however, is their primary objective, and here is where these organizations' weaknesses lie. A report by PwC suggests that while preparing for the combat of cybersecurity, most of financial organizations are not well equipped with security measures at their platform level. According to recent research by the consulting firm PwC, platform fraud accounts for 57% of all fraud events in India and costs more than 26% of Indian firms more than $1 million which is depicted below [42].

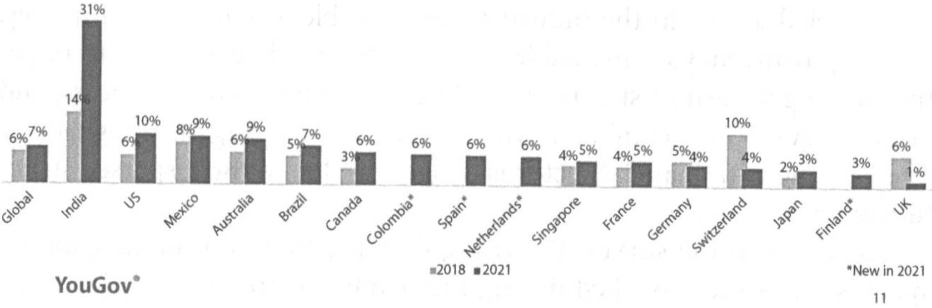

Figure 5.10 Graph showing a global number of people who lost money in bank-related fraud [44].

Further, this report elaborates that enterprise platforms are a top target for ransomware, phishing, malware, and money laundering. 89% of all platform scams involved financial fraud on transactions made to or from platforms. These scams range from simple identity theft and triangulation fraud to more sophisticated unauthorized digital purchases. For 92% of all consumer scams in India, payment fraud—particularly that using credit cards and digital wallets—was the cause. Different reasons exist depending on the type of attack [43].

It is important to keep in mind that the motivations and attribution of cyberattacks can be intricate and nuanced. In many instances, it may be challenging to determine the real causes of the crimes and the offenders with total confidence. Banks and cybersecurity experts continue to face difficulties in thwarting these assaults due to the continuously changing nature of cyber threats and the criminals' techniques.

Let us see in a summarized manner the different types of causes behind these attacks.

- **Financial Gain:** Financial gain to hackers means money lost to bank customers. Financial gain is one of the main drivers driving the cyberattacks on banks. Banks are a common target for cybercriminals who want to steal sensitive financial data including credit card numbers, login credentials, and personal information. They can then use this information to commit fraud, steal identities, or sell it on the dark web to get money. According to a separate Microsoft research, 31% of Indians lost money as a result of cyberattacks, while 70% were victims of tech support scams—the highest in the world.

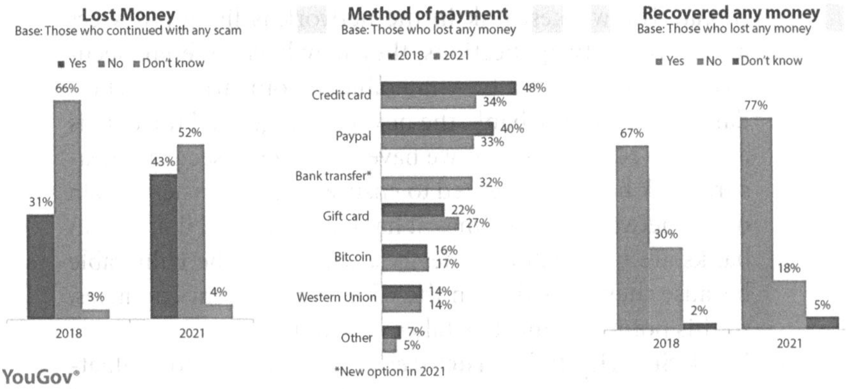

Figure 5.11 Graph showing the monetary loss in financial transactions [45].

Microsoft also monitored over 24 trillion danger signals for conceivable hostile activities for their research titled "Microsoft's Global Tech Support Scam Research." According to this survey, millennials or youngsters (those between the ages of 24 and 37) were the demographic most frequently targeted by tech support scams. A monetary loss was suffered by almost 58% of individuals who had been conned as depicted from the above Figure 5.11 [45].

From this report, it is evident that new generation (termed as Gen Z, Millennials) men were the most severely affected and most likely to have lost money; this is probably because younger generations are more "online" and participate in riskier activities, but lack of awareness about security measures.

It is interesting to note that all age groups now have less trust in using computers and the Internet, which presents opportunities for more education.

- **Easy Access to Data:** These days, almost all banks are interconnected to each other, termed a "core banking solution". Branches, ATMs, points of sale (PoS), and many other confidential devices are in the same network. Once a hacker has access to a computer system, they may be able to copy or transfer confidential financial records from clients as well as other personal data into a tiny portable device. Because information technology fuels the activities of banks, people, businesses, governments, etc., the insecure storing and processing of sensitive data on their computers pose a severe threat. The weakest link in the network is linking devices and third-party applications, they may have different security ratings and are a bit vulnerable in comparison to standard devices of the bank; the next challenge is all the data is available 24 × 7 × 365 so we have to see what security measure bank has implemented to ensure secure transfer of data over a network. Many times, it has been reported that Indian banks are using Chinese devices, which may be vulnerable because they store data in the Cloud in different countries, so this point also must be taken care of [46].

- **Weak Security Infrastructure:** When it comes to evaluating cybersecurity preparedness, spotting security issues, and respecting cybersecurity requirements even when compliance is optional, NIST has become the industry standard [47]. According to a second study-based poll, the majority of public sector bank workers are unaware of the NIST framework. The following Figure 5.12 shows the awareness ratio among bank employees about NIST framework.

In order to increase compliance and control in banks and other regulated organizations, the RBI has tightened regulations on digital payment security; however, a strict framework for digital currency is missing. In India's expanding digital economy, outages, security breaches, and fraud are becoming more frequent. It is the right time for RBI to establish the rules and regulations for a secure Internet banking framework, i.e., NIST over RBI's own created framework when we see the challenges of cybersecurity.

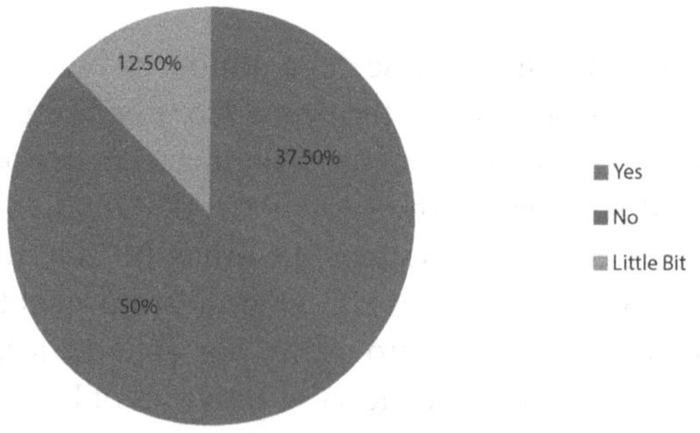

Figure 5.12 Awareness of NIST framework [48].

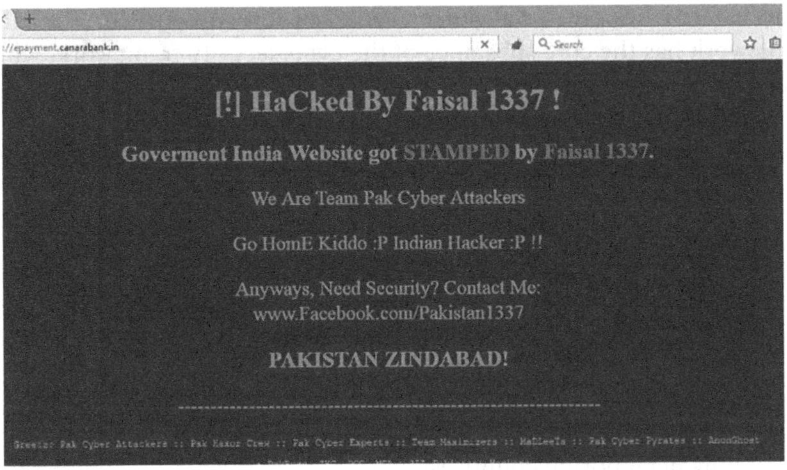

Figure 5.13 Canara bank e-payment page hacked and claimed by a Pakistani group.

The RBI instructed banks to follow specific regulations provided as instructions on information security, electronic banking, technology risk management, and cyber frauds (G. Gopalakrishna Committee) in its circular DBS.CO.ITC.BC.No.6/31.02.008/2010-11/April 29/2011 [49].

The guidelines state that implementation strategies cannot be static and that banks must actively develop, fine-tune, and adapt their procedures, technology, and policies in response to new developments and emerging problems in light of the RBI security framework. When measured against the NIST framework [50], it has been observed on certain facts that NIST has better scope to deal with cybersecurity-related challenges. The NIST Cybersecurity Framework provides a better way to deal with, i.e.,

- Describe the current cybersecurity posture of the organization in a regular manner.
- Describe and classify the target state of the systems.
- Identify and prioritize opportunities for improvement within the context of risk management.
- Assess progress toward the target state.
- Promote communication among internal and external stakeholders; organizations can use the NIST Cybersecurity Framework.

These aspects are not well explained and defined in the RBI framework as RBI has used a "Template-based framework" where the onus of cybersecurity lies on its subsidiary bank not directly on RBI. The NIST framework has the core substance of the cybersecurity framework, which is composed of three parts: (1) the framework core, (2) the framework implementation tiers, and (3) the framework profile, whereas this kind of classification is not discussed in the RBI Framework.

- **Sponsored Attack:** Indian banks have been the target of campaign-based targeted attacks potentially affecting millions of customers. Using the names, logos, and linked brands and services of actual banks to deceive victims into thinking their phishing sites are connected is a common practice in these activities. Some reports have been in the news where the defacing of the websites was also observed by neighboring countries.

These attacks may have political or economic objectives, seeking to destabilize the financial system or learn more about the nation's financial activities.

- **Corporate Espionage:** In rare instances, corporate espionage has been observed; however, it was not well established. Organizations or people with ideological motives may attack banks to express their opposition to specific laws, business practices, or governmental acts. These attacks can aim to harm the bank's reputation or interfere with its business.
- **CIPHER Framework for Privacy:** Digital information types, electronic systems, and methods for data sharing, processing, and maintenance are all covered under the CIPHER framework [51].

  The CIPHER methodological framework's primary goal is to provide recommendations and industry best practices for protecting privately held information systems (PHIS) online. The CIPHER methodological framework's main feature is its ability to protect data privacy. Technology independence (versatility) is the ability to work for any organization functioning in any field, even when existing technologies deteriorate or are replaced by newer ones. CIPHER's practicality offers prospective measures and practices to strengthen or verify if the company is safeguarding data from internet dangers. It is simple to use and does not need organizations or individuals to have specialized experience.

- **Hacktivism:** Hacktivism-based attacks or attacks just for fun have been observed in many public and private sector banks. In a recent alleged cyberattack, the "Mysterious Silent Force," a well-known hacking gang, is said to have targeted two important Indian institutions, the Federal Bank Limited and Indian Bank, according to reports from a new agency called Cyber Express. The cyberattacks on the Federal Bank and the Indian Bank serve as a reminder of the necessity for stronger cybersecurity measures. It is essential for the Indian financial sector to act proactively to stop future instances of these assaults. Customers would not be able to trust financial institutions or feel secure about the security of their hard-earned money until that happens.
- **Weak Security Controls:** In view of new services as a new endeavor by the bank, RBI keeps monitoring and informing banks to check and to have strong security control in a regular manner. An appropriate investment must be made in IT and ITES-based operations and services, as well as the necessary number of people, specialized officers for each service, emergency response teams, certified specialists, and tools and procedures.
- **Motivated Attack:** Many groups are working as per their ideological motivation to attack a campaign on banking organizations at the country level. Cybercriminals use a variety of tactics to steal money, such as creating phony online shopping sites, promising jobs in exchange for cash, and

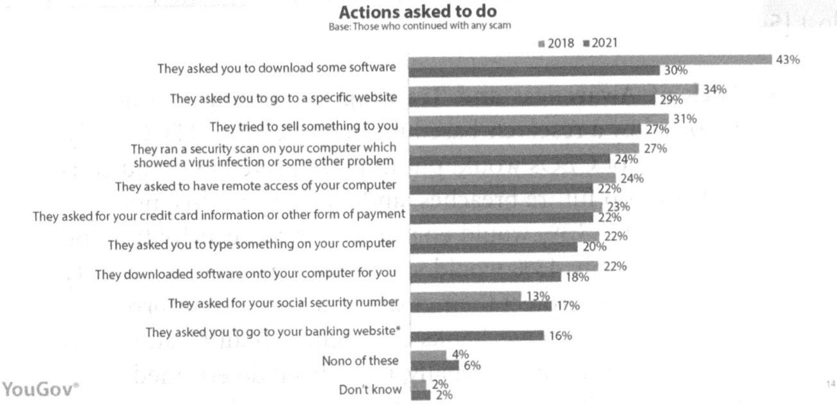

Figure 5.14 Different actions asked by scamsters to do for stealing sensitive data [53].

sending phishing URLs to mobile devices. Numerous gangs using identical tactics have been dismantled in Jamtara, Mewat, Mathura, Agra, etc. [52].

Additionally, Jamtara might be linked to 50% of cybercrimes in India, which keeps cyber police on their toes and causes sleeplessness at night. This city has been linked to fraudsters posing as bank executives; it is undoubtedly the underbelly of digital India. Smartphones help the young people of Jamtara who engage in cybercrime feel less unsafe in the world.

Cyber specialists also said that online fraudsters are buying phony SIM cards from other countries in order to place these swindling calls. In addition to this, people are also defrauded by simply an SMS. Several people receive an SMS directing them to a scratch card webpage and promising prizes ranging from money to a free night at a posh hotel and other freebies. So, this turns into a scheme to defraud others of their money.

- **Social Media–Based Attack:** Fraudsters also exploit social media sites like Facebook, where the creation of bogus profiles and a cry for assistance results in victims losing money to cyber fraud.

Financially sensitive data is still in danger. While 30% of customers reported computer troubles when requested to download software or visit a website by fraudsters, the percentage of consumers who were asked for their Aadhar Card number (a kind of SSN in India) has grown since 2018, and 16% were asked to visit their banking website. Unsurprisingly, more customers reported fraudulent use of credit/debit or store cards as well as fraudulent use of online retailers, which accounts for the rise in money lost [54].

- **Lack of Awareness and Training:** According to statistics reported by a research-based finding titled the DTCC study, only 28% of CEOs would put in place protections and controls to stop future breaches, and contrary to this, not even half but only 13% would engage in a cybersecurity training program. Only 43% would spend more money on security equipment to protect their customers' personal information and data. On average, banks experience about 85 attempted cyberattacks annually. Finally, it has been determined that a financial institution's entire cybersecurity risk is made up of around 70% of its own workers [55].

- **Ransomware:** Institutions all around the world have been impacted by the growth of ransomware attacks, and Indian institutions are not immune to this danger. Critical data is encrypted by ransomware assaults, and the attackers demand a ransom in exchange for the decryption key, affecting business operations and perhaps resulting in losses for the bank.
- **Bank Reputation:** The reputation of the bank is important. A large hack may certainly lead to a bank's failure. Almost all financial institutions have experienced some sort of cybercrime, and these assaults are happening more often. Financial institutions are 300 times more likely to confront them than other institutions, according to the Boston Consulting Group. This paper also highlights the fact that due to the interconnectedness of the banking sector, there is a substantial potential for cyberattack-related spillover consequences. According to the analysis, one of the five most active U.S. banks could be the target of a cyberattack that would damage 38% of the network. Major banks are also well-connected internationally, leaving them susceptible to greater security threats. Although banks have recently made significant investments in cybersecurity, there have nonetheless been instances where a bank's information security defenses behaved more like a dummy defense shield than an iron vault [56].

5.8 How to Reduce the "Security Threats" in the Banking Sector?

5.8.1 Team Management

Create and use a board that lists the necessary and relevant information as a cybersecurity attack vector: any information on any current concerns and risks; keeping track of historical information from any past cyberattacks (such as IP addresses, server, and domain data, etc.) in order to create profiles of any future cyberattacks.

5.8.2 Creation of R & D Board

Formation and placement of a "Managed Response" team, which consists of a group of people that train constantly to assist organizations and corporations in reducing any form of cyberattack. As a result, they are sometimes referred to as "As Service" offers. These teams are frequently considerably more prepared to assist a financial institution in recovering from a cyberattack than the internal response team itself due to their degree of complexity and skill.

5.8.3 Partnership

Partnerships are being established to strengthen security awareness and lines of defense. For instance, there is a very high likelihood that other companies will also be subject to the same type of cyberattack if a big financial institution is struck by one. Therefore, in order to raise the degree of security awareness overall, it is crucial for financial institutions to communicate what they know.

5.8.4 Framework Compliance

There are many frameworks globally that must be followed to secure the privacy of the person and the confidentiality of the data. Framework, i.e., National Institute of Standards and Technology (NIST) Framework, CBEST–CREST (the Council for Registered Ethical Security Testers) vulnerability testing framework, has been implemented well in many countries of the world. There may be unique security requirements of an individual bank according to the residing country and that bank may develop its own framework centrally, but that framework must be in equivalence to the global standard as security attacks are not launched locally but can come from any part of the globe [57].

5.8.5 Establish Strict Access Management Policies

Strict policies must be formed and should be implemented in a hierarchical manner. Check and control of implementation to assess its efficiency must also be tested well in a regular manner. intrusion detection systems (IDSs)–based policies should also be implemented following BIBA/Be-La-Padula rules. Policy not only for people but also for access control of data and devices must be controlled and regulated. A separate Identity and Access Management (IAM) software must be implemented to achieve the best access management policies [58].

5.8.6 Keep Business Continuity Plan/Disaster Recovery Plan

There is an old proverb that if you fail to plan means you plan to fail, it is true in the case of banking organizations where gain and loss are directly related to money. Business continuity plans must be drafted and implemented well in banking organizations. Major banks have more than two mirrors sever at their cold and hot sites and keep testing those sites in mock drills. Similarly, in a banking organization, a disaster recovery plan should also be ready and a dedicated emergency response team (ERT) should be ready to handle any casual situation [59].

5.8.7 Cybersecurity Training

One of the most crucial ideas to understand about cybersecurity is that upkeep is a never-ending task. Your security would be a nightmare if you simply updated your network equipment once a year, which also applies to your personnel [60].

5.9 Conclusion

The banking industry's main worry is cybersecurity. In order to save expenses, today's financial institutions frequently rely on outside parties to carry out routine job duties. They must be trained and subjected to the same level of scrutiny as normal workers, if not more.

Form alliances to strengthen security awareness and the lines of defense. For instance, there is a very high likelihood that other companies will also be subject to the same type of cyberattack if a big financial institution is struck by one. Therefore, in order to raise the general level of security awareness, it is crucial for financial institutions to communicate what they know. Today's cyber-based threats and attacks are incredibly sneaky and covert, so it is crucial to remember that the attackers aren't simply pursuing individual financial accounts.

In the FinTech industry, advanced technologies are essential to cybersecurity. Proactive threat identification is aided by AI, ML, and analytics. Additionally, they guarantee quicker examination of huge amounts of data. As a result, you can promptly identify, foresee, and take action against the threats: financial frauds, insider threats, known security threats, unknown vulnerabilities, known risks, emerging risks, unauthorized data access and usage, network-based problems, corporate espionage, and irregular activities.

References

1. Oruganti, S., What will it take for the Digital Rupee to be widely acceptable in India? 2023, March 17. https://www.ey.com/en_in/financial-services/what-will-it-take-for-the-digital-rupee-to-be-widely-acceptable-in-india
2. Andolfatto, D., Assessing the Impact of Central Bank Digital Currency on Private Banks. *Economic. J.*, *131*, 634, 525–540, 2020, https://doi.org/10.1093/ej/ueaa073.
3. Wang, C., Fan, X., Zhe, Y., Financing online retailers: Bank vs. electronic business platform, equilibrium, and coordinating strategy. *Eur. J. Oper. Res.*, *276*, 1, 343–356, 2019, https://doi.org/10.1016/j.ejor.2019.01.009.
4. Kannabiran, G. and Narayan, P., Deploying Internet banking and e-commerce—case study of a private-sector bank in India. *Inf. Technol. Dev.*, *11*, 4, 363–379, 2005, https://doi.org/10.1002/itdj.20025.
5. Huang, H., Xiong, Z., Kang, J., Zheng, Z., Fusing blockchain and AI with metaverse: a survey. *IEEE Open J. Comput. Soc.*, 3, 122–136, 2022. https://doi.org/10.1109/ojcs.2022.3188249
6. Alonso, S., Vázquez, J.J., Forradellas, R.F.R., Central Banks Digital Currency: Detection of Optimal Countries for the Implementation of a CBDC and the Implication for Payment Industry Open Innovation. *J. Open Innov.*, *7*, 1, 72, 2021, https://doi.org/10.3390/joitmc7010072.
7. Huang, Y. and Mayer, M., Digital currencies, monetary sovereignty, and U.S.–China power competition. *Policy Internet*, *14*, 2, 324–347, 2022. https://doi.org/10.1002/poi3.302.
8. Akinlo, A.E. and Odusola, A., Assessing the impact of Nigeria's naira depreciation on output and inflation. *Appl. Econ.*, *35*, 6, 691–703, 2003, https://doi.org/10.1080/0003684032000056823.
9. Raskin, M. and Yermack, D., Digital Currencies, Decentralized Ledgers, and the Future of Central Banking. Peter Conti-Brown & Rosa Lastra (eds.), *Research Handbook on Central Banking*, Edward Elgar Publishing, Spring 2017, Forthcoming, May 1, 2016, Available at SSRN: https://ssrn.com/abstract=2773973
10. Corbet, S., Lucey, B.M., Urquhart, A., Yarovaya, L., Cryptocurrencies as a financial asset: A systematic analysis. *Int. Rev. Financial Anal.*, *62*, 182–199, 2019, https://doi.org/10.1016/j.irfa.2018.09.003.
11. Choo, K.R., Cryptocurrency and Virtual Currency, in: *Elsevier eBooks*, pp. 283–307, 2015, https://doi.org/10.1016/b978-0-12-802117-0.00015-1.
12. Bhuvana, R. and Aithal, S., RBI Distributed Ledger Technology and Blockchain - A Future of Decentralized India. *Int. J. Manage. Technol. Soc. Sci.*, 5, 1, 227–237, 2015, https://doi.org/10.47992/ijmts.2581.6012.0091.
13. Ashish, D., Is e-RUPI a Cryptocurrency like Bitcoin? Stable Investor, 2021, August 17. https://stableinvestor.com/2021/08/erupi-not-cryptocurrency.html

14. Invest, T. and Invest, T., Time to decrypt cryptocurrency. *Help readers understand topics related to markets, economy, Pers. finance Focus ETFs*, 2021, https://tavaga.com/blog/time-to-decrypt-cryptocurrency/.
15. Ashish, D., What is Digital Rupee & How to use E-Rupee in India (2023)? *Stable Investor*, 2023, https://stableinvestor.com/2023/01/digital-rupee-e-rupee-india.html.
16. Moore, T.M., The promise and perils of digital currencies. *Int. J. Crit. Infrastruct. Prot.*, 6, 3–4, 147–149, 2013, https://doi.org/10.1016/j.ijcip.2013.08.002.
17. Ozili, P.K., Central bank digital currency research around the world: a review of literature. *J. Money Laund. Control.*, 26, 2, 215–226, 2022, https://doi.org/10.1108/jmlc-11-2021-0126.
18. Detragiache, E. and Tressel, T., Gupta, P., Foreign Banks in Poor Countries: Theory and Evidence. *J. Finance*, *63*, 5, 2123–2160, 2018, https://doi.org/10.1111/j.1540-6261.2008.01392.x.
19. Das, S.K. and Uppal, K., NPAs and profitability in Indian banks: an empirical analysis. *Future Bus. J.*, *7*, 1, 2021, https://doi.org/10.1186/s43093-021-00096-3.
20. Chakrabarti, S., Trehan, D., Makhija, M., Assessment of service quality using text mining – evidence from private sector banks in India. *Int. J. Bank Mark.*, *36*, 4, 594–615, 2018, https://doi.org/10.1108/ijbm-04-2017-0070.
21. Agrawal, S., Mittal, M., Gupta, R., Service Quality in Public and Private Sector Banks of India. *Int. J. Cust. Relat.*, *4*, 1, 2016, https://doi.org/10.21863/ijcr/2016.4.1.016.
22. Sharma, D., Nexus between financial inclusion and economic growth. *J. Financ. Econ. Policy*, *8*, 1, 13–36, 2016. https://doi.org/10.1108/jfep-01-2015-0004.
23. Kumari, J.M., Central Bank Digital Currency (CBDC) Can it Replace Notes and Coins in India. *Shanlax Int. J. Manage.*, *8*, S1-Feb, 21–28, 2021, https://doi.org/10.34293/management.v8is1-feb.3754.
24. Iqbal, B.A. and Sami, S., Role of banks in financial inclusion in India. *Contaduría Y Administración*, *62*, 2, 644–656, 2017, https://doi.org/10.1016/j.cya.2017.01.007.
25. *Future Direction of Indian Banking and Career Opportunities in Banking Sector By M.V Tanksale,CE,IBA*, 2022, https://slideplayer.com/slide/9217261/.
26. Brandt, M., Online Banking Rivals Physical Branch Banking. *Statista Daily Data*, 2012, https://www.statista.com/chart/467/channels-used-for-investment-transactions/.
27. Geeta, D.V., Online identity theft – an Indian perspective. *J. Financ. Crime*, *18*, 3, 235–246, 2011, https://doi.org/10.1108/13590791111147451.
28. Online, Et., *Public Sector Banks Were Much Easier to Defraud Than Private Sector Ones: Here's Why*, 29 Aug. 2018, The Economic Times, economictimes.indiatimes.com/wealth/personal-finance-news/public-sector-banks-are-much-easier-to-defraud-than-private-sector-ones-heres-the-proof/articleshow/65592437.cms?utm_source=contentofinterest&utm_medium=-text&utm_campaign=cppst.

29. Nidugala, G.K. and Pant, A., Lessons From NPAs Crisis in Indian Banks. *J. Public Aff.*, 17, 4, e1672, Aug. 2017, https://doi.org/10.1002/pa.1672.
30. Alonso, S., Fernández, M.A. *et al.*, Reasons Fostering or Discouraging the Implementation of Central Bank-Backed Digital Currency: A Review. *Economies*, 8, 2, 41, May 2020, https://doi.org/10.3390/economies8020041.
31. Agrawal, N., 5G And IoT Vs Cyber Security: Addressing the Elephant in the Room, 1 Dec. 2020, nopr.niscpr.res.in/handle/123456789/55721.
32. 10.2 Monetary and Financial Statistics, in: *Ministry Of Statistics and Program Implementation*, Government of India, mospi.gov.in/102-monetary-and-financial-statistics.
33. Peysieux, S., *Inventiva Reports Its 2022 Full-Year Results - Inventiva Pharma*, Inventiva Pharma, 29 Mar. 2023, inventivapharma.com/inventiva-reports-its-2022-full-year-results. https://inventivapharma.com/inventiva-reports-its-2022-full-year-results/
34. Gangwani, M., Suitability of Forensic Accounting in Uncovering Bank Frauds in India: An Opinion Survey. *J. Financ. Crime*, 28, 1, 284–99, Emerald Publishing Limited, Nov. 2020, https://doi.org/10.1108/jfc-07-2020-0126.
35. Adrian, T. and Griffoli, T.M., The Rise of Digital Money. *Fintech Notes*, 19, 01, International Monetary Fund, July 2019. https://doi.org/10.5089/9781498324908.063.
36. Kaspersky: The State of Industrial Cyber Security, in: *Network Security*, vol. 2019, p. 4, Elsevier BV, Sept. 2019, https://doi.org/10.1016/s1353-4858(19)30104-7.
37. Cyber Report. *CNBC*, 26 Jan. 2023, www.cnbc.com/cyber-report.
38. Jassal, R.K. and Sehgal, R.N.M., Study of Online Banking Security Mechanism in India: Take ICICI Bank as an Example. *IOSR J. Comput. Eng.*, 13, 1, 114–21, International Organization Of Scientific Research (IOSR), Jan. 2013, https://doi.org/10.9790/0661-131114121.
39. Suitability of Forensic Accounting in Uncovering Bank Frauds in India: An Opinion Survey. *J. Financ. Crime*, 28, 1, 284–99, Emerald Publishing Limited, Nov. 2020, https://doi.org/10.1108/jfc-07-2020-0126.
40. Alghazo, J. *et al.*, *Cyber Security Analysis of Internet Banking in Emerging Countries: User and Bank Perspectives*, 2017, https://doi.org/10.1109/icetas.2017.8277910.
41. Payandeh, M., The Concept of International Law in the Jurisprudence of H.L.A. Hart. *Eur. J. Int. Law*, 21, 4, 967–95, Oxford UP, Nov. 2010, https://doi.org/10.1093/ejil/chq065.
42. Fuller, L.L., Positivism and Fidelity to Law: A Reply to Professor Hart. *Harv. Law Rev.*, 71, 4, 630, Harvard Law Review Association, Feb. 1958, https://doi.org/10.2307/1338226.
42. Da Xu, L. *et al.*, Industry 4.0: State of the Art and Future Trends. *Int. J. Prod. Res.*, 56, 8, 2941–62, Taylor and Francis, Mar. 2018, https://doi.org/10.1080/00207543.2018.1444806.

43. Lee, I. and Shin, Y.S., Fintech: Ecosystem, Business Models, Investment Decisions, and Challenges. *Bus. Horiz.*, 61, 1, 35–46, Elsevier BV, Jan. 2018, https://doi.org/10.1016/j.bushor.2017.09.003.
44. Button, M. *et al.*, Online Frauds: Learning From Victims Why They Fall for These Scams. *Aust. N. Z. J. Criminol.*, 47, 3, 391–408, SAGE Publishing, Mar. 2014, https://doi.org/10.1177/0004865814521224.
45. Financial Services & Banking Reports and research. 2024, April 15. https://business.yougov.com/sectors/banking-insurance
46. Wazid, M. *et al.*, Mobile Banking: Evolution and Threats: Malware Threats and Security Solutions. *IEEE Consum. Electron. Mag.*, 8, 2, 56–60, Institute of Electrical and Electronics Engineers, Mar. 2019, https://doi.org/10.1109/mce.2018.2881291.
47. Suman, A. and Joshi, S., Impact Of Cyber-Attacks On Banking Institutions In India: A Study Of Safety Mechanisms And Preventive Measures. *Palarch's J. Archaeol. Egypt Egyptology*, 17, 6, ISSN 1567-214x.
48. Gupta, N., A Study to Analyze The Impact Of New Rbi Cyber Security Guidelines And Its Comparison With NIST Framework. *Int. J. Educ. Mod. Manage. Appl. Sci. Soc. Sci.*, 03, 03(I), 2581–9925, Sept. 2021, www.inspira-journals.com/uploads/Issues/1440414074.pdf.
49. RBI guidelines for banks to combat escalating cyber attacks - CloudSEK, 2020, Retrieved 13, June 2021, from https://cloudsek.com/rbi-guidelines-on-how-banks-can-be-resilient-in-the-face-of-escalating-cyber-attacks/.
50. NIST Framework, Retrieved from https://www.nist.gov/industry-impacts/cybersecurity-framework.
51. Top Cyber Security Assessment Frameworks for Banks Around the Globe. *CISO Platform*, 18 Aug. 2016, www.cisoplatform.com/profiles/blogs/top-security-frameworks-for-banks-around-the-globe.
52. Jamtara India: The Hub of Cyber Crime. www.legalserviceindia.com/legal/article-10200-jamtara-india-the-hub-of-cyber-crime.html.
53. State of Cybercrime. *Microsoft Secur.*, www.microsoft.com/en-in/security/business/microsoft-digital-defense-report-2022-state-of-cybercrime.
54. Bani-Hani, A. *et al.*, Online Authentication Methods Used in Banks and Attacks Against These Methods. *Proc. Comput. Sci.*, 151, 1052–59, Elsevier BV, Jan. 2019, https://doi.org/10.1016/j.procs.2019.04.149.
55. Das, R., Why Does the Finance Industry Need Security Awareness Training? *Infosec. Resour.*, 15 Oct. 2020, resources.infosecinstitute.com/topic/finance-industry-need-security-awareness-training.
56. Jung, J.H. *et al.*, Repackaging Attack on Android Banking Applications and Its Countermeasures. *Wirel. Pers. Commun.*, 73, 4, 1421–37, Springer Science+Business Media, June 2013, https://doi.org/10.1007/s11277-013-1258-x.
57. Barth, J.R. *et al.*, A Cross-Country Analysis of the Bank Supervisory Framework and Bank Performance. *Financ. Mark. Inst. Instrum.*, 12, 2,

Wiley–Blackwell67–120, May 2003, https://doi.org/10.1111/1468-0416.t01-2-00001.

58. Liu, Y.-H. and Chen, X., *A New Information Security Model Based on BLP Model and BIBA Model*, 2005, https://doi.org/10.1109/icosp.2004.1442325.
59. Ayadi, R. and *et al.*, Does Basel Compliance Matter for Bank Performance? *J. Financ. Stab.*, 23, 15–32, Elsevier BV, Apr. 2016, https://doi.org/10.1016/j.jfs.2015.12.007.
60. Tahir, N. *et al.*, The Impact of Training and Development on Employees Performance and Productivity a Case Study of United Bank Limited Peshawar City, KPK, Pakistan. *Int. J. Acad. Res. Bus. Soc. Sci.*, 4, 4, Apr. 2014, https://doi.org/10.6007/ijarbss/v4-i4/756.

6

Navigating the Legal Landscape of Green Finance and Responsible Investment in India: A Critical Analysis

Shikha Dimri* **and Anushka Srivastava**

School of Law, UPES, Dehradun, India

Abstract

The robust commitment to attain sustainable development goals requires a paradigm shift in the financial investment mechanism, leading to the introduction of green finance and responsible investment the picture. With the growing consciousness of the consumers, it has become imperative for the business houses to act sustainably. Therefore, to put that responsibility into practice, the concept of issuance of green finance emerged, certain sources of green finance are green bonds, and green corporate social responsibility is dedicated to financing green projects that intend to upgrade the environment. However, with green finance, the challenging problem of greenwashing pops up, which deceives customers and other stakeholders into believing that the operations of corporate houses are environmentally sustainable. The researchers have emphasized the role of legal provisions that are attempting to leave no stone unturned to engage corporate houses in environment preservation nevertheless, there are certain lacunae associated with those legislations. Such norms are thriving to pay attention to the environmental degradation caused due to business houses and further compelling them to address these challenges in various forms ranging from issuance of green debt securities, calling out greenwashing to mandatory corporate social responsibility. The impact of green debt securities in advancing sustainability is descriptively discussed thereby addressing the various challenges associated with it that call for legal acknowledgment such as the lack of internal capacity and regime to manage the green bond process, the complex rules that require compliance, and the

**Corresponding author*: shikha@ddn.upes.ac.in: ORCID: https://orcid.org/0000-0002-2973-3131

Anushka Srivastava: ORCID: https://orcid.org/0009-0002-7146-4729

Ernesto D.R. Santibanez Gonzalez, Vinay Kandpal, Peterson K. Ozili and Prasenjit Chatterjee (eds.) Fintech for ESG and the Circular Economy, (93–118) © 2024 Scrivener Publishing LLC

deceiving practices of companies such as greenwashing. Certain regulations dealing with green financing and responsible investment are critically examined concerning environmentally advanced countries in this study.

Keywords: Environment, green debt securities, SEBI, greenwashing, National Green Tribunal

6.1 Introduction

A significant surge has been witnessed in the realm of corporate sustainability. This shift has gone from companies freely engaging in sustainable operations to companies being required to do so to satisfy both community standards and legal pressure. Lately, global challenges such as climate change, environmental degradation, and emissions of carbon have risen to the forefront of public attention. A significant number of companies have implemented sustainability plans and released environmental, social, and governance (ESG) information, which has led to major shifts in management and business models. To ensure the capability of future generations to live a healthy life in a secure and wholesome setting, it is crucial that the judicious use of natural resources takes place. It is high time to strive toward restoring the environment and bringing certain practices into the loop that are sustainable in nature (Cortellini and Panetta, 2021) [1]. Given the fact that industrialization is a major factor contributing to the deterioration of the environment around us, business houses are required to own up and follow a triple-bottom-line approach. There are different forms in which the business houses can contribute to the upliftment of the environment such as the issuance of green debt securities, investing in green corporate social responsibility, and refraining from participating in greenwashing. Green finance has risen tremendously in the past 10 years, which signifies the rising consciousness and concern of the industries toward the environment and its welfare (Çalıyurt, 2019) [2]. Green bonds are regarded as a primary instrument of the initiatives that intend to finance environmentally friendly infrastructure, as they provide a method for assisting finance the expenses of transforming the Indian economy to zero emissions. To combat climate change and increase the availability of reliable electricity, India has set aspirational targets for the use of renewable energy. India has set a laudable goal of installing 175 GW of solar, wind, and other renewable energy capacity by 2022, which is expected to cost a whopping US$264 billion. Scaling up new banking vehicles like green bonds is essential if we are to raise the necessary capital to meet these global commitments (Freeburn and Ramsay, 2020) [3]. These goals call for the issuance of certain financial instruments so that the projects can be implemented However, with the issuance of green debt securities comes various challenges associated with it such as the inconveniently costly process, complicated rules, and norms, complex mechanisms for the issuance, and greenwashing. Greenwashing is the deceiving tactic followed by business houses that create an image that the process followed by them is environmentally sustainable, thus raising funds through green debt securities; however, the reality of the mechanism says otherwise. Hence, India needs strong legislation to govern green debt securities and their issuance, green corporate social responsibility, and eventually curb the practice of greenwashing.

Research Methodology of the Study

To achieve the objectives of this research study, a careful critical review of the existing literature on green finance and responsible investment has been undertaken. The researcher has referred to a structured literature review to extract and study the apt available literature for the study. Parallelly, this has also been contrasted with the way the subject of the research problem has been dealt with in advanced countries. In this study, the researchers have covered both the public and private sector investments more comprehensively and specifically. Given the choice and central theme of the subject, the research will primarily be based on secondary data and is qualitative in nature. Secondary sources of data shall be utilized by the researcher to conduct this study. The overall method of the research is analytical and descriptive. As for the comparative analysis, the researcher has referred to systematic content analysis. The researcher has referred to credible secondary sources such as textbooks, journal articles, reports, and case studies.

6.1.1 Green Financing in India

The adverse impact of climate change is irreversible and agriculture, food, water supplies, etc., are vulnerable to their potential implications on temperature, changes in precipitation, ocean level, and the occurrence of climate calamities (Kesharao, 2017) [4]. The livelihoods of inhabitants of developing nations, as well as current success in the battle against poverty, famine, and diseases, are at risk. To overcome such a formidable obstacle, it is essential to simultaneously emphasize its social aspects while engaging in two distinct but related strategies: abatement, to prevent the uncontrollable, and adaptability, to deal with the unpredictable (Camilleri, 2017) [5].

To combat climate change, countries around the world have begun to work together like never before. The World Bank Group is working to assist developing nations and advance global progress by aiding and adapting its methods to meet the specific requirements of its developing country (Khan *et al.*, 2022) [6]. The "Strategic Framework for Development and Climate Change" was introduced by the World Bank in 2008 to coordinate and boost the industries to address climate change globally and within this framework, the World Bank has launched initiatives like the World Bank Green Bonds (From India to Indonesia, Green Bonds Help Countries Move Toward Sustainability, 2023) [7]. Green debt securities are those financial instruments that are utilized to finance environmentally sustainable projects. The purpose of issuing green bonds is to mitigate climate change and meet sustainable goals by the end of 2030. In every economy, there is a segment of the corporate bond market that is referred to as the green bond market (Bachnik *et al.*, 2022) [8]. A green bond acts almost like a regular bond, namely, as an instrument of debt that is issued by a business to collect investment funds. Nevertheless, the line of demarcation between the two is that the issuance of green bonds in the market is earmarked to be used toward the funding of green initiatives. To increase energy availability and global security coupled with attaining India has established ambitious goals related to renewable energy, India has committed to 17 sustainable development goals (SDGs). To accomplish its goal of installing 175 gigawatts of capacity for solar, wind, and other forms of renewable energy by the year 2022, India has committed to a gigantic undertaking that requires an estimated significant financing of over US$264 billion (Ministry of New and Renewable Energy, 2018) [9]. As a result, to expand the mandatory and required financing to accomplish these goals, new and novel instruments raising finance, such as green bonds, need to be scaled up. As a result, the set goals shall be made stringent and the market for green debt securities shall be extended with the objective of (Krichewsky, 2019) [10]:

- Reducing the capital cost (Chen *et al.*, 2023) [11].
- Expanding the base of issuers and investors (Hay *et al.*, 2010) [12].
- Determining a flexible and balanced interest rate that inspires more investment.

6.2 Legal Framework Governing Green Finance and Investment in India

In India, both listed and unlisted companies can issue green debt securities. For the green bonds issued by unlisted companies, there are no hard and fast rules or specific guidelines, other than the principal requirements for the issuance of green bonds. As for raising green finance by the listed companies, the issuer needs to abide by the guidelines set under different regulatory frameworks listed below:

- The SEBI (Issue and Listing of Non-Convertible Securities) Regulations, 2021.
- The SEBI (Listing Obligations and Disclosure Requirements) Regulations, 2015; and
- Chapter IX of the SEBI Operational Circular for Issue and Listing of Non-convertible Securities.

In 2015, SEBI issued a consultation paper on its website detailing the issuance of green bonds in India. SEBI has begun the process of consulting with interested parties regarding the disclosure requirements for the issuance and listing of Green Bonds along with the issuance of green bonds by private industries. A detailed concept paper was posted on the official website of SEBI on December 3, 2015, to solicit feedback from the public. The disclosing requirements were formulated by the Green Bond Principles, 2015 (GBP) (Securities and Exchange Board of India, 2015) [13]. The briefs of the consultation paper are listed below (de Freitas Netto *et al.*, 2020) [14]:

- **Use of proceeds**: The party issuing the bonds is required to develop and properly disclose the criteria following which the eligibility of the proposed project, assets, or activities be determined. There shall be criteria identification for various kinds of projects.
- **Project evaluation**: Complete details and checklist following which a project would be evaluated for using the proceeds from the Green Bonds. The information concerning the process that shall be followed to examine the sustainability of specific projects or activities shall be disclosed.
- **Administration of the profits**: Specifics regarding the procedures and checks that will be carried out to guarantee that

the allocated cash will be put toward the "green" projects only.

- **Reporting**: It entails the examination of the progress made on the projects to which green bonds have been allocated, with respect to both its sustainability and finance utilization (Green Bond Principles » ICMA, n.d.) [15].

In accordance with the NCS Regulations, primarily, those bonds aiming to raise finance dedicated to activities and projects falling in the categories mentioned below shall be referred to as green bonds (2022) [16].

- Projects that promote renewable energy using clean technology.
- Projects endorsing clean and green transportation contributing to pollution reduction such as mass transportation.
- Projects including sustainable water management such as water recycling, and clean water.
- Projects mitigating climate change.
- Projects promoting energy efficiency and the development of green buildings.
- Projects endorsing sustainable waste management which further includes waste recycling, energy generation, and systematic waste disposal.
- Sustainable use of land further including sustainable agriculture and afforestation.
- Protection of wildlife.
- Further categories can be listed by SEBI at its discretion.

The SEBI operational circular assembled numerous circulars focused on non-convertible securities which has superseded the green bonds circular of 2017. Chapter IX of the SEBI operational circular (Securities and Exchange Board of India, 2021) [17] mentions certain supplemental requirements that are to be disclosed concerning the issuance of green debt securities. In addition to the disclosure necessities for a public or private placement of green bonds under the NCS regulations and current circular governing green bonds include:

- Statement of the project for which green debt securities are to be issued.
- Information shall necessarily be considered by the party issuing green bonds to examine the eligibility of the project

being green. The issuer shall mandatorily follow the process using which the sustainability and the nature of the project are determined whether it falls under the criteria issued by SEBI or not.

- Relevant information concerned with the procedure implemented for tracking the deployment of the proceeds.
- Relevant information regarding the project for which the issuance is being considered shall be disclosed. Whether the raised finance be invested in an already existing project shall be disclosed.
- Specifics of the impartial third reviewer/certifier assigned by the lender for evaluating the procedures, such as project assessment, project classifications qualified for funding by green debt securities, etc., if such a reviewer/certifier has been assigned by the issuer. The assigning of such a person is voluntary; however, the offer document must include all disclosures that are required in this respect if the person is chosen.

On a regular basis, the party issuing the green bonds shall also disclose these additional details:

- The details of the utilization of the raised finance shall be disclosed on a half-yearly and annual basis. The disclosed report shall be examined by an external auditor.
- It shall further disclose the annual report of the issuer and the information shall necessarily contain:
  a) List of the projects that will receive funding from green bonds along with the details and amount that is allocated to a particular project. Nevertheless, there is an exception for the projects that are confidential in nature, the locations of such projects or assets are sufficient.
  b) Metrics to measure the performance (quantitative/qualitative) of the environmental impact of the projects. In instances, where the quantitative advantages or impacts cannot be determined, the required declarations in this respect are required to be provided in addition to the primary motivations for the inability to determine the perks or impacts on the environment.
  c) The techniques and the primary underlying principles that were applied in the process of preparing the performance measures and predictors.

d) In addition, under the LODR regulations, the issuers of a listed debt security shall make necessary and consistent disclosures to the concerned stock exchange and, if required, to SEBI. These obligations shall necessarily be fulfilled (Securities and Exchange Board of India, 2021) [18].

Additional Legal Requirements

The projects that receive funding through the issuance of green bonds shall comply with the eligibility criteria not only initially but also during the execution and the entire duration of the project completion. The objectives of the project shall be disclosed in the offer document. The issuer party is further required to formulate a process that ensures the continuity of the project in alignment with its pre-conceived environmental objective (Labelled Green Bonds Data: Latest 3 Months) [19].

6.3 Certain Indian Companies Engaged in Green Financing and Responsible Investment

Table 6.1 shows the list of green bonds issued ini India till 2020. This table indicates the active participation of corporate houses in India to raise funds for the attainment of SDGs. The pursuit of ESG investment by businesses is encouraged by sustainable financing, which helps alleviate the shortage

Table 6.1 Certain companies issuing green bonds in India till 2020 (Bagaria, 2021) [25].

S. no	Issuer	Amount (US$ Million)	Year and month of issuance
1.	ReNew Energy Global (ReNew raises US$400 million by issuing green bonds | ReNew, n.d.) [20]	400	January 2022
2.	State Bank of India (2021) [21]	650	November 2021

(Continued)

Table 6.1 Certain companies issuing green bonds in India till 2020 (Bagaria, 2021) [25]. *(Continued)*

S. no	Issuer	Amount (US$ Million)	Year and month of issuance
3.	Adani Green Energy Limited [22]	750	September 2021
4.	ACME Solar (ACME Solar Holdings raises US$334 million via green bonds, 2021) [23]	334	July 2021
5.	Adani Electricity Mumbai Limited (2021) [24]	300	July 2021
6.	State Bank of India	100	March 2020
7.	ReNew Power	450	January 2020
8.	Adani Green Energy	362	October 2019
9.	State Bank of India	650	September 2019
10.	Azure Power	350	September 2019
11.	ReNew Power	300	September 2019
12.	Greenko	300	August 2019
13.	Greenko	950	July 2019
14.	Adani Green Energy	500	June 2019
15.	ReNew Power	375	March 2019
16.	Indian Railway Finance Corporation	500	December 2017
17.	Power Finance Corporation	400	December 2017
18.	IREDA	19.5 (Billion)	September 2017
19.	Azure Power	500	August 2017

(Continued)

Table 6.1 Certain companies issuing green bonds in India till 2020 (Bagaria, 2021) [25]. (*Continued*)

S. no	Issuer	Amount (US$ Million)	Year and month of issuance
20.	Rural Electrification Corporation	450	July 2017
21.	IREDA	7 (Billion)	March 2017
22.	ReNew Power	475	February 2017
23.	Greenko	500	August 2016
24.	NTPC	20 (Billion)	August 2016
25.	ReNew Power	5 (Billion)	August 2016
26.	Axis Bank	500	June 2016
27.	PNB Housing Finance	5 (Billion)	April 2016
28.	Hero Future Energies	3 (Billion)	February 2016
29.	IDBI Bank	350	November 2015
30.	CLP Wind Farms	6 (Billion)	September 2015
31.	EXIM Bank	500	March 2015
32.	YES Bank	10 (Billion)	February 2015

of capital that hinders the growth of a green economy. Green bonds, which are one of the most significant carriers of green finance, contribute favorably to the process of financing the shift toward a low-carbon economy. Since green bonds combine conventional financial qualities with an overarching commitment to addressing environmental concerns, they serve as an extraordinarily efficient link between the worlds of corporate finance and corporate sustainability.

6.4 Interface of Sustainable Development Goals and Green Finance

In 2015, the United Nations proposed and sought a commitment from several countries contributing to the establishment of several goals that align with sustainable development. The SDGs possess the capability to contribute to environmental justice. Though environmental justice is not specifically embedded into the language or spirit of the SDGs, it is apparent that certain goals such as life on land, life below water, and cleaner cities are the flag bearers of climate justice to which individuals are entitled. The establishment of these goals is a call to seek actions from countries to fight against climate change and encourage sustainability. This 2030 agenda lays down a blueprint for empowering peace and prosperity across the world. Most of the goals go hand in hand with each other, thus keeping the eventual target similar for all. The effective realization of the SDGs is dependent on prompt action being taken to both combat the negative impact of climate change and reduce the disruptions it causes. The most significant obstacle that stands in the way of progress is climate change. Among the 17 SDGs, 6 goals are specifically dedicated to environmental welfare and preservation which are listed below (Kroll *et al.*, 2019) [26]:

To transform these SDGs into reality, it is of essence to raise the required finance, and this is when green debt securities come into the picture. As per the Climate Bonds Initiative 2018, approximately US$409 billion has been raised through the issuance of green bonds (India, 2023) [27]. The finance raised by the green bonds has been effectively contributing to the attainment of these goals. The green bond market is an example of how climate change can be incorporated into the SDGs mentioned in Figure 6.1 to raise finances from investors. It is of the utmost importance to accelerate the integration of solutions addressing climate change across private and public sectors. At this point, the world economy is still lagging on the level of investments that are climate-aligned to attain the objectives of the Paris Agreement let alone reaching a target of 1.5 degrees Celsius. To achieve such targets, the issuance of bonds that are congruent with global climate targets certainly needs a boost. To realize the SDGs, it is predicted that the global community will require an annual contribution of US$5 trillion to

Figure 6.1 SDGs focused on climate mitigation.

US$6 trillion. The provision of this capital cannot be accomplished solely through public financing. Every sector, but especially the commercial sector, needs to contribute. Sustainable green finance is attracting attention from global financial and political actors, in addition to the public, as there is a rising awareness of the need for a transition in the financial industry. To close the funding gap of the SDGs, the financial sector needs to incorporate sustainability standards.

6.5 CSR Rules and Companies Act, 2013, and Environmental Justice

In the landmark case, "Vellore Citizens Welfare Forum v. Union of India" (Vellore Citizen v UOI) [28], the Supreme Court extensively adopted the notion of sustainable development as an adjusting concept. Simultaneously, the court overturned the long-held belief that growth and environmental protection cannot coexist. The apex court of India held the notion that sustainable development is now universally acknowledged as a feasible idea to alleviate poverty and enhance the living standards of humans within the range of supporting ecosystems. Therefore, the amount of pollution that is produced because of development needs to be proportionate to the capacity of our environment to support it. There are several provisions in the Indian constitution that promote environmental welfare, i.e., Article 48(a), Article 51(a)(g), and Article 253, which empower the parliament to make laws to implement international treaties and conventions.

In the context of sustainable development and maintaining the ecological balance, in "M.K Ranjitsinh v Union of India" (WPC 838 of 2019) [29], the court directed to preserve the environment and endangered species via CSR. To generate business in the direction of sustainable practices, SEBI has repeatedly issued sustainable reporting guidelines. One of the fundamental parts of the approach was the construction of a system for environmental management by corporations that would deter them from causing environmental damage while conducting official operations. The "Business Responsibility Report" is an additional reporting framework that attempts to ensure the ecologically sustainable operation of businesses. The framework provides a disclosure model that organizations can use to evaluate their performance in reporting categories. The entity must comply with eight rules for the environment's principles ranging from recyclable materials to reduction in the emission of greenhouse gasses. In 2021, SEBI made a bold step forward by proposing the Business

Responsibility and Sustainability Report to improve the disclosure of ESG standards. This reporting requirement applies to the top 1,000 enterprises commencing in 2022. The BRSR framework incorporates worldwide ESG standards such as the Global Reporting Initiative (GRI), and both qualitative and quantitative data are reported (Securities and Exchange Board of India, 2023) [30].

6.6 Greenwashing: A Challenge to Honest Implementation of Green Bond

Environmental activist, Jay Westerveld, was the first to introduce the concept of greenwashing by one to start accusing a hotel of greenwashing in 1986, when the hotel encouraged the customers to reuse towels under the illusion that it was part of a water conservation strategic plan, even though there were no environmental activities with serious environmental impact issues in place (Dey, 2022) [31]. Greenwashing in the true sense is the practice of creating a deceptive image about the sustainable and environmentally friendly practices of the organization by keeping the consumers under the assumption that the corporation is environment-friendly in nature.

When the term "Greenwashing" first emerged, it was not expected that the concept would stick for long and be practiced both domestically and globally. It has become a global concern given that thousands of business houses are indulging in it. The possibility of "greenwashing" is among the primary obstacles that must be overcome before the financial markets see a surge in the issuance of green bonds. Greenwashing is the practice of directing earnings from green bonds into projects that have either no environmental advantages at all or impacts that detract from the environment. It poses a huge risk to the credibility of socially aware investors who are looking to broaden their investment strategies by purchasing methods that are environmentally friendly, socially responsible, and democratically accountable. The developer of the Three Gorges Corp in China, which has been roundly criticized for causing pollution and harming the ecosystems in the surrounding areas, recently issued green bonds, which is one of the contentious instances (Collins and Northrup, 2022) [32].

The major challenge that comes with the issuance of green bonds in the market is greenwashing. The crashing environmental conditions have prompted businesses to pursue the development and enhancement of environmentally friendly products. However, a certain number of businesses have indulged themselves in a practice known as greenwashing, which encourages them to mislead their stakeholders. India is dealing with several environmental issues, including increasing air pollution, food insecurity, and pollution from e-waste disposal. 2.3 million metric tons of CO2 emissions were generated in 2017, placing them in third place behind only China and the United States, which has been a long-time polluter ace (Chateau and Dang, 2023) [33]. Corporate houses are under pressure in recent times due to their stakeholders, such as consumers, investors, governments, and corporate customers, to reveal details regarding their sustainability impact and to produce environmentally friendly products.

The greenwashing procedures have increased to epidemic compositions over the past few decades and are now widespread. As green markets emerge accompanied by the proliferation of greenwashing, the customers are confronted with difficulty, distinguishing between a genuine green claim and a greenwashing claim. With the rise of greenwashing, there has been an increase in green skepticism, which has the potential to impede green marketing. Genuine green claims are met with greater skepticism, as customers struggle to distinguish between the durability of green marketing initiatives and the reliability of other marketing initiatives. When it comes to the seven sins of greenwashing, TerraChoice has released a study to assist customers in identifying greenwashing practices by businesses. The seven sins vehemently emphasize hidden trade-offs, absence of proof, vagueness, false labels, less relevance, lesser of two evils, and lastly, fibbing (Singh, 2019) [34].

Environmental awareness has increased throughout society, particularly among consumers, who are increasingly interested in environmentally friendly products. It has been estimated that around 66% of global consumers intend to pay more for eco-friendly products, as per a study conducted by Nielsen Media Customers who think that a company is socially ethical, are generally willing to pay more ("Recent Study Reveals More Than a Third of Global Consumers Are Willing to Pay More for Sustainability as Demand Grows for Environmentally Friendly Alternatives," 2021) [35]. It is asserted that the companies must be self-sustaining and socially conscious, rather than simply profitable. Three bottom lines must be targeted by companies: financial performance, environmental performance, and social performance. Section 135 of the Companies Act states that profit-making corporations are required by Indian company law to allocate funds to CSR activities unrelated to their core business. As part of their CSR strategy, many corporations opt to sponsor environmental causes, such as afforestation or the development of solar parks. There is potential for more concerted use of CSR money to address climate change, and greater impact shall be attained by forming CSR fund pooling vehicles that target climate mitigation measures directly. However, certain CSR compliance requirements, specifically the necessity to transfer "unspent" CSR payments to designated government relief funds, may be incompatible with the needs of climate projects with long gestation times.

6.6.1 Renowned Brands Called Out for Greenwashing

Greenwashing refers to the practice of making products appear more environmentally friendly. The practice allows businesses to care while increasing overall profit margins, as they understand the environmental concerns of the consumers these days. The McDonald's controversy that erupted in 2019 was brought to public attention when it was discovered that the paper straws launched by the company were not recyclable. The tactic of applying a green label on a product to make it appear healthier is another example of greenwashing. Coca-Cola did this with Coca-Cola Life, which was not a healthy beverage due to its 6.6% sugar content (Robinson, 2022) [36].

6.6.1.1 H&M and Uniqlo ("USA: H&M faces 'greenwashing' class-action lawsuit over alleged misleading & false marketing of 'sustainable' clothing line - business & human rights resource centre," n.d) [37]

Brands like H&M, Zara, and Uniqlo were among those that have been trapped under greenwashing. These brands are huge contributors to the waste generated by the apparel industry. Fast fashion companies also have a habit of publicizing their environmental initiatives widely, even though they account for a small portion of their overall operations. Consider the case of H&M, which in 2019 debuted its very own line of environment-friendly clothing dubbed Conscious. Organic cotton and recycled polyester, according to the company, are used. The line, on the other hand, is nothing more than a marketing ploy to make themselves look to be more environmentally conscious.

6.6.1.2 Volkswagen (Pellegrino, 2023) [38]

Volkswagen admitted to defrauding pollution limits by installing a defective device in its automobiles. The device consisted of software that could recognize when the machine is going through an emission test and change its effectiveness to reduce the level of emission levels. It happened when the company was promoting the low-emissions and environmentally friendly characteristics of its vehicles to the public through marketing campaigns. These engines were excreting up to 40 times the maximum allowable limit for nitrogen oxide pollution, thus making it a classic example of greenwashing.

6.6.1.3 *Innocent Drinks*

Innocent Drinks, owned by the world's largest beverage company and the world's worst polluter of plastic, Coca-Cola, is a leading example of taking an implausible approach to solving a problem. In addition, the company makes use of single-use plastic, which is harmful to the environment. Nonetheless, someone, somewhere thought it would be a good idea to release TV cartoon commercials featuring pictures of animals singing songs about recycling and saving the environment to promote their products. To establish a connection between the brand and these opposed causes is, without a doubt, greenwashing in its most basic form. Following a complaint from Plastic Rebellion, the Advertising Standards Authority (ASA) intervened and banned the ludicrous advertisements.

6.6.2 Identification of Greenwashing

The act of greenwashing can be regarded and alleged in a variety of ways by onlookers in several ways. Product-level claims with environmental labeling to the firm-level nature-evoked ability to execute components in integrated reporting, the occurrence can be classified in a wide range of different ways, each with its own set of characteristics.

Because of the numerous forms in which greenwashing has been observed, it is difficult for consumers to distinguish between the different manifestations of the phenomenon. Identification of greenwashing is a challenge, even among consumers considered to be expert consumers, who are well-informed about greenwashing and the specific market in question. The accusation process is even more difficult to navigate in the case of consumers who are considered regulars but who are unaware of or have limited knowledge about the phenomenon. Corporate social responsibility is often used as a veil by big corporate houses to engage in greenwashing. Due to the absence of proper laws, it is difficult to trace the cases of greenwashing and punish the companies accordingly. To prevent greenwashing, the funds and operations of the companies must be operated with transparency, and in the absence of proper legislation for Greenwashing, the corporations will continue to damage the environment if they are minting profits.

6.6.3 Rules Governing Greenwashing in India

Greenwashing regulation is limited in developed countries possessing higher levels of environmental awareness than in developing countries. In the United States, the regulation of greenwashing is extremely limited with a high degree of uncertainty surrounding regulation enforcement. Researchers, activists, and environmentalists have expressed concern about the effectiveness of non-binding regulatory guidelines in protecting consumers from the harmful effects of the phenomenon of "greenwashing," which is the practice of misrepresenting products as "green." Even though most of the world's population is becoming conscious of the environment, governments in developing countries have either no or inadequate green regulations in place. The practice of recycling through waste sorting and collection, which appears to be a regular thing to do for millennials in developed countries, is considered a privilege in developing countries on the other hand.

As of now, in India, no trademark, competition, or environmental regulations exist that explicitly state greenwashing. In several cases involving advertising and promotion, the Indian Judicial system has ruled that advertisers must make valid claims and not mislead consumers. There are no specific regulations that govern or penalize the act of greenwashing, which not only deceives the consumers but also the investors if done through a green project with the help of finance raised through the issuance of green bonds. The SEBI of India has led to the emergence of an advisory committee concerned with ESG matters. It imposes a mandatory and continuous disclosure by companies specific to ESG schemes of mutual funds emphasizing particularly the mitigating risk associated with greenwashing and misleading sales. The Advertising Standards Council of India (ASCI), an autonomous organization that is accountable for the self-regulation of marketing by its representatives and the safeguarding of customer interests, mandates that advertisements adhere to its Code for Self-Regulation. The ASCI has brought on board certain mandatory requirements, which are that the advertisements shall necessarily be legal, decent, honest, and truthful and shall abide by fair and just competition. However, on the contrary, it is simply a code for self-regulation and no formulated body checks the reliability of the same. Greenwashing claims can fall within the ambit of ASCI guidelines for unsubstantiated false advertising claims. Nevertheless, set guidelines and concrete rules on green advertising or environmental claims might well assist in addressing the issue and discouraging businesses from claiming such things while preserving consumer confidence (Aggarwal and Kadyan, 2011) [39].

6.6.3.1 *French Climate and Resilience Law and European Union's Proposed Unfair Commercial Practices Directive: A Standard Model to Combat Greenwashing*

Currently, France is one of the nations that are effectively tackling greenwashing as it consists of different legal mechanisms to regulate greenwashing. These legal mechanisms include the Consumer Code (Act of Parliament of France, 1993) [40] and the Climate and Resilience Law. An essential requirement under the Consumer Code that prohibits deceptive business practices, along with misleading marketing, is included in the Consumer Code. This is frequently based on incorrect accusations and details that are misleading regarding the key attributes of a product or service, such as those that comprise greenwashing advertising.

It is prevalent for manufacturers to assert environmental claims that are not accurate, in part because there are very few standards available to determine what constitutes a precise sustainability assertion. When viewed as a whole, these laws produce a much more distinct picture of the procedures that businesses are required to implement to provide any sustainable claim without being at risk of greenwashing. What emerges is an outline of the new proposals in the legislation that is the most substantial, in addition to methodologies that businesses have already employed effectively to accomplish the new requirements. The Climate and Resilience Law includes a specific provision addressing greenwashing, the law has made the engagement in any practice that misrepresents the context of the marketer's responsibilities, particularly about the environment, the essence, the procedure, or the rationale for the selling or the rendering of facilities, illegal (Article 2 of the Climate Resilience Act, 2021) [41]. In case of violation of the provisions, offenders face a maximum imprisonment of two years and a fine of €300,000, which is about US$400,000. The law also contains a framework for "naming and shaming," which also allows a judge to direct that its judgment be articulated to the general populace using any method that the court deems appropriate.

In addition, the Climate and Resilience Law makes it mandatory for the Audiovisual and Digital Communication Regular Authority to develop "climate contracts" as codes of behavior to prohibit commercial information exchange that falsely publicizes the positive environmental impact of products or assistance that genuinely has an adverse effect on the environment.

The following five provisions are included in these climate contracts, which were signed with various advertising actors:

- What is measured?
- What is promoted?
- What is monitored?
- What is manufactured?
- What are the issues that are brought to the public?

Moreover, the French Environmental Code prohibits it from stating in a commercial that a service or product is carbon neutral unless the evidence supporting the same is easily available. A fine of 20,000 Euros is levied against natural persons who violate such a provision, while a fine of 100,000 Euros is levied against legal persons.

6.7 Implications of Regulating Sources of Green Financing on Policymakers, Business Houses, and Society

The regulating bodies, governments of several countries, financial organizations, and private and public sector organizations throughout the world come to realize the significance of acting against climate change; the notion of green financing is now gathering the necessary backing to move forward. The introduction of novel technology in conjunction with a strategy that emphasizes cooperation among all relevant parties may prove to be essential in helping India close its current deficit in green financing. In this segment of the study, the researchers have emphasized the implications of regulating the sources of green financing and responsible investment on the part of key players in the capital market on policymakers, business houses, and society.

6.7.1 Impact of Green Financing on Policymakers

Significant developments have been witnessed lately in the regulations governing green financing in India. In 2023, while addressing the parliament, the finance minister of India, Nirmala Sitaraman, emphasized the pivotal role of sovereign green bonds in attaining SDGs (Ministry of Finance, 2022) [42]. The Indian legislations and policies are being developed in such a manner that they align effectively with the commitments made under SDGs. Attainment of SDGs shall have a colossal global impact ranging from mitigation of climate change to global recognition of a country. Developing the regulations leads to innovation and creativity on the end of the policy framers. However, with the introduction of such laws, strong oversight and monitoring shall be required by the government agencies, leaving opportunities for employment. Regulating the laws governing green finance can enhance the economic growth of a country by stimulating investments by key players in the market in green business practices such as clean energy and sustainable manufacturing. It also aids in reducing the negative ecological effects associated with financial transactions. Investment in such projects leads to the creation of employment opportunities.

6.7.2 Impact of Green Financing on Business Houses

Effective green corporate governance practices result in brand recognition, enhancement in investment, etc. Green financing opens a new source of funding for companies. Financial institutions, private equity firms, and impact fund managers are all actively seeking investments in environmentally conscious ventures (Fu *et al.*, 2023) [43]. Investments and financing opportunities are more accessible to companies with a focus on environmental sustainability. Many green initiatives, such as energy-efficient technologies, renewable energy installations, and sustainable supply chain management, can lead to cost savings in the long run. Businesses that invest in these initiatives can reduce energy consumption, minimize waste, and lower operating costs. An organization actively engaged in green financing shall gain social recognition and company reputation leading to improved consumer loyalty and favorable public relations. When it comes to financing, green finance pushes companies to undertake a futuristic perspective and make decisions about how their actions will affect the world around them. This can aid businesses in becoming more robust in the face of fluctuating market conditions and new threats. Businesses can improve their relationships with employees, consumers, and vendors resulting in strong collaborations.

6.7.3 Impact of Green Financing on Society

Green financing has the potential to introduce a paradigm shift in society by promoting environmental sustainability, economic growth, employment opportunities, and a resilient future. The risk management capability of green financing is phenomenal in mitigating climate change, eliminating poverty, resource scarcity, and regulatory challenges, therefore leading to the eventual upliftment and well-being of society. Reduction in pollution will enhance the water and air quality, eventually resulting in enhanced health of the public, making it a powerful tool for positive change.

6.8 Conclusion and Recommendations

If India intends to attain the goals to which it has committed, it is essential to grow the green bond market. The required finance for achieving the standard goals shall be attained if the green bond market thrives and is strictly regulated so that there is no scope for greenwashing left. It is the need of the hour that not only the public sector but also the private sector emerges as the savior and contributes to raising the required finance. However, the existing laws and regulations are not sufficient to promote green bonds in India. The SEBI regulations along with Section 135 of the Companies Act, 2013, are not sufficient to address the issues and challenges that come with green bonds as technicalities, the complexity of the issuance process, greenwashing, etc., India must adopt the legal mechanism from certain countries that have strong legislation governing green bonds. Developing markets like India face numerous institutional and financial obstacles to the advancement of an advanced green bond market. Since specialist expertise in contemporary multilateral practices in the green bond market is a basic requirement for the issuing of green bonds, financial institutions and investors have steered away from these instruments. India requires a whopping amount of US$2.64 trillion to achieve the target, which it has committed to fulfilling by 2030. The green bonds market can pave the way to help implement renewable energy initiatives by improving accessibility to domestic and international capital and improving financing options, such as a balanced rate of interest, and comparatively longer lending tenures. The concept paper published by SEBI stated that the market for green bonds is a crucial instrument to assist in raising the financial support required to achieve the ambitious goals of India's Intended Nationally Determined Contribution for COP21, COP 26, and COP 27, which is India's climate change action plan. The foremost gap in the current framework is that the appointment of a third-party reviewer is optional, which is against the principles of natural justice "*Nemo Judex Causa sua*," meaning that no one shall be a judge in his own case. Further, the issues associated with the green bonds are way beyond the jurisdiction of the National Green Tribunal, which makes the offender go unscathed. With the help of a stringent legal framework in India, it is impossible to overestimate the advantages of obtaining financing through the granting of green debt securities. In addition to being a constructive step forward in the raising of green finance, the issuance of green debt securities is likely to pique the interest of international bodies and shareholders who have the intention of channeling capital into green projects. The issuance of green-debt securities will be of additional assistance to India's ambitious goals regarding the use of renewable energy and environmentally friendly development. The issuance of green debt securities and an effective legal regime for raising green finance is the first welcoming step to a green future and the attainment of SDGs. However, India could use a replicate of the France model to deal with the issuance and effective use of green bonds along with dodging greenwashing. The creation of a regulatory framework for the issuance of green debt securities in India could be a historic moment and a wave of transition given the essence of financial instruments required to fulfill SDGs and many more environmental concerns that India is struggling with. Further, it is essential to address regular uncertainties associated with the allotment of green projects, timely execution of green projects across various sectors, and bureaucratic hurdles in obtaining approvals and clarifications. Additionally, it is suggested that there should be the formulation of dispute resolution forums since the National Green Tribunal has limited jurisdiction and there is clearly a lack of policies and procedures for green projects. The issue of greenwashing, which comes tagged along with green bonds, is a challenging issue and shall be necessarily addressed at the earliest as the existing regime is not sufficient to tackle it.

References

1. Cortellini, G. and Panetta, I.C., Green Bond: A Systematic Literature Review for Future Research Agendas. *J. Risk Financ. Manage.*, 14, 12, 589, Dec. 2021, https://doi.org/10.3390/jrfm14120589.
2. Çalıyurt, K.T., *New Approaches to CSR, Sustainability and Accountability*, vol. I, Springer Nature, Singapore, 2019, https://doi.org/10.1007/978-981-10-3212-7.
3. Freeburn, L. and Ramsay, I., Green Bonds: Legal and Policy Issues. *Cap. Mark. Law J.*, 15, 4, 418–442, Oct. 2020, doi: http://dx.doi.org/10.2139/ssrn.3715969.
4. Kesharao, S., Greenwashing in India an alarming issue: misleading and deceptive environmental claims in advertising. *Int. J. Commerce Manage. Res.*, 3, 2, 91–97, 2017.
5. Camilleri, M., *Corporate Sustainability, Social Responsibility and Environmental Management*, 1st ed, Springer Cham, United Kingdom, 2018, doi: https://doi.org/10.1007/978-3-319-46849-5.

6. Khan, S., Akbar, A., Nasim, I., Hedvičáková, M., Bashir, F., Green finance development and environmental sustainability: A panel data analysis. *Front. Environ. Sci.*, 10, Nov. 2022, https://doi.org/10.3389/fenvs.2022.1039705.
7. *From India to Indonesia, Green Bonds Help Countries Move Toward Sustainability.* World Bank, Apr. 10, 2023, https://www.worldbank.org/en/news/feature/2023/04/10/from-india-to-indonesia-green-bonds-help-countries-move-toward-sustainability.
8. Bachnik, K., Kazmierczak, M., Rojek-Nowosieslska, M., Stefanska, M., Samolej, J., *Corporate Social Responsibility and Sustainability: From Values to Impact*, 1st ed, Routledge, New York, 2022, doi: https://doi.org/10.4324/9781003270768.
9. Ministry of New and renewable energy, *A target of installing 175 GW of renewable energy capacity by the year 2022 has been set. PIB*, May 2018. https://pib.gov.in/Pressreleaseshare.aspx?PRID=1539238 (accessed Oct. 13, 2023).
10. Krichewsky, D., *Corporate Social Responsibility and Economic Responsiveness in India*, Cambridge University Press, Cambridge, United Kingdom, 2019, doi: https://doi.org/10.1017/9781108756662.
11. Chen, D., Hu, H., Chang, C., Green finance, environment regulation, and industrial green transformation for corporate social responsibility. *Corp. Soc. Responsib. Environ. Manage.*, 30, 5, 2166–2181, Mar. 2023.
12. Hay, B.L.P., Stavins, R.N.P., Vietor, R.H.K.P., *Environmental Protection and the Social Responsibility of Firms*, Routledge, United Kingdom, 2010.
13. Securities and exchange board of India, *Concept paper for issuance of Green Bonds. SEBI*, Dec. 2015, https://www.sebi.gov.in/reports/reports/dec-2015/concept-paper-for-issuance-of-green-bonds_31167.html (accessed Feb. 21, 2024).
14. de Freitas Netto, S.V., Sobral, M.F.F., Ribeiro, A.R.B., da L. Soares, G.R., Concepts and forms of greenwashing: a systematic review. *Environ. Sci. Eur.*, 32, 1, 1–12, Feb. 2020, https://doi.org/10.1186/s12302-020-0300-3.
15. *Green Bond Principles*, ICMA, https://www.icmagroup.org/sustainable-finance/the-principles-guidelines-and-handbooks/green-bond-principles-gbp/ (accessed Oct. 16, 2023).
16. J., *Growing Green Finance in India: A Review of Green Bond Principles, Indian Green Debt Securities and ESG. JSA*, 2022, May 13, https://www.jsalaw.com/banking-financial-services/growing-green-finance-in-india-a-review-of-green-bond-principles-indian-green-debt-securities-and-esg/ (accessed Oct. 15, 2023).
17. Securities and exchange board of India, *Operational Circular for issue and listing of Non-Convertible Securities (NCS), Securitised Debt Instruments (SDI), Security Receipts (SR), Municipal Debt Securities and Commercial Paper (CP). SEBI*, Aug. 2021, https://www.sebi.gov.in/legal/circulars/aug-2021/operational-circular-for-issue-and-listing-of-non-convertible-securities-

ncs-securitised-debt-instruments-sdi-security-receipts-sr-municipal-debt-securities-and-commercial-paper-cp-_51761.html (accessed Feb. 21, 2024).
18. SEBI, *Securities and exchange board of India. SEBI*, Feb. 06, 2023, https://www.sebi.gov.in/legal/circulars/feb-2023/revised-disclosure-requirements-for-issuance-and-listing-of-green-debt-securities_67837.html (accessed Feb. 19, 2024).
19. Labelled Green Bonds Data: Latest 3 Months, in: *Climate Bonds Initiative*, https://www.climatebonds.net/cbi/pub/data/bonds (accessed Sep. 17, 2023).
20. *ReNew raises $400 million by issuing Green Bonds. ReNew.*, https://investor.renewpower.in/news-releases/news-release-details/renew-raises-400-million-issuing-green-bonds (accessed Sep. 16, 2023).
21. Pti, *SBI lists $650 mn green bonds on India INX, Luxembourg Stock Exchange. Mint*, Nov. 22, 2021, https://www.livemint.com/industry/banking/sbi-lists-650-mn-green-bonds-on-india-inx-luxembourg-stock-exchange-11637592802184.html (accessed Sep. 13, 2023).
22. *Adani Green Energy lists $750 million green bonds*, Sep. 09, 2021, BusinessLine, https://www.thehindubusinessline.com/money-and-banking/adani-green-energy-lists-750-million-green-bonds/article36377560.ece (accessed Sep. 25, 2023).
23. *ACME Solar Holdings raises $334 million via green bonds*, Jul. 30, 2021, BusinessLine, https://www.thehindubusinessline.com/companies/acme-solar-holdings-raises-334-million-via-green-bonds/article35623414.ece (accessed Sep. 19, 2023).
24. Pti, *Adani Electricity Mumbai raises $300 million through sustainability bonds*, Jul. 23, 2021, Business Today, https://www.businesstoday.in/latest/corporate/story/adani-electricity-mumbai-raises-300-million-through-sustainability-bonds-302194-2021-07-23 (accessed Sep. 16, 2023).
25. Bagaria, R., *Everything You Need to Know About Green Bonds in India*, Apr. 09, 2021, Green Clean Guide, https://greencleanguide.com/everything-you-need-to-know-about-green-bonds-in-india/ (accessed Sep. 9, 2023).
26. Kroll, C., Warchold, A., Pradhan, P., Sustainable Development Goals (SDGs): Are we successful in turning trade-offs into synergies? *Palgrave Commun.*, 5, 1, 140, Nov. 2019, https://doi.org/10.1057/s41599-019-0335-5.
27. *India*, Jan. 09, 2024, Climate Bonds Initiative, https://www.climatebonds.net/market/country/india (accessed Sep. 6, 2023).
28. *Vellore Citizens Welfare Forum v. Union of India*, AIR 1996 Supreme Court 2715.
29. *M.K Ranjitsinh v Union of India*, Writ Petition Civil No. 838 of 2019.
30. Securities and exchange board of India, *BRSR Core - Framework for assurance and ESG disclosures for value chain. SEBI*, 2023, July 12, Retrieved February 21, 2024, from https://www.sebi.gov.in/legal/circulars/jul-2023/brsr-core-framework-for-assurance-and-esg-disclosures-for-value-chain_73854.html (accessed Sep. 3, 2023).

31. Dey, S., *Sustainability in the spotlight: decoding India's ESG regulatory landscape*, May 26, 2022, The Economic Times, https://economictimes.indiatimes.com/prime/corporate-governance/sustainability-in-the-spotlight-decoding-indias-esg-regulatory-landscape/primearticleshow/91796559.cms (accessed Oct. 16, 2023).
32. Collins, S. and Northrup, L.M., *The Legal Risks of Greenwashing Are Real*, Jul. 25, 2022, Bloomberg Law, https://news.bloomberglaw.com/environment-and-energy/the-legal-risks-of-greenwashing-are-real (accessed Oct. 3, 2023).
33. Chateau, J. and Dang, G., A Framework for Climate Change Mitigation in India. IMF Working Papers, 2023, 218, 9798400247002, Oct. 2023, doi: https://doi.org/10.5089/9798400247002.001.
34. Singh, P., *Greenwashing: When Brands Pretend To Care About The Environment*, Nov. 12, 2019, Feminism in India, https://feminisminindia.com/2019/11/13/greenwashing-brands-pretend-care-environment (accessed Sep. 4, 2023).
35. *Recent Study Reveals More Than a Third of Global Consumers Are Willing to Pay More for Sustainability as Demand Grows for Environmentally Friendly Alternatives*, Oct. 14, 2021, Businesswire, https://www.businesswire.com/news/home/20211014005090/en/Recent-Study-Reveals-More-Than-a-Third-of-Global-Consumers-Are-Willing-to-Pay-More-for-Sustainability-as-Demand-Grows-for-Environmentally-Friendly-Alternatives (accessed Feb. 19, 2024).
36. Robinson, D., *10 Companies Called Out For Greenwashing* | Earth.Org. *Earth.Org.*, https://earth.org/greenwashing-companies-corporations/ (accessed Aug. 6, 2023).
37. *USA: H&M faces 'greenwashing' class-action lawsuit over alleged misleading & false marketing of 'sustainable' clothing line - Business & Human Rights Resource Centre. Bus. Hum. Rights Centre*, https://www.business-human-rights.org/en/latest-news/usa-hm-faces-greenwashing-class-action-lawsuit-over-alleged-misleading-false-marketing-of-sustainable-clothing-line/ (accessed July. 7, 2023).
38. Pellegrino, S., *Explainer: Household brands accused of greenwashing*, Mar. 10, 2023, Capital Monitor, https://capitalmonitor.ai/sector/consumer/explainer-household-brands-accused-of-greenwashing/ (accessed Nov. 12, 2023).
39. Aggarwal, P. and Kadyan, A., Greenwashing: The Darker Side Of CSr. *Indian J. Appl. Res.*, 4, 3, 61–66, Oct. 2011, doi: http://dx.doi.org/10.15373/2249555X/MAR2014/20.
40. Consumer Protection laws and regulations, 1993. Act of Parliament of France.
41. French Climate and Resilience Law, 2021. Act of Parliament of France.
42. Ministry of Finance, *Union Finance Minister Smt. Nirmala Sitharaman approves India's First Sovereign Green Bonds Framework*, Nov. 09, 2022, Pib.Gov, https://pib.gov.in/PressReleaseIframePage.aspx?PRID=1874788#:~:text=

Nirmala%20Sitharaman%20approves%20the%20final,investments%20in%20eligible%20green%20projects (accessed Sep. 21, 2023).

43. Fu, C., Lu, L., Pirabi, M., Advancing green finance: a review of sustainable development. *Digital Econ. Sustain. Dev.*, 1, 1, 20, Oct. 2023, https://doi.org/10.1007/s44265-023-00020-3.

7

Impact of Environmental, Social, and Governance (ESG) and the Circular Economy (CE) on Financial Decision-Making

Jeanne-Marie Lawrence

Department of Technology Systems, East Carolina University, Greenville, NC, USA

Abstract

This chapter examines the influence of environmental, social, and governance (ESG), and circular economy goals on (i) the policies of organizations guiding sustainability reporting and financial governance; (ii) the financial decisions of owners and managers of financial assets; (iii) the credit/lending decisions of banks and financial intermediaries providing capital for ESG and circular economy projects; and the investment and operational financial decisions of manufacturers and service providers implementing ESG and circular economy projects in their organizations and supply chains. Beginning with the global goals for sustainable development and climate risk mitigation, each category is discussed, and a cascading relationship approach is used to explain how financial decisions filter down to other categories of decision-makers, eventually impacting the financial decisions of firms undertaking ESG and circular economy capital projects. The chapter concludes with the impact of ESG on decisions to use emerging financial technologies (FinTech) to improve the availability and delivery of financial products and services to entities undertaking ESG and circular economy projects.

Keywords: Environmental, social, and governance, financial decision-making, green finance, FinTech

Email: lawrenceje@ecu.edu

Ernesto D.R. Santibanez Gonzalez, Vinay Kandpal, Peterson K. Ozili and Prasenjit Chatterjee (eds.) Fintech for ESG and the Circular Economy, (119–148) © 2024 Scrivener Publishing LLC

7.1 Introduction

The maximization of shareholder profits at the expense of other stakeholder expectations is a notion that has gradually been eroded over the course of the past two decades. Increasingly, organizations are realizing that the financial decisions they make must be grounded in, and aligned with, the values embraced by their investors, customers, and wider stakeholders. Concepts, such as environmental, social, and governance (ESG), and circular economy, which were once considered peripheral to operational and organizational strategy, are now hitting mainstream executive agenda in the race to secure long-term profitability and growth. Today, firms are looking to increase revenue, reduce costs, and invest their assets to generate returns that are consistent with stakeholder sustainability values and beliefs.

While it would be noble of organizations to pursue sustainability and circular economy goals for the planet's sake, a McKinsey & Company report states that "leading companies pursue sustainability because it has a material financial impact" [1]. A study undertaken by Deutsche Bank [2] reiterates this perspective, as results have revealed that companies with strong ESG ratings tend to have a lower cost of debt and equity. The Deutsche Bank study also indicated that these enterprises outperform the market in both the medium and long term. As ESG and circularity become a channel for improving enterprise competitiveness, understanding how these concepts impact financial decision-making at all levels is both relevant and timely.

Financial decision-making that incorporates ESG and circular economy goals is not a simple process. It is influenced by several external factors and conditions, including international organizations' goals, legal and regulatory requirements, voluntary and required disclosures, the availability of "green" finance, and the impact of customer and other stakeholder perspectives and behaviors. Producers of goods and services are faced with the task of examining the potential negative impacts of ESG- and climate-related risks that stem from their operations and supply chains, assessing the possible impacts of these risks, and devising suitable ways to mitigate the outcomes. They must invest in innovative technologies to mitigate risks and develop new products and processes to maintain continued market competitiveness. As preferences for sustainably designed products and processes increase in consumer markets, firms that fail to seize the opportunities to offer more desirable goods and services risk reducing future revenue streams by alienating both current and future customers.

In the financial sector, the decisions of asset owners and managers are impacted by ESG and circular economy trends. Firms that sell marketable securities to the public seek ESG investments as a long-term strategy to increase their returns, reduce downside risk, minimize the negative effects of rare catastrophic events, and create more diversified portfolios that balance risk and return. Funds that offer green finance for large-scale projects must, therefore, allocate these funds to maximize returns and minimize risk. To put these issues in perspective, it is useful to examine the global trends in sustainable investing over the past decade. In 2012, assets managed by entities that integrated ESG metrics into financial analyses were estimated at US$13.6 trillion; by 2020, this figure had risen to US$35 trillion [3]. Investments in assets that contributed to ESG solutions also climbed - from US$0.276 trillion in 2016 to US$1.948 trillion in 2020 [3].

ESG and circularity concepts also impact the policies of governing bodies and regulators that guide the operations of financial institutions - for example, banks, asset managers, institutional investors, and others providing debt and equity. These policies impact the availability and allocation of funds to firms that require capital to undertake ESG and circular economy projects.

7.2 The Mandate for ESG and Circular Economy Global Goals

The concept of environmental sustainability refers to the use of the earth's natural resources for current needs in a manner that also allows future generations to meet their own needs. Life is a natural cycle that can only be regenerated and sustained if the earth's resources are in balance with its ongoing needs. Since natural cycles to replace resources used in production and manufacture are slow, incomplete, or simply do not exist, thoughtful human interventions are necessary to ensure that the resources extracted from the earth are returned at a rate and in a form commensurate with the ongoing needs of life.

To substantiate this point, the degradation of high-density polyethylene (HDPE)—a carbon-based synthetic polymer or plastic used to manufacture bottles, pipes, and other products—can be examined. A recent publication of the American Chemical Society [4] reported that in a marine environment, the estimated half-life of HDPE ranges from 58 years for bottles to 1,200 years for pipes. These degradation rates are ill-aligned with the rate at which carbon and hydrogen (the constituent elements of HDPE) need to be replenished in the atmosphere to support life. The concept of circularity recognizes this problem and seeks to couple the use of resources with a deliberate obligation to return them to nature. In a circular economy, the markets incentivize customers to reuse and recycle products, rather than discard them and extract new materials to be used in production operations [5]. To support circularity efforts, scientific research is expanding to find innovative ways to expedite the return of used resources back to the earth.

Another example is the mounting quantities of electronic waste from discarded electronic items, such as smart phones and laptops, after a few years of use. Researchers at Johannes Kepler University in Austria have developed a biodegradable material from mushrooms to produce computer chips that degrade quickly, losing over 90% of their mass within a few days of being placed in a composting bin [6, 7]. Technologies like these, when scaled at a reasonable cost, can be useful to humanity in solving the electronic waste problem. However, developing these solutions is cost-intensive and requires significant outlays of capital, particularly when undertaken in industry.

The mandate for ESG and circularity stems from the global goals that have been set to counter the adverse effects of human activities on climate change, and the environment, economy, and society. The Paris Agreement and the United Nations (UN) Sustainable Development Goals are two of the best-known international endeavors where nations have joined to support the goals of climate risk and sustainability. The Paris Agreement's main goal is to prevent global average temperatures from rising by more than 2 degrees Celsius (and more recently 1.5°C) above that of the pre-industrial era. It is a goal that requires deliberate actions to combat the rise in greenhouse gas (GHG) emissions by 2025 to achieve a decline to 60% of current levels by 2030. In contrast, the UN Sustainable Development Goals consist of 17 environmental, social, and economic goals adopted by all UN member states. Each goal consists of several sub-goals. Combined, these goals seek to achieve approximately 170 targets.

ESG and circular economy impact financial decision-making through direct and indirect inter-organizational relationships and stakeholder influences. Figure 7.1, which depicts the relationships between several critical entities, demonstrates how decisions filter down to firms making financial decisions regarding investments in ESG and circular economy projects. At the highest level, global initiatives, such as the Paris Agreement and the UN Sustainability Goals, steer governments, corporations, and other organizations toward achieving the stipulated goals. In turn, regulators and governing bodies develop standards, policies, laws, and guidelines to steer the financial activities of the entities they govern toward initiatives

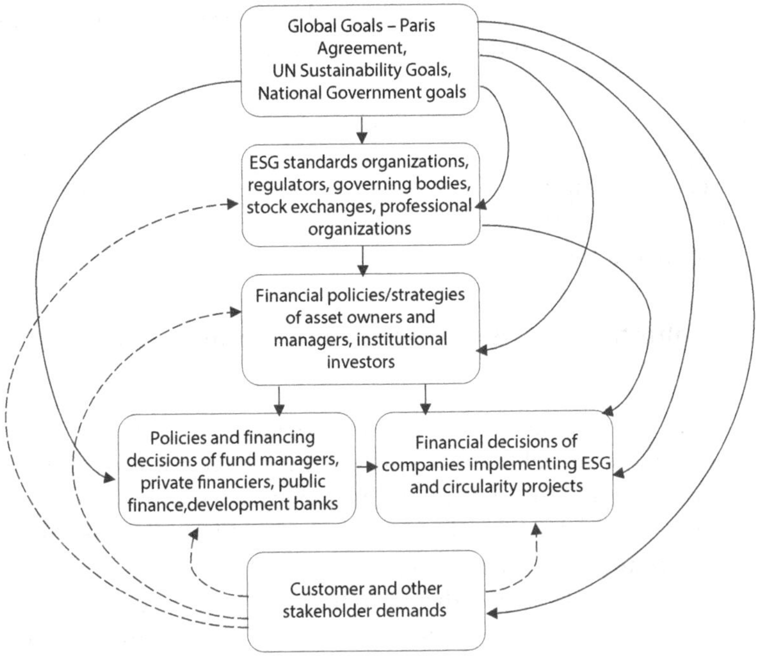

Figure 7.1 Relationships driving ESG and circular economy in financial decision making.

that support global goals. These entities include banks, lenders, and institutional investors, as well as producers of goods and services. The guidance and mandates impact organizations that are dependent on debt and equity by requiring financed projects to be compatible with ESG and circularity priorities. At the other end of the spectrum are customers and stakeholders who have tremendous power to impact financial decisions by boycotting products, lobbying for change, and raising awareness of the negative impacts of human activities on the environment, society, and economy.

7.3 Organizations Impacting Sustainability Reporting and Financial Governance

Given the critical role of information in evaluating ESG risks and opportunities, several organizations have proposed reporting frameworks, requirements, and metrics to standardize the information available to investors. In doing so, these organizations play vital roles in making relevant information available for evaluation, comparison, and financial planning. By setting voluntary standards, the organizations aim to create greater transparency and efficiency and, thereby, help investors to better understand how a firm's ESG and circularity risks and opportunities are likely to impact future financial performance. The recommended disclosures also help the reporting firm to identify areas for sustainability growth, influencing management financial decisions pertaining to investments in ESG and circular economy capital projects. The following is a summary of the major entities involved in setting these standards along with a discussion of the impact on financial decision-making.

7.3.1 Voluntary ESG and Sustainability Frameworks and Metrics

Several systems have been developed to provide a standardized approach for organizations to voluntarily disclose their ESG risks, opportunities, actions, and results. Through the transparency of information, investors are able to gain a better idea of where funds should be allocated to obtain the highest returns. Reporting organizations also benefit as they can see firsthand the types of projects that need to be implemented (and financed) to reduce ESG and climatic risk and support the requirements of the reporting frameworks. Some of the commonly known systems include the Global Reporting Initiative (GRI); the Carbon Disclosure Project (CDB); the International Sustainability Standards Board (ISSB); the Sustainability Accounting Standards Board (SASB); the Taskforce on Climate-Related Disclosures (TCFD); the World Economic Forum International Business Council (WEF IBC); and the Dow Jones Sustainability Indexes (DJSI). The standards vary in scope, with some requiring reports only on a single aspect of ESG (e.g., GHG emissions), while others facilitate reporting on a full range of environmental and social initiatives. Additionally, some standards focus on reporting information that is specifically relevant to financial decision-making as in the case of the DJSI and the SASB.

7.3.1.1 The Global Reporting Initiative

Among the most well-known and widely used voluntary standards for reporting on sustainability is the Global Reporting Initiative (GRI). The GRI is an independent organization that provides a reporting standard for all three dimensions of sustainability—environmental, social, and economic—through detailed guidelines on what should be assessed and reported. To date, over 10,000 organizations spanning more than 100 countries use the GRI standards for sustainability reporting, and according to a recent KPMG report, 78% of the largest global corporations have adopted the GRI standards [8].

The GRI addresses sustainability and, where relevant, circularity. For example, included in the GRI Standards for environmental sustainability is GRI 306: Waste 2020, Disclosures 306-1 through 306-5. These guidelines provide several suggestions for reporting on waste along the entire value chain of an organization. In particular, Disclosure 306-2 provides guidelines on reporting circularity initiatives to prevent the creation of waste.

The standards make detailed suggestions on how each aspect of each dimension of sustainability should be reported. Using GRI 306 as an example, the guidelines recommend the use of flow charts for identifying and reporting on the inputs, outputs, and activities that produce waste along the value chain of an organization. The standards also advise including a description of the type of waste generated, the materials present in the waste, the methods of recycling, the types of recovery operations, and the methods of disposal (e.g., incineration or landfilling). From these recommendations, it is easy to understand how the GRI standards impact financial decision-making. For example, if data collection on the types and quantities of waste streams is important, then investment in technologies that monitor waste in real time would be valuable. Therefore, by way of the GRI standards, ESG and circularity impact the financial decisions of firms seeking to align their activities to meet the recommended sustainability reporting standards.

7.3.1.2 The Carbon Disclosure Project

The Carbon Disclosure Project (CDP) is the premier global disclosure reporting system on environmental impacts. It is an affiliate of the Task Force on Nature-related Financial Disclosures (TNFD) and the owner of the largest Taskforce on Climate-Related Financial Disclosures (TCFD). Its aim is to help countries make progress toward the Paris Agreement and the UN Sustainability Goals. The organization has offices in 50 countries and aims to achieve the following:

- Engage with regional and national governments to develop standards for reporting on environmental sustainability; and to help implement standards developed by other organizations, such as the International Sustainability Standards Board (ISSB), the European Sustainability Reporting Standards (ESRS), and the US Securities and Exchange Commission (SEC).

- Partner with national and local government and corporate leaders to tackle issues such as global emissions, climate change risk, water consumption, deforestation, and supply chain environmental impacts, by increasing awareness through measurement and disclosure.
- Maintain a comprehensive database on self-reported country-level emissions, climate actions, climate risks, forests, and water-security issues for use in developing environmental policies and identifying areas for improvement.
- Mobilize investors, such as asset owners and managers, banks, and insurance companies to use its environmental database to gain insights into ESG issues and craft financial strategies that aim to reduce environmental impacts.

To date, over 90 jurisdictions have disclosed sustainability data through the CDP. By making annual disclosures, these countries and regions have the opportunity to examine how ESG and circularity can be integrated into their long-term plans and determine where and how financial investments need to be made to achieve global goals.

7.3.1.3 The International Sustainability Standards Board (ISSB)

Recognizing the critical role of sustainability disclosures in rational investment decisions, the International Sustainability Standards Board (ISSB) was formed at the United Nations Summit on Climate Change in Glasgow, Scotland, in 2021 (COP26). The ISSB is an entity under the International Financial Reporting Standards (IFRS), a non-profit organization that was created to develop accounting and sustainability disclosure standards that can easily be interpreted and enforced globally. The ISSB aims to develop sustainability disclosure standards that are compatible with the IFRS Accounting Standards and, thereby, serve as a minimum standard for reporting on material issues internationally. The main goals of the ISSB can be summarized as follows:

- To create a set of guidelines that serve as a minimum standard for sustainability disclosures.
- To provide relevant information to investors to facilitate sound financial decisions.
- To guide corporations in providing information on sustainability initiatives and results to global capital markets.
- To facilitate information sharing and disclosures pertinent to specific jurisdictions and stakeholders.

Along with the International Accounting Standards Board (IASB), the ISSB shares responsibility for the Integrated Reporting Framework. The framework aims to provide a broad reporting standard that supports decision-making and value creation by providing high-quality material information to stakeholders. Through access to information on the factors that are integral in creating sustainability value, organizations can make informed decisions on how best to allocate available finances.

7.3.1.4 Sustainability Accounting Standards Board (SASB)

The SASB is a non-profit organization that falls under the International Financial Reporting Standards (IFRS) Foundation and the oversight of the ISSB. The SASB has developed over 75 industry-specific standards that comprise a set of global standards to facilitate the minimum reporting requirements of financial-material information. For example, there is a standard reporting framework for the consumer goods sector and specifically for the household and personal product industry within that sector. The standards prescribe accounting metrics for evaluating materials and processes in each ESG area and indicate whether evaluation is to be conducted in quantitative or qualitative terms.

In some ways, the SASB standards are similar to that of the GRI. They both define metrics for evaluating specific areas of sustainability. They also provide comprehensive technical guidance for assessing sustainability actions and results for each metric. However, while the GRI focuses on environmental, economic, and social impacts, the SASB specifically emphasizes the issues of financial materiality. With this focus, the SASB plays a critical role in influencing the financial decisions of firms as any decision that has a material negative impact on financial performance will reduce the firm's value.

7.3.1.5 Taskforce on Climate-Related Financial Disclosures (TCFD)

The TCFD has developed a framework to assist publicly traded companies and other enterprises with revealing climate-related opportunities and risks within their existing reporting mechanisms. The TCFD divides climate-related issues into two categories: those that affect the transition to a low-carbon economy and those that result from the consequences of climate change. The first group includes risks relating to policy, litigation, markets, technology, and reputation. The second includes risks that are a consequence of the increasing severity of weather events (e.g., hurricanes, floods) and looming risks due to gradual shifts in climatic patterns (e.g., seawater rise, higher average temperatures).

The TCFD also aims to identify opportunities that can benefit organizations financially—for example, through cost savings or revenue streams resulting from improved management of resources, energy efficiency, new products, markets, and supply chain resilience. The TCFD recognizes that the opportunities and risks associated with climate change impact a firm's strategic plans and the approaches used to strengthen a firm's income statement and balance sheet in the long term. Revenues are impacted by product demand and by trends such as the use of carbon pricing to offset carbon emissions. Costs are reduced by mitigating risks and making prudent investment decisions. The value of a firm's assets and liabilities are impacted by policy and market changes relating to technology, supply, and demand. From these impacts, it can be seen that climate-related risks have the potential to alter the debt and equity structure of a firm since capital expenditures are incurred to develop new products or processes and these projects need to be financed with debt or equity. Climatic risks also affect an organization's ability to acquire or refinance debt. Since ESG and climatic risks are intimately connected, the disclosures encouraged by the TCFD impact an organization's ESG plans, and ultimately, its financial decisions.

7.3.1.6 World Economic Forum International Business Council (WEF IBC)

The WEF IBC is an international entity that believes that organizations have a responsibility to deliver value to all stakeholders—what it describes as "profit and purpose". To this end, the organization has created a set of metrics for reporting on environmental and social factors. The metrics can be used within a firm's existing reports to standardize reporting, ensure consistency, and build trust. Metrics have been developed to measure and quantify financial losses resulting from unprincipled behavior, GHG emissions, the level of protection of ecologically sensitive areas, water usage in water-deficient regions, diversity and inclusion, compensation equality, employment of children, health and safety, and economic impacts to the firm and other stakeholders.

7.3.1.7 Dow Jones Sustainability Indexes (DJSI)

The DJSI is a family of indices that was introduced in 1999 to assess the returns of large publicly traded companies (as a group) in the areas of environmental, social, and economic sustainability. The indices are a weighted average of the stock prices of major corporations that meet specific sustainability criteria, e.g., crisis management, supply chain standards, mitigation of climate change, environmental efficiency of operations, labor practices and human rights, and development of human capital. The DJSI World is the overall global index, and several indices fall under the DJSI umbrella. There are also specific indices such as the DJSI Europe or Eurozone and the DJSI North American and United States Index. In the case of the latter, the index comprises the top 20% of the 600 largest North American companies with the highest sustainability ratings in the S&P Global Broad Market Index (BMI). The data reported to the S&P is compiled from information self-reported by the companies.

The DJSI impacts financial decision-making by influencing investor purchase of stock in a DJSI fund as companies that make up the index consistently strive to attain the highest sustainability results. Companies that are part of the index benefit by leveraging index performance to advertise their company's efforts in the area of sustainability, and thereby, attract greater investment funds for ongoing sustainability projects. Decisions to embrace and implement ESG and circular economy impact the performance of the DJSI indices, which in turn impacts the decisions to implement the said projects.

Table 7.1 provides a summary of the organizations leading the ESG agenda and the contribution of each. The organizations all have an impact on the financial decisions of firms by influencing the selection, investment, and management of ESG and circular economy projects.

7.3.2 National Governments and Regulatory Authorities

Beyond voluntary reporting and organizational commitment, laws that protect the environment and human rights are also emerging, forcing mandatory action in the ESG and circularity areas. Various authorities have proposed greater enforcement of ESG and circular economy through legal and regulatory enforcement. At the country level, Germany has long been a pioneer in enforcing ESG and circular economy requirements. The Closed Substance Cycle and Waste Management Act was enacted in 1996 to avoid production waste, promote products that generate minimal waste, and require environmentally friendly disposal at the end of a product's life cycle. More recently, in January 2023, the "Act on Corporate Due Diligence to Prevent Human Rights Violations in Supply Chain" (Lieferkettensorgfaltspflichtengesetz or LkSG) was enacted and is expected to impact German companies employing 3,000 or more people. By 2024, companies with 1,000 or more employees [9, 10] are expected to be impacted. The act also requires small- and medium-sized companies that

Table 7.1 Summary of organizations leading the ESG and circularity agenda.

	Framework	Standards	Metrics	Index
Global Reporting Initiative (GRI)		x		
Carbon Disclosure Project (CDP)	x			
International Sustainability Standards Board (ISSB)		x		
Sustainability Accounting Standards Board (SASB)		x	x	
Taskforce on Climate-Related Financial Disclosures (TCFD)	x			
World Economic Forum International Business Council (WEF IBC)			x	
Dow Jones Sustainability Indexes (DJSI)				x

are not required to adhere to the stipulations of the law to consider ways to incorporate the requirements in their operations. In 2012, the German Circular Economy Act (Kreislaufwirtschaftsgesetz) was implemented, with basic tenets and objectives reflecting a revision of the prior LkSG.

Another recent development is a supply chain law that is meant to harmonize the laws across the European Union (EU) pertaining to environmental and social sustainability. In February 2022, the Corporate Sustainability Due Diligence Directive (CSDD) was proposed, and in December 2022, the EU countries agreed to move forward with a supply chain law. The next step will be to present the law to the European Parliament in May 2023. The law will impact companies operating in the EU with over 50 employees, as well as foreign companies operating in the EU. Although small- and medium-sized companies do not fall under the law, they could also be impacted if they supply materials or services to larger companies that are required to operate in adherence to the law. The fundamental goal of the law is to require companies to manage the environmental and social impacts of their operations along the entire value chain.

Enforcement of these laws will no doubt impact corporate financial decision-making pertaining to ESG and circularity. At the heart of most social sustainability violations is the cost of materials and labor. The stipulations obligate companies to direct financing to those areas of their operations that need to be in compliance with the law. For example, investment in due diligence may be necessary to ensure that child labor or human trafficking is absent in supply chains.

7.3.3 Financial Governing Institutions

7.3.3.1 United States Security and Exchange Commission (SEC)

Mutual funds and other securities have become an attractive choice for individuals and entities interested in investing in ESG. However, both risks and opportunities need to be considered when making investment choices. Investment decisions should minimize the risks due to climate change, ESG non-compliance, reputational harm, and other sustainability risks. Good investment decisions are, therefore, heavily dependent on the type of data accessible to the investor.

Recognizing the importance of information, the U.S. Security and Exchange Commission (SEC) recently proposed new rules for disclosing climate-related risks. To ensure investors have adequate knowledge of both risks and opportunities to make informed investment decisions, a new set of rules for ESG-related disclosures was proposed in 2022. The rules will require public companies to disclose the quantity of direct GHG emissions, as well as indirect emissions and other GHGs along a company's value chain. With the expectation that these rules will be implemented in 2023, companies are likely to invest in new technologies to track GHG emissions data.

7.3.3.2 European Banking Authority (EBA)

In December 2022, The European Banking Authority (EBA) published a roadmap detailing the goals and deadlines for meeting legislative requirements pertaining to sustainable finance and ESG risks. While the mandates support ESG and sustainability goals, the greater interest is in ensuring the stability and resilience of the financial system. The framework addresses issues of transparency and disclosures; risk management and supervision; prudent treatment of exposures; stress testing; standards and labels; greenwashing; supervisory reporting; and ESG risks and sustainable finance monitoring. In particular, the EBA is concerned with integrating ESG criteria into financial services and incorporating ESG criteria into the regulatory and supervisory frameworks of financial institutions. The key milestones pertaining to these issues are expected to be accomplished by 2025.

7.3.3.3 The Monetary Authority of Singapore (MAS)

Singapore has taken significant steps in the journey toward green finance. The Monetary Authority of Singapore (MAS) has taken the lead in establishing a Green Finance Industry Taskforce (GFIT) consisting of financial institutions, corporations, and other stakeholders. The task force aims to develop a taxonomy for green finance that is compatible with that developed in other parts of the world, such as the EU and ASEAN. It also hopes to strengthen the environmental risk management practices of financial institutions, improve disclosures, and promote green finance solutions.

As a first step, the task force has proposed a taxonomy for categorizing activities that mitigate climate change using a color-coded scale - with green signifying environmentally sustainable activities that contribute significantly to climate change mitigation; amber representing activities edging closer to a green state or facilitating significant emission reductions; and red identifying activities that are detrimental or incompatible with a carbon neutral or net zero carbon state. The task force is currently working on defining the threshold limits and criteria for industrial activities in each of these categories. Projects will be assessed holistically to ensure that they not only support climate change mitigation but that peripheral project activities are also in harmony with sustainability goals (e.g., they do not destroy biodiversity or endanger safe housing). Such requirements will increase the information needed to qualify a project for funding, by including additional requirements such as an environmental impact assessment [11]. Certainly, these information requirements will impact the financial decisions of firms interested in implementing ESG and circular economy projects.

7.3.4 Professional/Trade Organizations

Several organizations encourage their members to integrate sustainability and circular economy principles in their operations, by setting guidelines, developing codes of conduct, and distributing awards for innovative ideas. One of these is The Business Roundtable, an organization in the United States that consists of chief executive officers (CEOs) in several industries. In 2019, the organization redefined the purpose of a corporation and issued a statement signed by 181 CEOs. The statement laid out a new direction for corporate performance, affirming that the role of a corporation is larger than profit generation for shareholders. The statement sought to formalize the decisions taken by a growing number of firms to commit to creating value for all stakeholders and not just for shareholders. Stakeholders identified include employees, suppliers, customers, investors, and the society at large. Through this statement, The Business Roundtable created an avenue for executive leaders to address long-term ESG issues within their organizations while simultaneously balancing shorter-term profits.

Several other organizations recognize sustainability efforts at a global, national, sectoral, or industry level by offering awards for outstanding performance. Two examples are Sustainability Leaders and the Business Intelligence Group. Sustainability leaders focus on recognizing performance related to environmental and social sustainability. Awards include the Chief Sustainability Officer (CSO) of the Year, the Carbon Reduction Award, the Circular Economy Award, the Sustainable Supply Chain Award, the Profit with a Purpose Award, the Sustainability Excellence Award, the Sustainable Technology Award, and the Diversity and Inclusion Award. The Business Roundtable offers similar awards to organizations that have made significant strides in the implementation of sustainability concepts in their organizations. In 2022, the organization presented the awards of the Sustainability Champion of the Year (Non-executive), the Sustainability Hero of the Year (Executive), the Sustainability Initiative of the Year (Project), the Sustainability Leadership (Organization), the Sustainability Product of the Year, and the Sustainability Service of the Year.

Many other organizations offer recognition for sustainability and circular economy efforts in areas such as supply chain management, construction, and tourism. By recognizing the long-term importance of sustainability, these organizations encourage entities to implement ESG and circular economy projects in their organizations. In doing so, they encourage organizations to take ESG and circular economy seriously and to recognize success in this area as a long-term strategy for growth.

7.4 Financial Policies and Strategies of Asset Owners, Banks, and Other Financial Firms

Given the urgency of the ESG and climate risk mitigation agenda, asset owners and managers recognize that failure to support global initiatives will only serve to increase the financial risk of firms in the long term. Asset owners manage investments on behalf of their organizations or other entities and include institutional investors, such as pension funds, insurance companies, endowments, and foundations. To meet client requirements, asset owners and managers continually seek to invest in lucrative projects and companies. They set policies on the types of projects that will be covered, the technical assistance that will be provided, and how ESG risks will be managed. Recognizing the role of credit in generating revenue for banks and many firms, these investors direct the flow of capital to those projects that align with global goals. Since green investments have proven to yield high rates of return, asset owners, managers, and institutional investor groups set policies on the percentage of their portfolios that will be invested in ESG projects to minimize portfolio volatility and balance returns. As traditional sources of finance become less available, asset owners play an increasingly vital role in the realization of global goals [12]. For instance, the California State Teacher's Retirement System in the United States became the first North American pension fund to include ESG risk analysis in its investment decisions [13].

Among asset owners seeking investment in ESG and climate risk mitigation, several have organized into groups. One example is the Institutional Investors Group on Climate Change (IIGCC) which is composed of European investors that hold a combined asset base of over €6 trillion and are interested in investing in a low-carbon economy. Another example is the Investor Network on Climate Risk in the United States with US$9 trillion in assets [13]. Institutional investors such as ATP and PGGM in Europe have invested in renewable energy infrastructure and technology, such as wind farms, hydropower generation, biofuels, and biomass. These asset owners develop policies that filter down to banks, financial institutions, and private organizations interested in investing in ESG ventures. For example, prior to COP 16 in Cancun, Mexico, IIGCC affirmed the following: "Private investment will only flow at the scale and pace necessary if it is supported by clear, credible, and long-term policy frameworks that shift the risk-reward balance in favor of less carbon-intensive investment".

The reasons that institutional investors invest in ESG and circular economy projects vary and include the following: potential returns; portfolio diversification; reduction of long-term risks (rare events with monumental negative impacts); and responsible leadership. Investment decisions of institutional investors impact the availability of finance for green projects—e.g., whether in green equity funds, fixed-income securities (green bonds), venture capital, or other financial vehicles [12].

As the availability of financing increases, and consumer demand for products and services that support ESG and circularity initiatives intensifies, organizations offering goods and services to the public increasingly make financial decisions to support green projects.

Several leading financial organizations have taken steps to develop green finance products to support ESG and climate-related goals. Global goals, regulatory stipulations, and best practices promoted by governance organizations impact the credit decisions and practices of banks and financial firms. Development banks, green banks, and commercial banks all play a role in mobilizing finance for ESG and circularity initiatives. Development banks are financial institutions that provide capital and technical assistance to developing countries, while green banks are niche financial institutions that are capitalized by public funds to support private sector investment in low-carbon and climate-resilient development. Commercial banks differ from green banks in that they offer a broader array of financial products and services related to both green and non-green initiatives. Worldwide, the promotion and development of green banks and green finance products to support ESG and circularity initiatives have escalated. Green finance encompasses all financing instruments, investments, and mechanisms that contribute to a "climate-plus" approach, impacting both climate and environmental sustainability goals [14]. Green finance products include green loans, green bonds, public finance, renewable energy equity financing, green securities, and renewable energy carbon credits.

7.4.1 Development Banks

The ultimate goal of green finance offered by development banks is to augment the scale-up and flow of finance, particularly from the private sector, and to close financing gaps between available finance and that needed to implement sustainable projects [14, 15]. Following are examples of the role of development banks in providing finance for ESG projects, particularly in developing countries.

- **Africa:** The shortfall in finance to mitigate climate change impacts in Africa has been estimated at between US$100 billion and $130 billion [16]. To increase and accelerate financial flows to support green and climate-resilient initiatives, the African Development Bank (AfDB) recently launched the African Green Bank Initiative (AGBI) to serve as a model for accessing and deploying green finance in Africa. This AfDB initiative is backed by the African Green Finance Fund (AG3F), which provides technical assistance to financial entities and governments to create and fund green facilities, invest in green projects in collaboration with the private sector, and apply de-risking strategies to encourage private sector investment in low-carbon and climate-resilient projects. The AGBI is expected to reduce the gap in funding by supporting green banks in obtaining the required funds to support a strong pipeline of sustainable and climate-resilient projects for private sector investment.

- **Asia:** The Asian Development Bank uses several approaches to support green finance initiatives [14]. The ACGF developed eligibility criteria tailored for the ASEAN region to link green indicators to financing. Innovative loan products have also been developed whereby a two-step pricing mechanism is applied.
- **Latin America and the Caribbean:** To encourage and support green finance and climate-resilient projects in Latin America and the Caribbean, the Green Finance Latin America and Caribbean (GFL) platform was created as a portal for accessing green finance information. The platform shares information on topics such as green finance products; carbon markets; green, social, and thematic bonds; climate risks, and financial mechanisms for sustainable energy to assist national development banks, private sector financial institutions, and other entities in learning about and accessing information on green finance. The platform is promoted by the Inter-American Development Bank (IDB), which in turn, works with national development banks and other stakeholders to develop and market green financial instruments in Latin America and the Caribbean.

The Inter-American Development Bank (IDB) has structured various financial instruments, such as concessional loans, green bonds, energy savings insurance, contingent grants, performance contracts, and project validation schemes. Emphasis is placed on assisting national financial institutions in investing in private sector green/sustainable projects and implementing and strengthening regulatory mechanisms in areas relating to energy efficiency, renewable energy, sustainable transportation, and others. An example of a de-risking product provided by the IDB is energy savings insurance (ESI), which uses various instruments to eliminate risk and increase investor confidence. The IDB's ESI is an insurance policy that (i) guarantees project implementation and compliance in terms of energy savings; (ii) offers insurance coverage to compensate investors in the event that the green project fails to yield the promised energy savings benefits; (iii) supports validation of energy savings through the use of an independent audit entity; and (iv) provides finance to support green projects through national financial institutions.

7.5 Impact of ESG and Circular Economy on Financial Decisions of Banks and Financial Intermediaries

Banks and other financial intermediaries bid for available funds, which they then repackage and offer to companies interested in investing in ESG and circular economy projects. These funds are sought from development banks, public finance, and institutional investors. The conditions for acquiring the funds are defined by the asset owners and managers, and banks and other lending institutions set criteria for obtaining the loans by linking their criteria to the stipulations of the asset owners.

7.6 Impact of ESG and Circular Economy on Financial Decisions of Firms

Several forward-thinking enterprises are aware that the new market reality demands responsible leadership and investment. Companies are aware that ESG and circular economy regulatory requirements are tightening, and it is only a matter of time before voluntary disclosures become mandatory. The recent proposal of the SEC, for instance, calls for increased disclosures on climate-related risks, prompting investors and customers to intensify their examination of a company's operations management and investment strategies. As a result, companies that are focused on driving long-term growth are embedding ESG and circular economy criteria in their investment and operational decisions to close the gaps between current reporting guidelines, investor expectations for ESG solutions, and sustainability progress made by their organizations [17].

Since ESG and circular economy have a significant impact on the financial growth and competitiveness of an organization, decisions to implement these initiatives are assessed for both short-term and long-term financial impact. Firms base their short-term decisions on the effect of financial ratios measuring profitability, efficiency, liquidity, and solvency. Long-term investment decisions are based on a thorough capital

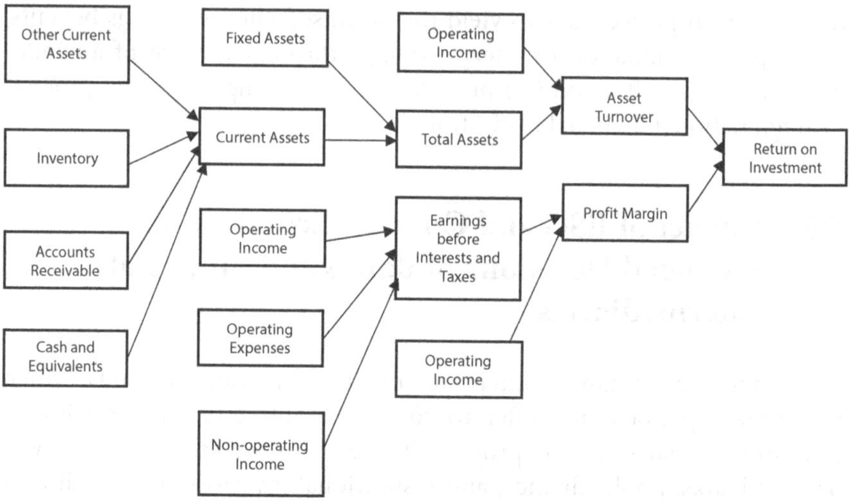

Figure 7.2 Breakdown of the DuPont model.

investment analysis and the availability of funds. Large companies tend to have adequate resources to invest in ESG and circular economy initiatives, while smaller enterprises lack the funds and, therefore, depend on external financing.

The DuPont model in Figure 7.2 provides a schematic of the financial ratios used to measure a firm's return on investment. The diagram indicates how different financial statement categories impact ESG and circular economy decisions.

7.6.1 Impact of ESG and Circular Economy on Operational Financial Decisions of Firms

Financial ratios are calculated based on information on the income statement, balance sheet, and cash flow statement. Depending on the results of these ratios, investor confidence in the firm is increased or decreased. When investor confidence decreases, the ability to raise capital in financial markets through the sale of equity (stock) is reduced. Figure 7.3 provides a summary of the categories of these ratios and the financial statement items that have an impact on these ratios.

7.6.1.1 Profitability Ratios

Profitability ratios indicate an enterprise's ability to combine inputs, such as materials, labor, and overhead to generate a profit. These ratios include

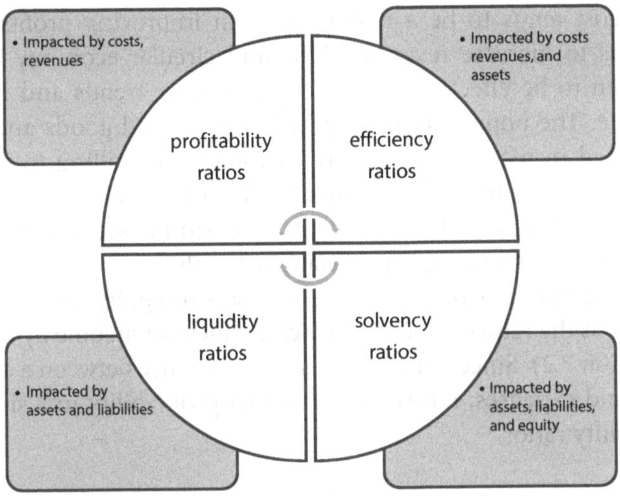

Figure 7.3 Financial ratios impacted by ESG and circular economy projects.

(i) margin ratios and (ii) return ratios. Examples of margin ratios are gross profit margin, operating profit margin, and net profit margin; while return ratios include return on assets, return on invested capital, and return on equity. All profitability ratios are impacted by ESG and circular economy projects as the ratios incorporate revenue and cost. A profitability ratio such as gross profit margin (see Equation 7.1), improves when revenue increases and cost decreases.

$$Gross\ Profit\ Margin = ((Revenue - Cost\ of\ Goods\ Sold) / Revenue) \times 100 \tag{7.1}$$

Since the value chain has been recognized as one of the major sources of ESG risk, firms frequently consider how to increase value through risk mitigation and improvement of products and processes. ESG projects that improve efficiency, recycle, or reuse materials help to reduce the value chain's cost and risk. PepsiCo is a prime example of a company that has simultaneously reduced cost and risk. The company targeted the wastewater at its bottling operation in Fresno, California, and selected Aquacycl to provide an innovative treatment technology that uses bacteria to break down organic solids in the wastewater, producing electrons that are subsequently used to generate energy. The system reduced wastewater treatment costs by 30% while simultaneously removing over 100 tons of GHG emissions per month and discharging cleaner water into the sewage system [18].

While cost tends to be a major factor in improving profits, another approach is to increase revenues. ESG and circular economy initiatives have proven to be effective in meeting consumer trends and increasing brand value. The popularity of responsibly produced goods and services has increased in recent years. Many customers are willing to pay a premium for eco-friendly products. High-performing companies include ESG in product development decisions by using customer scorecards, engaging with vendors, and sourcing appropriate materials.

Return ratios compare net income to assets or equity. An example of a return ratio is the return on assets, which divides net income by total assets (see Equation 7.2). Since net income is the difference between a company's revenues and expenses, return ratios impact profitability in a similar way to profitability ratios.

$$Return\ on\ Assets = (Net\ Income \div Total\ Assets) \times 100 \tag{7.2}$$

ESG and circular economy projects can impact return on assets by reducing operational costs and increasing revenue streams. Additionally, ESG and circular economy can impact the value of the asset base by deciding on appropriate levels of capital investment in innovative technologies.

7.6.1.2 Efficiency Ratios

Efficiency ratios are financial measures of a company's ability to use its assets effectively. Common efficiency ratios include inventory turnover, asset turnover, accounts receivable turnover, and accounts payable turnover. Asset turnover, for example (see Equation 7.3), divides total sales (revenue) by total assets. The greater the revenue generated by the asset base, the higher the efficiency ratio, and the greater the improvement in financial performance.

$$Asset\ Turnover = Total\ Revenue \div Average\ Total\ Assets \tag{7.3}$$

It is obvious from the asset turnover formula that if a company is able to increase its revenue or reduce the value of the assets used to generate a given amount of revenue, the company will improve its efficiency. Using the example discussed in 7.6.1.1, PepsiCo was able to reduce its total assets by partnering with Aquacycl to provide wastewater technology as a service. Instead of purchasing the technology, the company reduced its ownership of wastewater treatment assets by operationalizing the expense associated with the treatment. If PepsiCo was successful in reducing its asset base, then it likely generated a higher return on assets. While this may not result in a large difference when one project is considered, several ESG projects, when combined, could increase the return on assets.

7.6.1.3 *Liquidity Ratios*

Liquidity ratios evaluate a company's ability to pay its short-term debts as they become due. Four commonly used liquidity ratios are the current ratio, the quick (acid-test) ratio, the cash ratio, and the working capital ratio. These ratios are calculated using balance sheet items, with assets in the numerator and liabilities in the denominator. For example, the current ratio measures the ratio of current assets to current liabilities. Current assets include cash, marketable securities, accounts receivable, and inventories, while the quick ratio does not include inventories (see Equation 7.4).

$$Current\ Ratio = Current\ \ Assets \div Current\ \ Liabilities \tag{7.4}$$

Firms desire a current ratio above 1. From both formulas, it can be seen that if current assets are held constant, an increase in current liabilities (e.g., through increased debt incurred to execute ESG and circular economy projects) will result in a lower current ratio. This is obviously not a desirable situation. Firms, therefore, need to evaluate how the implementation of an ESG project will impact liquidity.

7.6.1.4 *Solvency Ratios*

Solvency ratios are measures of a firm's long-term financial health. These metrics provide insights into how well a firm can meet its debt obligations and interest expenses and remain profitable. The metrics are also used to evaluate how well a firm uses its assets to finance its operations. The four commonly used solvency ratios are interest coverage ratio, debt-to-asset ratio, equity ratio, and debt-to-equity ratio. Using the example of the debt-to-equity ratio (Equation 7.5), we see that the amount of debt a company incurs relevant to its equity can impact its attractiveness.

$$Debt\ to\ Equity\ Ratio = Total\ Debt \div Total\ Shareholders'Equity \tag{7.5}$$

Solvency ratios are typically used by investors and creditors to assess the sustainability of a business before lending or investing in a project.

7.6.2 Impact of ESG and Circular Economy on Capital Investment Decisions of Firms

To derive any meaningful benefit from ESG and circular economy projects, substantial capital outlays are often necessary. As an example, investments made by GE in wind, solar, and renewable energies across 17 countries approximated US$15 billion. Consequently, firms must make financial decisions that support ESG and circular economy projects in ways that return the highest possible value. Large-scale ESG and circular economy projects require a thorough capital project analysis that examines the potential impact on future cash flows. Financial managers are expected to justify the viability of a project using traditional financial methods such as net present value (NPV) [see Equation 7.6], internal rate of return (IRR), benefit/cost ratio, and payback methods.

$$Net\ Present\ Value\ (NPV) = R^t \div (1+i)^t \tag{7.6}$$

where $R^t = net\ cash\ flow\ at\ time\ t, i = discount\ rate, and\ t = time\ of\ cash\ flow$

These methods, however, are often limited in the ability to properly assess the value of ESG and circular economy projects as some benefits and costs cannot be expressed in monetary terms—projects that impact the society, for instance, or projects that have a long interval between investment and potential returns. To address these limitations, some organizations have proposed alternative assessment methods.

Up to this point, a few examples have been given of ESG and circular economy initiatives. However, there are several areas of potential investment. Some examples are provided in Table 7.2. Additionally, Figure 7.4 depicts the circularity concept and identifies areas of potential investment to meet ESG and circularity goals.

7.7 Impact of ESG and Circular Economy on Decisions to Use Financial Technology (FinTech)

The financial technology (FinTech) market has ballooned in the past few years, with a compound annual growth rate of 20% projected for the next

Table 7.2 Examples of ESG and circular economy projects.

ESG	Circular economy
• Green buildings	• Recycling of materials
• Renewable energy generation	• Recycling of water
• Pollution control	• Refurbishment of materials
• Smart agriculture	• Reuse of packaging materials, finished goods
• Protection of watersheds	• Repair of equipment, materials, and goods
• Protection of terrestrial and marine biodiversity	• Landfill waste reduction
• Clean transportation	• Waste separation and management
• Development of biodegradable materials	• Design of barter networks
• Design of processes to reduce the consumption of energy, water, and resources	• Extraction of materials from wastewater
• Resilient homes	• Traceability as a service
• Affordable health care	• Designing closed-loop supply chains

decade. By 2030, the global FinTech industry is expected to reach a market value of almost US$700 billion [19]. FinTech utilizes emerging technologies such as artificial intelligence, blockchain, application programming interfaces, distributed computing, data analytics, and robotic process automation to provide a range of financial services that offer convenience, flexibility, and more diverse connections.

In the ESG space, FinTech companies have sought to align their financial service offerings to projects that promote the attainment of ESG and circular economy goals. In addition to the services offered, many FinTech firms have embraced ESG principles within their own firms. For firms interested in implementing sustainability projects, FinTech services can be used to reduce transaction costs, improve revenues, acquire assets, and obtain more favorable lending terms and conditions than can be acquired

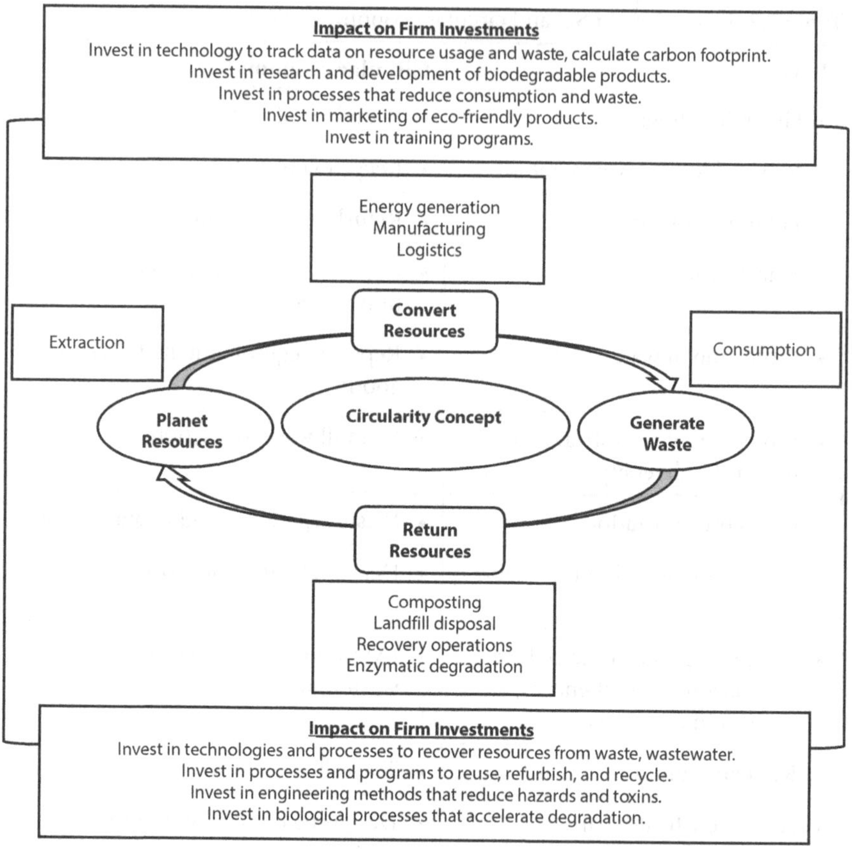

Figure 7.4 Impact of ESG and circular economy on a firm's investments.

from other financial firms. Areas in which ESG goals influence FinTech applications are discussed below.

- **Banking transactions:** FinTech has streamlined and improved the efficiency and transparency of the process of making payments, particularly for people without access to a bank account. E-wallets, for example, are examples of FinTech services that increase the speed and efficiency of banking transactions. Services that improve payments can also help to improve liquidity, particularly in the case of small firms implementing ESG projects in rural areas.
- **Purchases/payments:** Some FinTech firms help shape purchases (and by extension, the types of ESG products that are

developed and offered to customers) by providing data to customers on how spending habits advance or hinder the attainment of ESG goals. An example is Ecountabl [20], a climate risk mitigation and social sustainability enterprise that was recently purchased by Climate First Bancorp [21]. The company developed a database on the ESG impacts of over 10,000 companies and allows customers to link a bank account or credit card to its platform to determine how the brands they purchase impact ESG goals.

- **Investment:** FinTech firms provide the opportunity for organizations interested in implementing ESG initiatives to connect directly to financiers via their digital platforms. These FinTech firms offer a range of financing products, such as flexible loans, green bonds, and pooled securities such as sustainable exchange-traded funds. An example of such a company is Mosaic, Inc., which offers contractors and home improvement material suppliers the opportunity to become a partner in its financing network. Mosaic offers flexible financing to firms interested in undertaking projects to improve sustainability and resilience in the built environment. The company specializes in financing solar panels; battery storage (including bundled solar panels and battery storage); efficient HVAC systems, windows, and doors with low emissions, high energy efficiency, noise reduction materials; EV charging stations; and more. Through its digital portal, prospective clients can apply for a loan and connect with a network of potential lenders. Loans are finalized quickly and efficiently using an electronic device. The company also offers flexible financing terms, such as deferred interest loans with no payments for up to a year, which better align with the returns on ESG projects compared to traditional loans [20, 22].

7.8 Concluding Remarks

ESG and circular economy principles are rapidly impacting the financial decisions of organizations at all levels. Beginning with the global institutions that define the ESG goals, the cascading effect of financial decisions made by a series of intermediary organizations in the finance supply chain eventually filters down to impact the financial decisions of firms desiring to implement ESG and circular economy projects. Organizations that set legal, regulatory, voluntary reporting, and governance mandates and guidelines; asset owners and managers; banks and financial intermediaries; and customers ultimately impact the financial decisions of enterprises that pursue ESG projects to mitigate long-term financial risk and increase financial returns. The risk and returns of company stocks and asset portfolios are in turn impacted by these decisions, ultimately resulting in a feedback effect between the financial decisions of enterprising firms and those of investors.

Emerging technologies, such as FinTech, strengthen the opportunity to implement ESG projects. These technologies, when integrated into financial services, automate operations and facilitate inclusivity, and use of financial services. FinTech also simplifies financial processes, improving transactional efficiency.

References

1. Bonini, S. and Swartz, S., Profits with Purpose: How Organizing for Sustainability Can Benefit the Bottom Line. *McKinsey Company*, 2014, Retrieved at https://www.mckinsey.com/~/media/McKinsey/Business%20Functions/Sustainability/Our%20Insights/Profits%20with%20purpose/Profits%20with%20Purpose.ashx.
2. Fulton, Mark and Kahn, Bruce and Sharples, Camilla, Sustainable Investing: Establishing Long-Term Value and Performance (June 12, 2012). Available at SSRN: https://ssrn.com/abstract=2222740 or http://dx.doi.org/10.2139/ssrn.2222740.
3. Global Sustainable Investment Alliance, *Global Sustainable Investment Review*, Global Sustainable Investment Alliance, 2021, https://www.gsi-alliance.org/wp-content/uploads/2021/08/GSIR-20201.pdf.
4. Chamas, A., Moon, H., Zheng, J., Qiu, Y., Tabassum, T., Abu-Omar, M., Scott, S.L., Suh, S., Degradation Rates of Plastic in the Environment. *ACS Sustain. Chem. Eng.*, 8, 3494–3511, 2020, https://pubs.acs.org/doi/pdf/10.1021/acssuschemeng.9b06635.
5. United Nations Conference on Trade and Development (UNCTAD), Circular Economy, https://unctad.org/topic/trade-and-environment/circular-economy#:~:text=A%20circular%20economy%20entails%20markets,economy%20or%20used%20more%20efficiently.
6. Szal, A., *Mushrooms Could Lead to Biodegradable Computer Chips*, Thomas, 2023, https://www.thomasnet.com/insights/mushrooms-to-biodegradable-computer-chips/?utm_content=featuredstory&position=1&linktype=read-more&channel=email&campaign_type=thomas_industry_update&cam-

paign_name=tiu230413&utm_campaign=tiu230413&utm_medium=email&utm_source=thomas_industry_update&tinid=226799979. 2023.

7. Bonderud, D., Mushrooms May Lead to the Development of a Biodegradable Computer Chip, *Now*, 2023, https://now.northropgrumman.com/mushrooms-may-lead-to-the-development-of-a-biodegradable-computer-chip/.
8. International, K.P.M.G., Big Shifts, Small Steps, in: *Survey of Sustainability Reporting 2022*, 2022, Retrieved at https://assets.kpmg.com/content/dam/kpmg/xx/pdf/2023/04/big-shifts-small-steps.pdf.
9. Rödl & Partner, The new German Supply Chain Due Diligence Act (LkSG) – what needs to be done, *Rodl & Partner*, 2023, Retrieved at https://www.roedl.com/insights/supply-chain-act-due-diligence-obligations.
10. Davies, P.A., Bartz, S., Wilhelm, A., New German Law Aims to Strengthen Global Human and Environmental Rights, *Latham & Watkins*, LLP, 2023a, Retrieved at https://www.globalelr.com/2021/06/new-german-law-aims-to-strengthen-global-human-and-environmental-rights/.
11. Davies, P.A., Bartz, S., Wilhelm, A., Singapore's Green Finance Industry Taskforce Luanches Final Consultation on Green and Transition Economy, *Latham & Watkins*, LLP, 2023b2023, https://www.globalelr.com/2023/03/singapores-green-finance-industry-taskforce-launches-final-consultation-on-green-and-transition-taxonomy/.
12. OECD, Defining and Measuring Green Investments: Implications for Institutional Investors' Asset Allocations, in: *OECD Working Papers on Finance, Insurance, and Private Pensions, No. 24*, 20122012, https://www.oecd.org/environment/WP_24_Defining_and_Measuring_Green_Investments.pdf.
13. Della Croce, R., Kaminker, C., Stewart, F., *The Role of Pension Funds in Financing Green Growth Initiatives*, OECD Publishing, Paris, 2011, https://www.oecd.org/finance/private-pensions/49016671.pdf.
14. Mehta, A. and Andrich, M.L., *The Asian Development Bank's Green Finance Initiatives and Their Impacts*, Asian Development Bank, 2021, https://www.adb.org/sites/default/files/institutional-document/691951/ado2021bn-adb-green-finance-initiative.pdf.
15. Green Finance for Latin America and the Caribbean (GFL), 2022. https://www.greenfinanceplatform.org/platforms/green-finance-latin-america-and-caribbean-platform-gfl.
16. All Africa, *African Development Bank Launches Catalytic Initiative for Green Banks in Africa on the Sidelines of COP 27*, All Africa Info Wire, 2022, https://allafrica.com/stories/202211170458.html.
17. Jaros, N.D., Lee, M., Li, J., Munson, R., *Can Resilience Shape a Shifting Landscape?*, Ernst and Young (EY), 2022, https://www.ey.com/en_us/wealth-asset-management/global-alternative-fund-survey?WT.mc_id=10820940&AA.tsrc=paidsearch&gclid=EAIaIQobChMIyKyl4fy1_gIVwgplCh22WA-bEAAYASAAEgKze_D_BwE.

18. Gursahaney, R., Case Study: How PepsiCo reduced costs and addressed climate and water goals through onsite wastewater treatment. *Water Technol.*, September/October 2022, 10–13, https://www.watertechonline.com/wastewater/article/14282336/how-a-leading-cpg-company-reduced-costs-and-addressed-climate-and-water-goals-through-onsite-wastewater-treatment.
19. Adroit Market Research, *With 20.5% CAGR, Fintech (Financial Technology) Market to hit USD 699.50 Billion by 2030 – Top Companies, Growth Rate, Recent Trends, Business Opportunities and Forecasts Analysis – Adroit Market Research*, Global News Wire, 2022, https://www.globenewswire.com/news-release/2022/09/20/2518804/0/en/With-20-5-CAGR-Fintech-.
20. Grutman, S., Papdemetriou, D., Madhok, R., *ESG and Fintechs: How Firms are Benefiting from an ESG Focus*, Fintech Futures, North American Edition, 2022, https://www.fintechfutures.com/2022/04/esg-and-fintechs-how-firms-are-benefiting-from-an-esg-focus/.
21. Saulsbery, G., *Climate First Bancorp acquires ESG data fintech Ecountabl*, Banking Dive, 2022, https://www.bankingdive.com/news/climate-first-bancorp-acquires-esg-data-fintech-ecountabl/636743/.
22. Mosaic, *The 100% Clean Energy Home. We're Here to Make it Happen*, vol. 2022, Mosaic, p. 22, 2022, https://joinmosaic.com/.

8

Institutions and Crowdfunding Success in Africa

Isaac Appiah-Otoo

College of Management Science, Chengdu University of Technology, Chengdu, China

Abstract

Financial resources play an essential role in the growth of firms; nevertheless, providing small- and medium-sized businesses with financial resources is still difficult, particularly in Africa. Recently, crowdfunding has emerged as a solution for these firms that were previously neglected by traditional banks; however, crowdfunding development in Africa stays low as compared to their counterparts in advanced countries. Similarly, the institutional environment in Africa remains underdeveloped. This motivates this study to assess whether institutional quality influences crowdfunding development in Africa. By using a sample of 29 African countries from 2013 to 2020 and the two-step system generalized method of moments (sys-GMM) estimator, the findings show that institutions advance crowdfunding development in Africa. The country-level findings show that Kenya, Ghana, Nigeria, South Africa, and Uganda have the highest impact of institutions on crowdfunding development, while Lesotho, Algeria, Gambia, Guinea, and Benin have the least impact of institutions on crowdfunding development in Africa. The study also finds that institutions indirectly boost crowdfunding via economic growth. Policies that support strong institutions were proposed to boost crowdfunding development in Africa.

Keywords: Crowdfunding, institutional quality, Africa

Email: appiahotooi@yahoo.com; ORCID: https://orcid.org/0000-0002-3683-0634

Ernesto D.R. Santibanez Gonzalez, Vinay Kandpal, Peterson K. Ozili and Prasenjit Chatterjee (eds.) Fintech for ESG and the Circular Economy, (149–172) © 2024 Scrivener Publishing LLC

8.1 Introduction

African countries' economic growth relies heavily on small- and medium-sized enterprises (SMEs), which account for about 80% of the total workforce [1, 2]. However, these businesses often struggle due to inadequate funding, with estimates suggesting a funding gap of US$140 billion to US$160 billion for SMEs in Africa [2]. Traditional banking systems have failed to address this issue, primarily due to the challenge of insufficient collateral [2]. Fortunately, crowdfunding has emerged as a viable solution for SME financing, thanks to the rapid technological revolution [3, 4]. Crowdfunding eliminates middlemen, offers reasonable interest rates, and speeds up the process of acquiring loans for SMEs [5]. This approach reduces transaction costs and information asymmetry problems, often using cutting-edge technologies like blockchain and big-data analytics [5].

Transaction costs comprise the money and time expended to connect borrowers and lenders, as well as legal fees [6]. Problems with information asymmetry pertain to the uneven sharing of information among borrowers and lenders [6]. This is not surprising global crowdfunding investment stood at US$12.3 billion in 2019 and is expected to increase to US$25.8 billion in 2026[1]. Conversely, crowdfunding may also retard SMEs' growth by driving credit risks [6–9]. For instance, China reported the failure of 5,433 peer-to-peer lending platforms from 2014 to 2019 with over 2 million investors and RMB 117.21 billion (US$26.9 billion) in outstanding debts [6]. Thus, the current moment has witnessed an avalanche of studies assessing the antecedents of successful crowdfunding with the empirics establishing that the entrepreneur's social network ties, age, gender, location, place of residence of the fundraiser, meeting specifications, team experience, religion, economic policy uncertainty, ease of use, and project planning affect crowdfunding success [10–12], however, research is scarce on the contributions of institutional quality to crowdfunding development.

Institutions play an essential role in all facets of the economy [13, 14]. A developed institutional quality is the backbone of a stable economy, and equitable distribution of resources, thus likely to enhance crowdfunding development while a lackluster institutional environment reinforces underdevelopment, inequitable distribution of resources, and persistent backwardness, which is likely to impede the development of new financial products and markets resulting in underdeveloped crowdfunding.

[1]https://reports.valuates.com/reports/QYRE-Auto-1598/global-crowdfunding retrieved 23-07-2022

Accordingly, this study's purpose is to examine the effect of institutional quality on crowdfunding development in Africa.

Africa is the subject of this study for the aforementioned purposes. First, the majority of African countries have immature financial systems hindering easier access to finance for SMEs growth in Africa [15, 16]. Also, crowdfunding development in Africa remains low as compared to its counterparts in advanced countries. For instance, according to Statista, the volume of crowdfunding in Africa stood at US$1.21 billion in 2020 as compared to US$73.93 billion in the US and Canada and US$22.6 billion in Europe[2]. Furthermore, one of the world's lowest institutional-quality environments is found in Africa [14]. This is not surprising as Africa has recently witnessed an avalanche of coups. For instance, Mali, Chad, Guinea, Sudan, and Burkina Faso have all had coups, thus, likely to influence crowdfunding development. Finally, recent African governments have begun regulating crowdfunding platforms. Among some of the regulatory strategies are "wait-and-see," "test-and-learn," regulatory laws and reforms, and innovation facilitators [17], thus, knowing that the role of institutions in crowdfunding development will facilitate effective crowdfunding policies.

The following are new additions to the scholarship made by the present investigation. First, this research offers the first empirical estimate of the impact of institutional quality on crowdfunding development and finds that institutions enhance crowdfunding development in Africa. As argued previously, most of the prior studies have centered on the role of the entrepreneur's social network ties, age, gender, location, place of residence of the fundraiser, meeting specifications, team experience, and religion on crowdfunding success. Thus, by exploring the role of institutions in crowdfunding development, this study expands the existing literature on the drivers of crowdfunding development. Also, this study estimates the country-specific impact of institutions on crowdfunding development and finds that Kenya, Ghana, Nigeria, South Africa, and Uganda have the highest impact of institutions on crowdfunding development, while Lesotho, Algeria, Gambia, Guinea, and Benin have the least impact of institutions on crowdfunding development in Africa. Finally, this study explores the economic growth pathway via which institutions influence crowdfunding development and finds that beyond the threshold value of 6.242 (about US$514 billion), 5.446 (about US$232 billion), 5.197 (about US$181 billion), 5.018 (about US$151 billion), 6.067 (about US$432 billion), and

---

[2]https://www.statista.com/statistics/946659/global-crowdfunding-volume-worldwide-by-region/ retrieved 21-09-2022

6.199 (about US$492 billion) of economic growth will ensure control of corruption, government effectiveness, political stability, regulation quality, rule of law, and voice and accountability boosts crowdfunding development in Africa.

The study continues with the review of the literature and hypothesis formulation in Section 8.2. It also presents the data and methods used in Section 8.3. The results and discussion are presented in Section 8.4, while the policies and conclusion are disclosed in Section 8.5.

8.2 Literature Review and Hypothesis Development

8.2.1 Literature Review

This section reviews selected studies on crowdfunding development. Fu *et al.* [18] examined the effect of trade openness, economic growth, government spending, domestic credit, and Internet development on digital finance development in China. The study applied the system generalized method of moment (sys-GMM) technique and a sample of 29 Chinese provinces from 2014 to 2016 and found that trade openness, economic growth, government spending, domestic credit, and Internet development drive digital finance development in China. Hou *et al.* [19] found that project goal, initiation and experience, duration, the sources of followers, and the number of platform visitors drive crowdfunding project success. Zheng *et al.* [20] found that the entrepreneur's social network ties, the shared meaning of the crowdfunding project between the entrepreneur and the sponsors, and obligations to fund other entrepreneurs drive crowdfunding performance in China. Ba *et al.* [21] found that age, location, place of residence of the fundraiser, and social capital influence crowdfunding project success. Zheng *et al.* [22] also found that meeting specifications, team experience, and project planning are significant drivers of crowdfunding success. Zheng *et al.* [23] showed that trust management plays a significant role in crowdfunding project success usually through entrepreneurs' creditworthiness and entrepreneur-sponsor interactions. They also found that entrepreneurs' prior success moderates the impact of entrepreneur-sponsor interactions on crowdfunding success. Wang *et al.* [24] used the signaling theory to access the drivers of crowdfunding projects' success and found that the creator's previous experience, the creator's replies, and the backer's comments significantly affect funding success. Qian and Lin [25] established that the funder's credibility, project description, and pictures of the projects facilitate funding success, while too many words and an excessive target amount hamper funding success. Di Pietro and Butticè [26] found that market capitalization, uncertainty avoidance, protecting minorities, and individualism improve crowdfunding development, while ease of doing business, starting business procedures, indulgence, masculinity, power distance, and enforcing contracts impede crowdfunding development for a sample of 27 countries. Focusing on Ghana, Djimesah *et al.* [10] concluded that the ease of use of crowdfunding platforms influences their perceived usefulness, while perceived usefulness also influences users' intention to use crowdfunding platforms.

From the literature review, there are scarcity of studies on the impact of institutional quality on crowdfunding development. Subsequently, this study aims to fill this vacuum in research.

8.2.2 Hypotheses Development

Institutions are defined as the "rules of the game" of a society that governs and shapes the way humans interact [13]. Institutions encompass regulatory structures, government effectiveness, rules, and laws and are characterized as a social structure that puts influences, demands, and limits on companies' activities [27]. The activities of a company are usually constrained by a range of external factors because they possess similar and interrelated surroundings, and they must react to various needs and expectations to exist [28]. A weak institutional environment provides fertile ground for the prosperity of corruption, and this requires entrepreneurs to act to overcome the attendant uncertainties. In the context of developing countries, informal corruption exists when bureaucrats collect bribes to perform their basic public functions. This results in inequitable distribution of resources, lax protection of property rights, unfair competition, lack of trust and confidence to invest, and brain drain, thereby creating problems for entrepreneurs in the conduct of their businesses [29, 30]. Conversely, institutional relationships can improve wealth generation, thus boosting business performance [31]. Thus, this study hypothesizes:

Hypothesis 1: Institutional quality enhances crowdfunding development in Africa.

It is commonly known that institutional quality plays a crucial role in economic development [13]. A sophisticated institutional environment lowers risk and uncertainty while ensuring equal resource distribution thereby driving economic growth [13, 32]. Empirically, it is found that institutions influence economic growth [33–38]. For instance, Boateng *et al.* [33] found that institutions enhance SSA countries' economic growth. Other scholars such as Lee and Kim [34] for low-income countries, Kant [35] for developing countries, Siddiqui and Ahmed [36] for 84 countries, Slesman *et al.* [37] for 39 countries, Nedić [38] for 5 countries also found institutions to enhance economic growth, while economic growth is also found to enhance crowdfunding development [18]. Accordingly, we derive the second hypothesis:

Hypothesis 2: Institutional quality and economic growth are complementary drivers of crowdfunding development in Africa.

8.3 Methodology and Data

8.3.1 Data

This study evaluates the influence of institutional quality on the growth of crowdfunding in Africa. The study uses a panel of 29 countries, covering the 2013 to 2020 period. The countries employed in this study are Algeria, Benin, Botswana, Burkina Faso, Cameroon, Congo, Cote d'Ivoire, Egypt, The Gambia, Ghana, Guinea, Kenya, Lesotho, Madagascar, Mali, Morocco, Mozambique, Namibia, Nigeria, Rwanda, Senegal, Sierra Leone, South Africa, Tanzania, Togo, Tunisia, Uganda, Zambia, and Zimbabwe. Crowdfunding's data availability influenced the period and country selection.

We employed the parameters crowdfunding, GDP per capita to denote economic growth, trade openness which is the summation of export and import as a share of economic growth, domestic credit to the private sector, gross fixed capital formation as a measure of investment, and institutional quality (measured by control of corruption, rule of law, regulation quality, voice and accountability, political stability, and government effectiveness) for the empirical analysis. The Centre for Alternative Finance of the University of Cambridge[3] served as the source of the crowdfunding data. We also sourced the institutional quality data from the World Bank, Worldwide Governance Indicators Database, 2021[4]. The estimate ranges from approximately -2.5 to 2.5 with 2.5 indicating a strong institutional quality setting and vice versa. Finally, we derived the economic growth, trade openness, domestic credit, and investment data from the World Development Indicators Database [39].

[3]https://www.jbs.cam.ac.uk/faculty-research/centres/alternative-finance/ retrieved 20-07-2022
[4]https://databank.worldbank.org/source/worldwide-governance-indicators retrieved 22-07-2022

Crowdfunding is defined as "the efforts by entrepreneurial individuals and groups cultural, social, and for-profit to fund their ventures by drawing on relatively small contributions from a relatively large number of individuals using the Internet, without standard financial intermediaries" [40]. The three parties involved in crowdfunding are typically the creator, an intermediary (such as a platform provider), and donors [41]. Equity, reward, donation, and loan are the four main subcategories of crowdfunding [42]. Through online platforms, entrepreneurs can sell bonds or shares in their company to several small investors using equity-based crowdfunding [43]. Individuals who engage in reward-based crowdfunding make modest financial contributions to a campaign in exchange for non-cash benefits, but they run the risk of not obtaining the campaign incentives they were promised [44]. Donation-based crowdfunding allows people to donate money without expecting to receive anything in return in exchange for their contributions, but they do receive indirect advantages including a sense of accomplishment and mental satisfaction [45]. Examples of crowdfunding platforms include GoFundMe, Kickstarter, Indiegogo, Lending Club, and Prosper.

Table 8.1 Variable definition.

Variables	Definition	Justification	Unit of measurement
lncfd	Crowdfunding	[46]	Million US$
lngfcf	Investment	[6, 16, 18]	Percentage of GDP
lngdp	Economic growth	[6, 16, 18]	Constant 2015 US$
lntrade	Trade openness	[6, 16, 18]	Percent
lndcps	Domestic credit	[6, 16, 18]	Percentage of GDP
cc	Control of corruption	[14]	Scalar
rl	Rule of law	[14]	Scalar
va	Voice and accountability	[14]	Scalar
ge	Government effectiveness	[14]	Scalar
rq	Regulatory quality	[14]	Scalar
ps	Political stability	[14]	Scalar

Table 8.1 displays the variables, code, definition, and unit of measurement. All the variables, except the institutional quality measures, were log-transformed to present the results as elasticities.

8.3.2 Empirical Model

To examine the impact of institutions on crowdfunding development, this study estimates the following model (Equation 8.1).

$$lncfd_{it} = b_o + b_1 \ln gdp_{it} + b_2 \ln to_{it} + b_3 \ln dc_{it} + b_4 \ln gfcf_{it} + b_5 inst_{it} + e_{it} \tag{8.1}$$

Where cfd is crowdfunding, gdp is economic growth, to is trade openness, dc is domestic credit, $gfcf$ represents investment, $inst$ denotes institutional quality which is measured by control of corruption (cc), rule of law (rl), regulation quality (rq), voice and accountability (va), political stability (ps), and government effectiveness (ge), t and i denote time and country, and e is the error term.

To explore the economic growth channel via which institutions influence crowdfunding, we estimate the following model (Equation 8.2).

$$\begin{aligned} lncfd_{it} &= b_o + b_1 \ln gdp_{it} + b_2 \ln to_{it} + b_3 \ln dc_{it} + b_4 \ln gfcf_{it} + b_5 inst_{it} \\ &\quad + b_6 inst_{it} \times \ln gdp_{it} + e_{it} \end{aligned} \tag{8.2}$$

From Equation 8.2, we estimate the following marginal effect of institutions on crowdfunding development (Equation 8.3).

$$\frac{\Delta lncfd_{it}}{\Delta inst_{it}} = b_5 + b_6 lngdp_{it} \tag{8.3}$$

This study aims to compute b_5 of Equation 8.1 and b_6 of Equation 8.2. We expect b_5 and b_6 to have a statistically significant positive effect on crowdfunding development in Africa. That is, institutions directly and indirectly via economic growth improve crowdfunding development in Africa.

The sys-GMM model is used in this research for analysis. Because it tackles endogeneity by eliminating fixed effects and converts all predictors via differencing, this model yields efficient results [47]. When the time (T) is short and the number of cross-sections (N) is large, this model is suitable [48]. That is, $T<N$, similar to this research $T (8) < N (29)$.

8.4 Results and Discussion

Crowdfunding has an average of 13.6% with a maximum of 20.2% according to Table 8.2. Kenya leads in crowdfunding development in Africa, thanks to leading platforms such as M-Changa and Mpesa. Other notable countries are Ghana, Uganda, South Africa, and Nigeria, while The Gambia, Guinea, and Benin are the countries with the least crowdfunding development. Loan-based crowdfunding is the dominant crowdfunding model in Africa, contributing about 54% of the total crowdfunding volume [49]. Thus, crowdfunding is boosting entrepreneurial finance in Africa, thereby facilitating employment, and improving the quality of life [2]. Equity- or reward-based crowdfunding is typically used by entrepreneurs with relatively high potential for growth to launch creative, artistic, and innovative projects [2]. The economic growth average stood at 7.2% with a maximum of 8.9%. Botswana, South Africa, Namibia, Algeria,

Table 8.2 Descriptive statistics.

Variables	Obs.	Mean	Std. dev.	Min	Max	I (0)	I (1)
lncfd	232	13.561	2.920	4.677	20.188	51.540	100.008***
lngdp	232	7.244	0.774	6.118	8.886	59.667	101.784***
lnto	228	4.106	0.379	3.031	5.027	77.331**	129.918***
lndc	222	3.023	0.734	1.562	4.859	32.325	140.994***
lngfcf	227	3.095	0.329	2.002	3.959	66.420	161.293***
cc	232	-0.504	0.547	-1.572	0.930	94.842***	174.116***
ge	232	-0.595	0.490	-1.693	0.530	62.141	132.705***
ps	232	-0.596	0.737	-2.302	1.111	56.334	162.314***
rq	232	-0.516	0.464	-1.903	0.585	76.699*	121.121***
rl	232	-0.525	0.499	-1.791	0.634	61.345	125.744***
va	232	-0.378	0.584	-1.508	0.697	52.494	123.529***

$^{*}p < 0.1$, $^{**}p < 0.05$, $^{***}p < 0.01$.

Egypt, Tunisia, and Morocco are rich countries, while countries such as Congo, Madagascar, and Togo have low levels of income. Trade openness, domestic credit, and investment have averages of 4.1%, 3%, and 3.1%, respectively, while all the institutional quality proxies have negative averages. Lesotho, Mozambique, Botswana, Tunisia, and Guinea are more open to the outside world compared to countries such as Nigeria, Tanzania, and Uganda. South Africa has the strongest financial sector, while Sierra Leone has the weakest financial sector. Algeria has the largest infrastructure investment, while Zimbabwe has the lowest infrastructure investment. All the countries (except Botswana, Namibia, and South Africa) have weak institutional quality.

The Augmented Dickey-Fuller [50] unit root test indicates that all the variables are stationary at the first difference I(*1*) level, except trade openness, control of corruption, and regulation quality, which were stationary at both the log I(*0*) and first difference levels.

The study runs a correlation analysis and a variance inflation factor (VIF) test to see if the variables are multicollinear. This test is essential since the presence of multicollinearity influences the exact outcomes of the covariates. The results of Table 8.3 indicate that this study is devoid of multicollinearity since the highest correlation coefficient is 0.6. The VIFs are also below 10, suggesting that this study is free from the presence of multicollinearity.

The findings as disclosed in Table 8.4 show that previous crowdfunding volume influences the current crowdfunding volume. It was also found that economic growth, domestic credit, and investment have an

Table 8.3 Matrix of correlations and VIF[5].

Variables	VIF	lncfd	lngdp	lnto	lndc	lngfcf	rl
lncfd		1.000					
lngdp	1.83	0.067	1.000				
lnto	1.10	-0.385	-0.007	1.000			
lndc	1.96	0.086	0.621	0.173	1.000		
lngfcf	1.14	-0.128	-0.001	0.225	0.102	1.000	
rl	1.76	0.130	0.528	0.156	0.580	0.256	1.000

[5]In Table 8.3, we presented the results when the rule of law was used as the institutional quality proxy to preserve space. The other measures show similar results and are available as supplementary material.

Table 8.4 Crowdfunding and institutions.

Variables	Model 1	Model 2	Model 3	Model 4	Model 5	Model 6
l.lncfd	0.970***	0.984***	0.926***	0.968***	0.967***	0.983***
	(0.068)	(0.062)	(0.060)	(0.067)	(0.065)	(0.055)
lngdp	0.041	-0.016	-0.034	0.114	0.026	0.030
	(0.141)	(0.129)	(0.108)	(0.095)	(0.099)	(0.116)
lnto	-0.386	-0.147	-0.742**	-0.191	-0.241	-0.363
	(0.377)	(0.289)	(0.321)	(0.282)	(0.274)	(0.267)
lndc	-0.141	-0.258	0.049	-0.208	-0.153	-0.093
	(0.181)	(0.215)	(0.182)	(0.201)	(0.195)	(0.175)
lngfcf	0.234	0.145	0.048	0.237	0.183	0.409
	(0.356)	(0.402)	(0.368)	(0.343)	(0.353)	(0.333)
cc	0.449*					
	(0.236)					
ge		0.602**				
		(0.291)				
ps			0.504***			
			(0.138)			
rq				0.526***		
				(0.181)		
rl					0.523**	
					(0.204)	
va						0.331***
						(0.128)
Time dummies	Yes	Yes	Yes	Yes	Yes	Yes
Constant	2.156	2.198	4.780*	1.110	1.929	1.126
	(3.572)	(3.134)	(2.680)	(2.664)	(2.773)	(2.299)
Observations	190	190	190	190	190	190
AR (1) prob. value	0.030	0.029	0.027	0.028	0.027	0.033
AR (2) prob. value	0.554	0.452	0.542	0.557	0.513	0.457
Number of instruments	19.000	19.000	19.000	19.000	19.000	19.000
Hansen test prob. value	0.111	0.113	0.180	0.099	0.102	0.116

Standard errors are shown via brackets, * $p < 0.1$, ** $p < 0.05$, *** $p < 0.01$. In this table, the lag form of the independent variables, as well as the time dummies, was treated as instruments. The collapse option was also used.

insignificant impact on crowdfunding development in Africa, while trade openness significantly hampers crowdfunding development in Model 3. The statistically significant negative impact of trade openness on crowdfunding could be attributed to the fact that most of the countries under study are import-dependent and this reduces the demand for alternative finance, thus the negative impact of trade openness on crowdfunding. The significant negative impact of trade openness on crowdfunding conflicts with the outcomes of [18] for China.

Focusing on the essential variables, control of corruption, government effectiveness, political stability, regulation quality, rule of law, and voice and accountability are significant enablers of crowdfunding development in Africa. A 1% rise in control of corruption, government effectiveness, political stability, regulation quality, rule of law, and voice and accountability increases crowdfunding by 0.449%, 0.602%, 0.504%, 0.526%, 0.523%, and 0.331%. Governments in Africa have been actively involved in crowdfunding development. For instance, Ghana recently introduced mobile money interoperability to easily facilitate funds transfer across different mobile telecommunication platforms. The government of Ghana has also developed regulations guiding the safe development of crowdfunding platforms [10]. In Kenya, the government has allowed crowdfunding platforms to freely operate while rendering less supervision. Nigeria has also implemented deposit insurance for mobile money transactions. Countries such as Cote d'Ivoire and Tanzania have recently withdrawn their electronic money tax due to public outcry. These justify the statistically significant positive links between the institutional quality measures and crowdfunding, validating our hypothesis 1.

In Figures 8.1 to 8.6, we explored the country-specific impact of institutions on crowdfunding development in Africa. The results also show that all the institutional quality measures have a positive impact on crowdfunding development in Africa. However, Kenya, Ghana, Nigeria, South Africa, and Uganda have the highest impact of institutions on crowdfunding development, while Lesotho, Algeria, Gambia, Guinea, and Benin have the least impact of institutions on crowdfunding development in Africa. These are all original discoveries to the drivers of crowdfunding success literature.

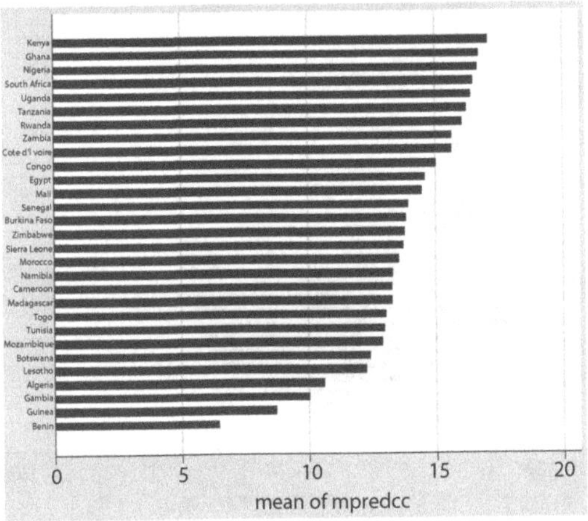

Figure 8.1 Control of corruption.

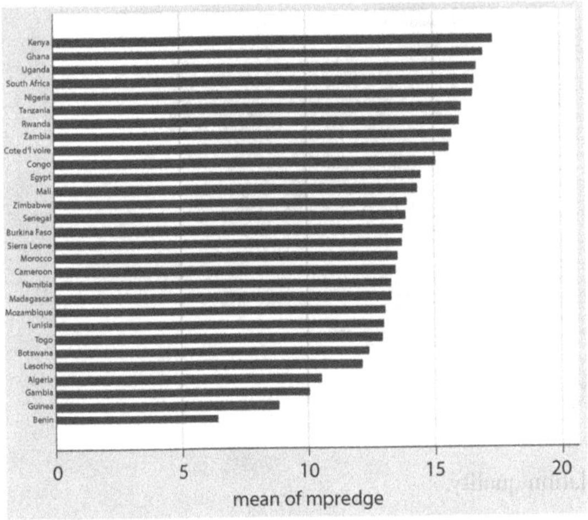

Figure 8.2 Government effectiveness.

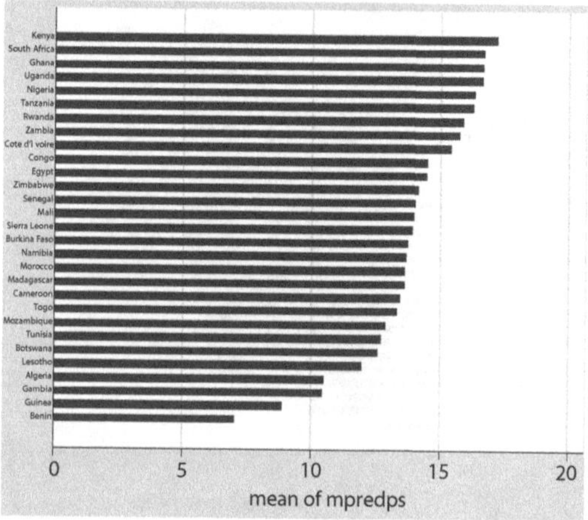

Figure 8.3 Political stability.

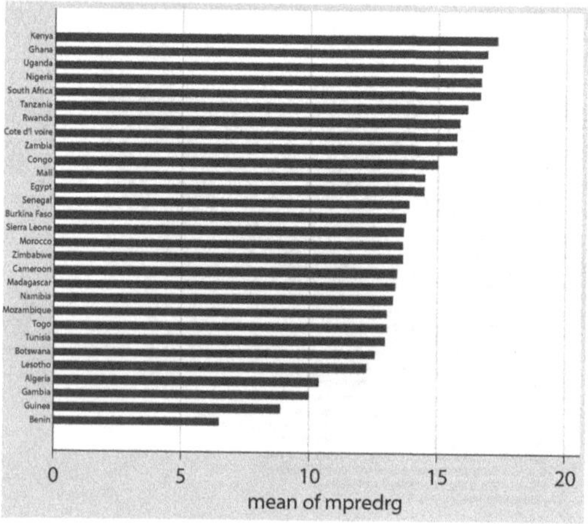

Figure 8.4 Regulation quality.

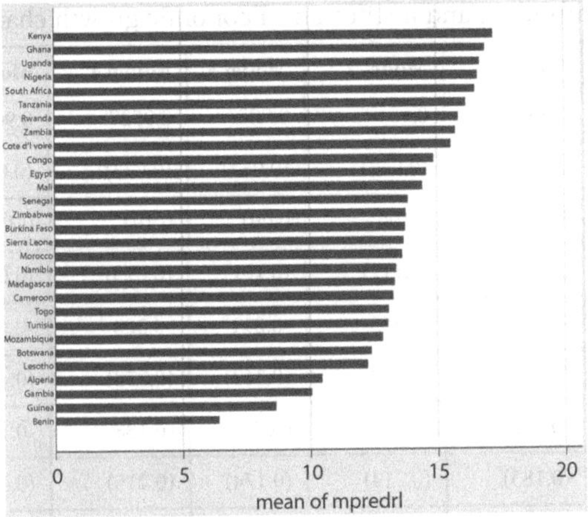

Figure 8.5 Rule of law.

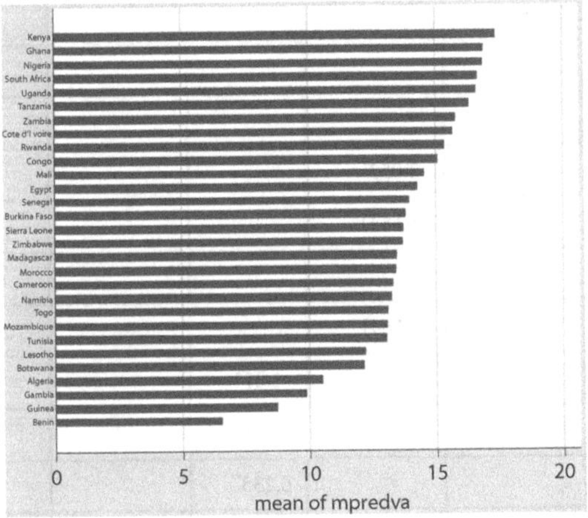

Figure 8.6 Voice and accountability.

Table 8.5 presents the results of the economic growth mechanism via which institutions influence crowdfunding development in Africa. The results show that the interaction effect of the institutional quality measures and economic growth on crowdfunding is statistically significant, except for regulation quality. Thus, institutions indirectly influence crowdfunding through economic growth. This approves our hypothesis 2. These are unique discoveries in the literature on the drivers of crowdfunding success.

Table 8.5 Crowdfunding and institutions: Economic growth channel.

Variables	Model 1	Model 2	Model 3	Model 4	Model 5	Model 6
l.lncfd	0.887***	0.951***	0.907***	0.952***	0.906***	0.940***
	(0.085)	(0.072)	(0.067)	(0.073)	(0.079)	(0.072)
lngdp	0.156	0.105	0.091	0.191***	0.173**	0.094
	(0.112)	(0.112)	(0.101)	(0.073)	(0.079)	(0.104)
lnto	-0.933*	-0.355	-0.811**	-0.308	-0.685*	-0.515
	(0.489)	(0.412)	(0.362)	(0.370)	(0.403)	(0.357)
lndc	-0.082	-0.263	0.033	-0.188	-0.128	-0.098
	(0.183)	(0.214)	(0.174)	(0.215)	(0.197)	(0.172)
lngfcf	0.184	0.232	0.055	0.329	0.241	0.463
	(0.357)	(0.369)	(0.350)	(0.338)	(0.322)	(0.327)
cc	-3.745***					
	(0.996)					
cc×lngdp	0.600***					
	(0.144)					
ge		-2.053*				
		(1.184)				
ge×lngdp		0.377**				
		(0.164)				
ps			-1.211			
			(0.755)			
ps×lngdp			0.233**			
			(0.099)			
rq				-1.104		
				(1.247)		
rq×lngdp				0.220		
				(0.160)		
rl					-3.155***	
					(1.056)	

(Continued)

Table 8.5 Crowdfunding and institutions: Economic growth channel. (*Continued*)

Variables	Model 1	Model 2	Model 3	Model 4	Model 5	Model 6
rl×lngdp					0.520***	
					(0.146)	
va						-1.742
						(1.115)
va×lngdp						0.281*
						(0.154)
Time dummies	Yes	Yes	Yes	Yes	Yes	Yes
Constant	4.572	2.285	4.436	0.850	3.160	1.654
	(4.203)	(3.349)	(2.841)	(2.738)	(3.357)	(2.735)
Observations	190	190	190	190	190	190
AR (1) prob. value	0.028	0.027	0.023	0.027	0.024	0.028
AR (2) prob. value	0.593	0.368	0.470	0.574	0.481	0.445
Number of instruments	20.000	20.000	20.000	20.000	20.000	20.000
Hansen test prob. value	0.150	0.142	0.121	0.103	0.129	0.119

Standard errors are shown via brackets, * $p < 0.1$, ** $p < 0.05$, *** $p < 0.01$. In this table, the lag form of the independent variables, as well as the time dummies, was treated as instruments. The collapse option was also used.

Table 8.6 shows the marginal effect results. The results indicate that institutions have a positive impact on crowdfunding at both the mean, minimum, and maximum levels of economic growth, except at the minimum values of economic growth in Models 1 and 6. Comparatively, institutions have a higher impact on crowdfunding at high levels of economic growth. The results further show that beyond the threshold value of 6.242 (about US$514 billion), 5.446 (about US$232 billion), 5.197 (about US$181 billion), 5.018 (about US$151 billion), 6.067 (about US$432 billion), and 6.199 (about US$492 billion) of economic growth will ensure control of corruption, government effectiveness, political stability, regulation quality, rule of law, and voice and accountability boosts crowdfunding

Table 8.6 Marginal effect.

Indicators	Model 1 Control of corruption	Model 2 Government effectiveness	Model 3 Political stability	Model 4 Regulation quality	Model 5 Rule of law	Model 6 Voice and accountability
Zero	3.745***	-2.053*	-1.211	-1.104	-3.155***	-1.742
Mean	0.601	0.678	0.477	0.490	0.612	0.294
Minimum	-0.074	0.253	0.214	0.242	0.026	-0.023
Maximum	1.587	1.297	0.859	0.851	1.466	0.755
Unconditional effect	3.745***	-2.053*	-1.211	-1.104	-3.155***	-1.742
Conditional effect	0.600***	0.377**	0.233**	0.220	0.520***	0.281*
Threshold value	6.242	5.446	5.197	5.018	6.067	6.199
Threshold amount	US$514 billion	US$232 billion	US$181 billion	US$151 billion	US$432 billion	US$492 billion

* $p < 0.1$, ** $p < 0.05$, *** $p < 0.01$.

development in Africa. All the studied countries have economic growth above US$514 billion, except Congo and Mozambique. Accordingly, these countries should improve their level of income for institutions to indirectly boost crowdfunding.

8.5 Conclusion and Policy Implications

Entrepreneurs in Africa are turning to crowdfunding to address their funding gap, nevertheless, the level of crowdfunding development in the region is still limited. To address this issue, this study examined the role of institutions in fostering crowdfunding development across 29 African countries from 2013 to 2020. Additionally, the study investigated the economic growth channel through which institutions influence crowdfunding. The findings, obtained through the sys-GMM technique, indicated that institutions, as measured by control of corruption, government effectiveness, political stability, regulation quality, rule of law, and voice and accountability, play a critical role in enhancing crowdfunding development in Africa. Furthermore, the study revealed that Kenya, Ghana, Nigeria, South Africa, and Uganda have the highest impact of institutions on crowdfunding development, while Lesotho, Algeria, Gambia, Guinea, and Benin have the least impact. Finally, the study found that institutions indirectly facilitate crowdfunding development by promoting economic growth. The study established that beyond the threshold value of 6.242 (about US$514 billion), 5.446 (about US$232 billion), 5.197 (about US$181 billion), 5.018 (about US$151 billion), 6.067 (about US$432 billion), and 6.199 (about US$492 billion) of economic growth will ensure control of corruption, government effectiveness, political stability, regulation quality, rule of law, and voice and accountability boosts crowdfunding development in Africa.

The following theoretical contributions have been made by the current research: First, this research has identified the channels via which institutions impact crowdfunding development. These will form the basis for future studies on the impact of institutions on crowdfunding development. This study also looked at the economic growth channel by which institutions impact crowdfunding development. The statistically significant positive interaction impact of institutions and economic growth on crowdfunding adds to the body of knowledge on the factors that influence crowdfunding success.

The study's results indicated that the success of crowdfunding in Africa depends on institutional quality. Therefore, it is recommended that policies that improve institutions should be prioritized. Policymakers in Africa are advised to digitalize their economies, promote gender equality, provide free and universal education to enhance human capital development, ensure equal opportunities in civil service employment, and promote accountability. Additionally, strategies to improve the financial sector, economic growth, trade openness, and infrastructure investment should be given priority. Policymakers can remove the obstacles to investment by providing easier access to credit, granting tax incentives, and subsidizing the cost of using information and communication infrastructure. It is also suggested that collaboration between civil societies and the private sector should be encouraged to bridge the investment gap confronting the continent.

The major weakness of this research is that it relied on macro data due to data availability, accordingly, future studies should use enterprise data. Also, this study concentrated on Africa; however, crowdfunding is a global development, thus future research can extend the analysis to other regions. Finally, this study focused on 29 African countries because of data challenges. To this end, future research can test the robustness of these findings by using the 54 African countries when the data becomes available.

References

1. Appiah, E., Agbeko, K.Y.M., Moumbark, T., Dunya, R., What Makes Firms Perform Well? Evidence from Ghana Retail Shops. *Theor. Econ. Lett.*, 10, 01, 250–271, 2020, doi: 10.4236/tel.2020.101016.
2. Noëlle N'guessan, M., Canela, M. Á., Alegre, I., Crowdfunding in Africa: an empirical study of kiva platform users in sub-Saharan Africa, WP-1172-E, 05/2017. IESE, 2017, https://media.iese.edu/research/pdfs/WP-1172-E.pdf.
3. Abbasi, K., Alam, A., Anna, M., Luu, T., Huynh, D., FinTech, SME efficiency and national culture : Evidence from OECD countries. *Technol. Forecast. Soc. Change*, 163, May 2020, 120454, 2021, doi: 10.1016/j.techfore.2020.120454.
4. Appiah-Otoo, I. and Chen, X., Is crowdfunding the solution ? Appraising the environmental contributions of crowdfunding. *Environ. Dev. Sustain.*, 2023, doi: 10.1007/s10668-023-03875-w.
5. Appiah-Otoo, I. and Song, N., The impact of fintech on poverty reduction: Evidence from China. *Sustain.*, 13, 9, 5225, 2021, doi: 10.3390/su13095225.
6. Song, N. and Appiah-Otoo, I., The Impact of Fintech on Economic Growth: Evidence from China. *Sustain.*, 14, 10, 6211, May 2022, doi: 10.3390/SU14106211.
7. Li, Y., Jin, X., Tian, W., Econometric analysis of disequilibrium relations between internet finance and real economy in China. *Int. J. Comput. Intell. Syst.*, 12, 2, 1454–1464, 2019, doi: 10.2991/ijcis.d.191128.001.
8. Cheng, M. and Qu, Y., Does bank FinTech reduce credit risk ? Evidence from China. *Pacific-Basin Financ. J.*, 63, December 2019, 101398, 2020, doi: 10.1016/j.pacfin.2020.101398.
9. Wei, S., Internet lending in China : status quo , potential risks and regulatory options. *Comput. Law Secur. Rev. Int. J. Technol. Law Pract.*, 31, 6, 793–809, 2015, doi: 10.1016/j.clsr.2015.08.005.
10. Djimesah, I.E., Zhao, H., Okine, A.N.D., Li, Y., Duah, E., Kissi Mireku, K., Analyzing the technology of acceptance model of Ghanaian crowdfunding stakeholders. *Technol. Forecast. Soc. Change*, 175, 121323, Feb. 2022, doi: 10.1016/J.TECHFORE.2021.121323.
11. Hsieh, H.C. and Vu, T.H.C., The impact of economic policy uncertainty on crowdfunding success. *J. Int. Financ. Mark. Institutions Money*, 75, 101418, Nov. 2021, doi: 10.1016/J.INTFIN.2021.101418.
12. Rama, A., Jiang, C., Johan, S., Liu, H., Mai, Y., Religious and social narratives and crowdfunding success. *J. Int. Financ. Mark. Institutions Money*, 80, 101595, Jun. 2022, doi: 10.1016/J.INTFIN.2022.101595.
13. North, D.C., *Institutions, institutional change and economic performance*, Cambridge University Press, UK, 1990, doi: 10.1017/cbo9781139175302.016.
14. Appiah-Otoo, I., Chen, X., Song, N., Dumor, K., Financial development, institutional improvement, poverty reduction: The multiple challenges in West Africa. *J. Policy Model.*, 44, 6, 1296–1312, Nov. 2022, doi: 10.1016/J.JPOLMOD.2022.11.002.

15. Appiah-Otoo, I. and Song, N., Finance-growth nexus: New insight from Ghana. *Int. J. Financ. Econ.*, 27, 3, 2682–2723, 2022, doi: 10.1002/IJFE.2294.
16. Appiah-Otoo, I., Acheampong, A.O., Song, N., Obeng, C.K., Appiah, I.K., Foreign aid—Economic Growth Nexus in Africa: Does Financial Development Matter? *Int. Econ. J.*, 36, 3, 418–444, 2022, doi: 10.1080/10168737.2022.2083653.
17. World Bank Group, *How Regulators Respond To FinTech*, World Bank, USA, 2020, doi: 10.1596/33698.
18. Fu, J., Liu, Y., Chen, R., Yu, X., Tang, W., Trade openness, internet finance development and banking sector development in China. *Econ. Model.*, 91, 670–678, May, 2019, doi: 10.1016/j.econmod.2019.12.008.
19. Hou, J., Wang, N., Ge, S., Antecedents of Crowdfunding Project Success: An Empirical Study. *WHICEB 2015 Proceedings*, vol. 52, 2015, http://aisel.aisnet.org/whiceb2015/52.
20. Zheng, H., Li, D., Wu, J., Xu, Y., The role of multidimensional social capital in crowdfunding: A comparative study in China and US. *Inf. Manage.*, 51, 4, 488–496, 2014, doi: 10.1016/j.im.2014.03.003.
21. Ba, Z., Zhao, Y.C., Song, S., Zhu, Q., Understanding the determinants of online medical crowdfunding project success in China. *Inf. Process. Manage.*, 58, 2, 102465, Mar. 2021, doi: 10.1016/J.IPM.2020.102465.
22. Zheng, H., Wan, N., Chen, D., Wang, T., Antecedents of project implementation success in crowdfunding. *PACIS 2014 Proceedings*, vol. 318, Available: http://aisel.aisnet.org/pacis2014/318.
23. Zheng, H., Hung, J.L., Qi, Z., Xu, B., The role of trust management in reward-based crowdfunding. *Online Inf. Rev.*, 40, 1, 97–118, 2016, doi: 10.1108/OIR-04-2015-0099.
24. Wang, N., Liang, H., Ge, S., Xue, Y., How to Crowdfund More: A Signaling Perspective. *DIGIT 2015 Proceedings*, vol. 15, Dec. 2015, https://aisel.aisnet.org/digit2015/15.
25. Qian, Y. and Lin, J., Antecedents of Project Success in Donation-based Crowdfunding-based on Tencent LeJuan Platform in China. *Proc. Sci.*, 300, 018, Mar. 2018, doi: 10.22323/1.300.0018.
26. Di Pietro, F. and Butticè, V., Institutional characteristics and the development of crowdfunding across countries. *Int. Rev. Financ. Anal.*, 71, 101543, Oct. 2020, doi: 10.1016/J.IRFA.2020.101543.
27. DiMaggio, P.J. and Powell, W.W., The Iron Cage Revisited: Institutional Isomorphism and Collective Rationality in Organizational Fields. *Am. Sociol. Rev.*, 48, 2, 147, Apr. 1983, doi: 10.2307/2095101.
28. Barroso, R.M.R., Ferreira, F.A.F., Meidutė-Kavaliauskienė, I., Banaitienė, N., Falcão, P.F., Rosa, Á. A., Analyzing the determinants of e-commerce in small and medium-sized enterprises: A cognition-driven framework. *Technol. Econ. Dev. Econ.*, 25, 3, 496–518, 2019, doi: 10.3846/TEDE.2019.9386.
29. Lin, J., Luo, Z., Luo, X., Understanding the roles of institutional pressures and organizational innovativeness in contextualized transformation toward

e-business: Evidence from agricultural firms. *Int. J. Inf. Manage.*, 51, 102025, Apr. 2020, doi: 10.1016/J.IJINFOMGT.2019.10.010.
30. Stenholm, P., Acs, Z.J., Wuebker, R., Exploring country-level institutional arrangements on the rate and type of entrepreneurial activity. *J. Bus. Ventur.*, 28, 1, 176–193, Jan. 2013, doi: 10.1016/j.jbusvent.2011.11.002.
31. Hertwig, M., Institutional effects in the adoption of e-business-technology: Evidence from the German automotive supplier industry. *Inf. Organ.*, 22, 4, 252–272, Oct. 2012, doi: 10.1016/J.INFOANDORG.2012.06.002.
32. Marcelin, I. and Mathur, I., Financial development, institutions and banks. *Int. Rev. Financ. Anal.*, 31, 25–33, Jan. 2014, doi: 10.1016/J.IRFA.2013.09.003.
33. Boateng, E., Agbola, F.W., Mahmood, A., Foreign aid volatility and economic growth in Sub-Saharan Africa: Does institutional quality matter? *Econ. Model.*, 96, August 2019, 111–127, 2021, 2019, doi: 10.1016/j.econmod.2020.12.032.
34. Lee, K. and Kim, B.Y., Both Institutions and Policies Matter but Differently for Different Income Groups of Countries: Determinants of Long-Run Economic Growth Revisited. *World Dev.*, 37, 3, 533–549, Mar. 2009, doi: 10.1016/J.WORLDDEV.2008.07.004.
35. Kant, C., Are institutions in developing countries malleable? *J. Policy Model.*, 38, 2, 272–289, Mar. 2016, doi: 10.1016/J.JPOLMOD.2016.01.002.
36. Siddiqui, D.A. and Ahmed, Q.M., The effect of institutions on economic growth: A global analysis based on GMM dynamic panel estimation. *Struct. Change Econ. Dyn.*, 24, 1, 18–33, Mar. 2013, doi: 10.1016/J.STRUECO.2012.12.001.
37. Slesman, L., Baharumshah, A.Z., Ra'ees, W., Institutional infrastructure and economic growth in member countries of the Organization of Islamic Cooperation (OIC). *Econ. Model.*, 51, 214–226, Dec. 2015, doi: 10.1016/J.ECONMOD.2015.08.008.
38. Nedić, V., Despotović, D., Cvetanović, S., Djukić, T., Petrović, D., Institutional reforms for economic growth in the Western Balkan countries. *J. Policy Model.*, 42, 5, 933–952, Sep. 2020, doi: 10.1016/J.JPOLMOD.2020.04.002.
39. WDI, World development indicators database, 2023. https://databank.worldbank.org/data/source/world-development-indicators.
40. Mollick, E., The dynamics of crowdfunding: An exploratory study. *J. Bus. Ventur.*, 29, 1, 1–16, 2014, doi: 10.1016/j.jbusvent.2013.06.005.
41. Xiang, D., Zhang, Y., Worthington, A.C., Determinants of the Use of Fintech Finance Among Chinese Small and Medium-Sized Enterprises. *IEEE Trans. Eng. Manage.*, 68, 6, 1590–1604, 2021.
42. Tuo, G., Feng, Y., Sarpong, S., A configurational model of reward-based crowdfunding project characteristics and operational approaches to delivery performance. *Decis. Support Syst.*, 120, 60–71, May 2019, doi: 10.1016/j.dss.2019.03.013.

43. Ahlers, G.K.C., Cumming, D., Günther, C., Schweizer, D., Signaling in Equity Crowdfunding. *Entrep. Theory Pract.*, 39, 4, 955–980, Jul. 2015, doi: 10.1111/etap.12157.
44. Shneor, R. and Munim, Z.H., Reward crowdfunding contribution as planned behaviour: An extended framework. *J. Bus. Res.*, 103, August 2018, 56–70, 2019, doi: 10.1016/j.jbusres.2019.06.013.
45. Zhao, L. and Li, Y., Crowdfunding in China: Turmoil of Global Leadership, in: *Advances in Crowdfunding*, pp. 273–296, Springer International Publishing, Switzerland, 2020, doi: 10.1007/978-3-030-46309-0_12.
46. Appiah-Otoo, I., Song, N., Acheampong, A.O., Yao, X., Crowdfunding and renewable energy development: What does the data say? *Int. J. Energy Res.*, 46, 2, 1837–1852, 2022, doi: 10.1002/er.7301.
47. Arellano, M. and Bond, S., Some tests of specification for panel data: Monte Carlo evidence and an application to employment equations. *Rev. Econ. Stud.*, 58, 277–297, 1991.
48. Appiah-Otoo, I., Chen, X., Ampah, J.D., Does financial structure affect renewable energy consumption? Evidence from G20 countries. *Energy*, 272, 127130, Mar. 2023, doi: 10.1016/J.ENERGY.2023.127130.
49. World Bank Group, Crowdfunding in Emerging Markets: Lessons from East African Startups, 2015, http://documents.worldbank.org/curated/en/820101468186856874/Crowdfunding-in-emerging-markets-lessons-from-East-African-startups.
50. Dickey, D.A. and Fuller, W.A., Distribution of the estimators for autoregressive time series with a unit root. *J. Am. Stat. Assoc.*, 74, 366, 427–431, 1979, doi: 10.1080/01621459.1979.10482531.

9

Legal Aspects of Smart Contracts and Application of Blockchain Technology in FinTech

Gioia Arnone[1,2]

[1]Department of Managerial and Quantitative Studies, University of Naples Parthenope, Napoli, Italy
[2]Department of Private and Economic Law, Vrije Universiteit Brussel, Brussels, Belgium

Abstract
The use of technology in finance has altered how stakeholders conduct financial transactions. Blockchain technology is emerging as a financial technology (FinTech) paradigm change that promises to improve the effectiveness of financial transactions and fundamentally disrupt the global financial network, much to how the digital wave transformed the financial industry. The FinTech sector needs blockchain technology because it provides data privacy, asset verification, record keeping, and transition cost. The focus of the current study is an investigation of the legal implications of smart contracts and how blockchain technology is being used in the FinTech sector because smart contracts are one of the most active areas of blockchain technology development, also exploring the potential impacts of blockchain technology on new regulations of FinTechs such that the interests of stakeholders can be better served.

Keywords**:** Smart contracts, blockchain technology, financial technology, FinTech, financial industry

Email: gioia.arnone@vub.be; ORCID: https://orcid.org/0000-0002-6787-7283

Ernesto D.R. Santibanez Gonzalez, Vinay Kandpal, Peterson K. Ozili and Prasenjit Chatterjee (eds.) Fintech for ESG and the Circular Economy, (173–192) © 2024 Scrivener Publishing LLC

9.1 Introduction

Under the current banking system and financial technologies (FinTechs), records for financial transactions are held in centralized ledgers that are neither connected nor open to the public. People or organizations employ middlemen (trusted third parties) to link various ledgers so they can use numerous ledgers at once. However, the deployment of these is expensive and time-consuming. Computers could collaborate online and build a sizable shared ledger using a blockchain. This massive ledger is not owned by anyone and is not under the control of anyone or anything. The computers connected to the blockchain serve as nodes in a massive, interconnected, dispersed, and decentralized network [1]. This is vastly different from the present centralized ledger used by FinTech. This decentralized network allows any computer in the blockchain to view the online ledger that is updated in real time. This suggests that the nodes must interact with one another and reach a consensus to carry out a transaction between two parties utilizing the blockchain [2]. In other words, anytime a transaction takes place, every computer in the blockchain "talks" to one another and compares its ledgers to the real world. A consensus cannot be achieved and the transaction is rejected if there are any inconsistencies. This widespread comparison is feasible because the blockchain's ledger is accessible to everyone and makes all transactions visible. As a result, the blockchain is referred to as a single, open-source truth. A trading system that is 100% trustworthy and emanates confidence is incredibly beneficial because it enables a more democratic setting for social and commercial interaction [2].

The money on the blockchain is an additional benefit. The favored payment mechanism currently is Bitcoin, a currency that is encoded into others but has no intrinsic worth [3]. Any "social construct of value," such as euros, dollars, house titles, stock certificates, votes, energy, and contracts, can be used to link these currencies to other assets. Thus, on the blockchain, Bitcoins represent a diverse range of kinds of ownership or property. Because Bitcoins and the blockchain can be programmed, the financial sector has the opportunity to completely reinvent itself. Generalized automated compliance can be implemented by FinTech using blockchain technology before transactions or other actions [4]. In contrast to their current strategy, where compliance and audits take place after the fact, this is much different. The use of blockchain technology has several advantages, including improved productivity, more transparency, and reduced bureaucracy. Blockchain technology can alter how the world's economy functions [5].

The goal of the current study is to examine the legal implications of smart contracts, the application of blockchain technology in the FinTech sector, and any potential effects that blockchain technology may have on the regulation of FinTechs.

It looks into how financial professionals perceive, believe, and think about the possible financial effects of blockchain technology. Thus, this study specifically focuses on regulations and on how blockchain technology can thwart, alter, or support initiatives to control and oversee the financial industry.

9.1.1 What is FinTech?

FinTech refers to financial technology. As the financial industry progresses toward modernity and globalization, technology cannot be avoided. The use of technology in finance has altered how stakeholders conduct financial transactions. In the 1990s, both the Internet and FinTech were developing at the same time, which is consistent with a reduction in transaction costs [6]. Banking processes and financial transactions have become faster because of the rise of the Internet and smartphones. A new area of the financial services industry called FinTech has evolved as a result of changes to conventional brick-and-mortar banking. As a result, it is known as a disruptive technology, which is a term for a technology that fundamentally changes how something is done. This suggests that customers would start using apps and mobile devices instead of traditional banks for their financial operations. According to Li and Shin [6], there are two types of FinTech: traditional FinTech and emergent FinTech. As opposed to new financial technology, which is more of a market disruptor, traditional financial technology businesses serve as market facilitators. The former is considered a continuation of the current financial industry, whereas the former is seen as an innovation in the financial sector. According to Zavolokina *et al.* [7], the FinTech phenomenon is not one that directly impacts entrepreneurs; rather, it is influenced by several economic, technological, and governmental variables [8].

9.1.2 What is Blockchain Technology?

From a business viewpoint, a blockchain is a distributed ledger or database that is shared across a public or private computing network. Every computer node in the network has a copy of the ledger, thus there is not a single point of failure. In the 2018 paper by Carson *et al.* [9], information can be stored in the extra blocks once it has been encrypted. The participants' unanimity can be maintained by using a variety of procedures. The blockchain runs without the assistance of a third party, and each user of a network possesses a copy of every transaction that has ever occurred. The network's entities engage in more transactions, which increases the amount of data shared and the number of blocks added to the chain. The advantage of blockchain technology is that it has made it unnecessary for businesses to need an intermediary, enabling direct business transactions. Blockchain ensures that every party to a transaction process has a copy of all previous transactions [9].

Blockchain technology has the advantage that, by eliminating the need for a middleman, it has enabled entities to trade directly with one another. Blockchain ensures that every party to a transaction process has a copy of every transaction that has taken place. As can be seen, this technology has already spent the vast bulk of its incubation period developing [10]. It is projected that not all of its applications will last, but, certainly, the underlying technology will quickly find its way into our daily lives. Especially when some consequences on consumers were expected, the European Union and its legislators have long been among the most tech-savvy. The decision to support blockchain technologies and participate in their implementation within the "digital single market" was made in addition to the start of an interpretation process to determine whether the various forms of the legal classifications offered by EU statute, starting in particular with the link between "cryptocurrency" and "blockchain" technology [11].

9.1.3 What is a Smart Contract?

Using software running on top of a blockchain, a smart contract outlines how the contract parties are expected to communicate with one another. The agreement is immediately enforceable if and when the pre-established rules are followed [12]. The protocol for communication between the parties to the contract is established by a smart contract. This is the most basic form of decentralized automation. Contract logic can be inserted into blockchain networks. Therefore, if a truckload of cement is ordered, a purchase order can be made. Both the procedure of returning an invoice and receiving the money are automated. It would be challenging to modify this to include a payment phase of bribery [13].

The blockchain stores a basic program known as a smart contract. This type of contract is one of the most recent innovations brought about by blockchain. Most often, it is designed to carry out the transaction between the parties to the contract digitally and without the aid of a third party. In a traditional contract, each party must have confidence that the other parties will uphold the terms of the agreement. Because smart contracts are executed automatically, the rules enforce the contract, and as a result, the parties apply their trust in a quantifiable manner [13].

American computer scientist and legal theorist Nick Szabo used the term "smart contract" in 1994 to describe computerized transaction protocols that carry out a contract's terms. Such a contract is a self-executing contract that is stored in the blockchain as a group of codes. Before payments or other contract obligations may be fulfilled automatically by the parties, a smart contract's pre-configured conditions must be met [13]. Due to the efficiency and customizability they contribute to transactions as well as the variety of options they offer for individuals and organizations, blockchain-based smart contracts are one of the most sought-after technologies in the context of smart cities. Smart contracts may potentially take off soon as a way to enhance a few areas of a smart city [14, 15].

The term "contract" has never had a single meaning throughout different ages and countries. Depending on the definition offered by the legislator and the objectives that the definition of a contract is intended to serve, the meaning of a contract may change. Private law, of which contract law is a component, has developed in Europe during the past two millennia in a way that enables it to self-adapt to the structures and characteristics of each given civilization. In particular, the expansion and complexity of business, whose development is usually accompanied by and made possible by technological improvements, as well as the objectives that successive legislators intended to give it, have all contributed to the development of private law [15].

9.1.4 Legal Aspects of Smart Contracts

A new technology called blockchain has recently grown in prominence. It must be kept apart from Litecoin and Bitcoin [13]. The following subjects ought to be covered in this section: What benefits could smart contracts and blockchain technology bring to legal contracts? What problems will be overcome as a result of new laws and technology being adopted slowly? How can legally constructed smart contracts that use blockchain technology be supported such that the interests of their participants are better served [16]?

9.1.4.1 Contractual Features of Smart Contracts

Smart contracts are one type of contract employee under contemporary contract law. However, smart contracts must first be studied at the legal level to be governed by contemporary contract law. The fundamental issues that blockchain smart contracts may have, such as how to regulate them, must be identified at the legal level [13].

Which legal repercussions could an attack on and damage to a Blockchain smart contract cause? Both the implementation path, which involves automated execution to prevent default, and the subjectivity of smart contracts are addressed in this. The key issue we face is how to create legislation that establishes the legal standing and character of smart contracts and how to set up a system of legal oversight for those contracts utilizing the new blockchain technology [17, 18].

9.1.4.2 Traditional Laws and Rules are Under Attack

Traditional contracts provide a firm, open, and upholdable legal framework for all significant elements of the activities that take place under their purview. But, there is no legal control whatsoever for blockchain-based smart contracts.

A smart contract's legal framework should consist of specific judicial, governmental, and system-level agreements. The system itself and both parties to the transaction must be informed of their respective contractual rights and obligations. A smart contract's agreement cannot be changed by any one party, including the transaction parties or third-party organizations, because blockchain technology is used as a platform for data exchanges. As a result, the agreement cannot be altered or processed without a centralized regulator's consent [13].

Any other agency may make changes, but they would not take hold until the majority of users agree on a certain plan. Contrarily, the supervisory authority has actual jurisdiction and the power to affect the contract's rules in a traditional contract. A smart contract's agreement does not contain information on the members' legal rights and obligations. The protocol substitutes a distributed, decentralized, intelligent contract system for the implementation procedure and legal framework currently used by the regulatory body, which serves as the framework for the payment ecosystem. Existing frameworks are unable to adequately govern the risks associated with contract execution due to the lack of a legal foundation given by present regulatory agencies for the use of smart contracts made possible by blockchain technology [13, 18, 19].

Due to the rapid development of blockchain technology, several legal frameworks now in place in China cannot or do not take into consideration the needs of smart contracts. The smart contract is different from the contractual provisions in the current contract system in that it violates the promise's withdrawal and cancellation rules (the smart contract cannot be revoked); second, it will be harder to determine whether the contract is valid; third, the execution of the contract is changed from the performance of the two parties to the platform's automatic execution; fourth, the smart contract is not subject to the promise's withdrawal and cancellation rules; and fifth, the contract change will take place. Instead of mechanically "defending" the conventional contract structure against smart contracts, the distinctive features of blockchain technology should be actively and objectively discussed, and we should make sure that both parties are ready to absorb information. Blockchain smart contracts should also consider any pertinent international laws and treaties in addition to the pertinent domestic legal framework. Any differences between the relevant laws in other countries will require regulators to evaluate the difficulties they pose. Regulators must be adaptable in how they approach these possible problems when determining whether a comprehensive legal framework is in place for regulating the risks associated with the deployment of blockchain technology to contract sectors. The concerns now extend to more jurisdictions, especially those with less developed legal systems, as a result of the decentralization of blockchain-based smart contracts [13, 19, 20].

9.1.4.3 *Smart Contracts May be Created Legally*

The usage of blockchain technology and smart contracts indicates widespread support for free markets and hostility to centralized authority. According to American academic Lawrence Lessig, "code is the law". Like other types of technology self-help, if smart contracts entirely evade legal restrictions and governmental oversight, some people might use them to engage in illegal activity. This goes against the purpose of their invention and disturbs public order. Because of this, the application of blockchain technology and smart contracts in the fields of law, governance, and public policy still necessitates the usage of associated technologies. Smart contracts must therefore be created in line with the law and secured by various complementary security solutions [13, 20, 21].

9.1.4.4 *Legal Ramifications of Smart Contracts*

Decentralized distributed smart contracts' fundamental architecture, which employs blockchain technology, may lessen many of the hazards that present regulation is attempting to prevent. For instance, due to the restricted access to financial market utilities, blockchain cross-border payment systems perform atomic transactions in real time and greatly reduce settlement and transaction risk, making the system safer and more effective for those who can use it. As more market participants become aware of the system's ability to lower adversary and settlement risk, they will be able to obtain real-time payment settlements. Because of this, the laws governing a smart contract have greater legal authority than those governing a standard contract [13].

Contrarily, the accepted legal principles and customary contracts are outlined in writing. In the lack of a precise interpretation by the legislator or the parties, it is vulnerable to conflicts over numerous interpretations of phrases. Consequently, the legal clauses and business dealings in typical contracts before the content is turned into code; there is an opportunity for interpretation. It is challenging to choose and successfully apply a smart contract if it cannot be stated precisely. To ensure that the terms of the contract are upheld and that the agreement has a major legal impact, all participants must agree on the code used as the expression in a smart contract [13, 22].

The smart contract has a certain problem as a result of a conversion error in the conversion between them. The smart contract deviates from a genuine contract even though it uses the word "contract" on the surface. According to the author, the smart contract is merely one of the several "contracts" that every transaction on the blockchain must follow. When the agreement between the two parties enters into force, both parties are expected to "automatically" execute by providing data and moving corresponding funds. The ability of the code to perform the obligations that both parties are obligated to fulfill is referred to as its "intelligence." Since the term "contract" refers to the "contract" under the guarantee of the transaction contract between the two parties, the smart contract cannot completely replace the contract. Smart contracts, on the other hand, protect the interests of both parties to the transaction as well as the efficiency and security of the goods being sold [13].

9.1.5 Application of Blockchain Technology in FinTech

Similar to how the digital wave altered the financial industry, blockchain technology is emerging as a FinTech paradigm shift that promises to enhance the efficiency of financial transactions and radically disrupt the global financial network [23, 24].

Leaders in the financial sector believe that technology will fundamentally change their sector. According to a McKinsey report from 2016 [24], more than 50% of financial industry executives think that blockchain technology will have a substantial influence within three years. By 2020, 66%

of banks will have scalable blockchain platforms, predicts IBM. These predictions imply that change is imminent and might materialize within the following several years. Furthermore, the financial industry has already begun to undergo a technological revolution [25]. To go beyond the underlying assumptions about how blockchain technology might affect financial transactions, it focuses on four issues that are essential to all financial transactions. Some of these include transaction costs, data privacy, asset verification, and record keeping. Workie and Jain's description of the three stages of any transaction earlier underlined the relevance [26]. Initially, (1) when a client signs up for the blockchain network to acquire or sell financial assets, (2) incorporating middlemen and other blockchain database participants to verify the existence of financial assets, and (3) entering the data into the blockchain ledger [25].

According to the transaction cost theory [27], "transaction costs" in this chapter refers to both production costs and transaction costs. We also discuss the costs involved in transitioning from the current financial transaction platforms to a blockchain-based environment.

9.1.5.1 Asset Verification

Verifying certain aspects of a financial item before exchanging it on a blockchain network is the first step [26]. It is necessary to verify the owners of the associated assets to ensure that the parties seeking an exchange are the rightful owners (FINRA, 2017). According to BitPay CEO, Stephen Pair, ownership is established when a third party recognizes, documents, and protects a third party's rights to an asset [28]. Due to the consensus process that has already been adopted by all participants [26], blockchain technology can therefore permit direct ownership verification. The asset information is contained in a block that is created by a single full node, which also performs the blockchain network's ownership confirmation process. Additional full nodes in the network then confirm this block, continuously verifying both the accuracy of every new block and the overall accuracy of the entire ledger. The blockchain is robust because no single full node (custodian) has complete control over the ledger at any given time [29]. More akin to majority rule, this issue appears to involve the possibility of a single business holding more than half of the network's custodians [29].

In either case, depending on the operating situation, information can be kept in a database for an infinite amount of time thanks to the immutability property of blockchain data. As a result, there is more trust in a blockchain's ability to accurately record asset information. As a result of the blockchain's verifiable timestamped records for every item ever exchanged, immutability also promotes traceability [30, 31]. Blockchain technology may therefore easily be used to verify assets due to its inherent audit trail that is built in [29]. Therefore, employing blockchain technology makes asset verification feasible and maybe more trustworthy. In contrast, immutability means that it is hard to change a mistake regarding an asset by updating the database, especially on a public blockchain. Instead, a new block with the asset's updated representation needs to be added to the document. Immutability provides traceability and dependability as a result, but it also makes it difficult to undo human errors and blunders.

It might be argued that, due to the design of the distributed ledger, the built-in redundancy of blockchain significantly reduces the risk of losing asset information [29]. The fact that several network nodes are maintaining copies of the database chain or ledger makes blockchain more dependable and fault-tolerant than centralized databases [30]. Since the database may be accessed from numerous other nodes and the consensus mechanism is independent of the number of fully functional nodes, the network will continue to validate records even if most of the nodes fail. Anyhow, a decentralized consensus method requires significant operational and infrastructure costs in the areas of communication networks, computation, and storage to run a noisy transactional financial system [32–34].

As well as expanding the capabilities of blockchain technology to suit the demands of the financial sector, scalable integration of blockchain-based asset verification with traditional financial systems and processes is required [32]. Blockchain technology must be able to manage these kinds of loads because financial institutions often require high throughput and speed stock exchanges to process over 100K transactions per second, some of which may require asset verification.

Furthermore, Zhu *et al.* [32] asserted that, despite the addition of more computational capacity, it is difficult to meet the expectations of the financial industry since blockchain protocols are sequentially implemented. This is particularly true given how slowly the blockchain network operates by design. Since it is peer-to-peer, each node is required to serve as both a client and a server. Others, such as Mougayar [35], disagree with the assertion that scalability is a shifting target that historically has been met by technology developments and the pressure of increasing demand.

In terms of compliance, broker-dealers must find ways to abide by several regulatory standards about asset verification before implementing a blockchain-based network. The Exchange Act Rules and FINRA both created some of these asset verification criteria (FINRA, 2017). Further complicating the process of asset verification from a legislative perspective is the fact that a global blockchain covered by many countries makes asset verification difficult [30].

9.1.5.2 *Record Keeping*

According to Witte [36], maintaining records requires reliably and accurately preserving historical data across time in a way that is acceptable to all parties. The ability to keep records is a feature of blockchain technology [37]. Technology may significantly affect record keeping because it changes centricity and governance [23, 25]. Instead of using a shared blockchain ledger, which offers a central repository where documents are accessible by all participating institutions, financial institutions now retain records across numerous databases [23], asserting that a number of the issues the financial sector encounters (KYC) are caused by the inability to share records, the underuse of external sources of records, such as Internet data, and the challenges associated with complying with laws governing customers' records [37]. They come to the conclusion that, in order to solve these issues, financial institutions should work with other interested parties to develop blockchain-based record-keeping systems. By aggregating data along the full financial value chain in an efficient computational manner, these permissioned blockchain networks allow financial organizations to increase trustworthiness, responsibility, and controllability [25]. Financial institutions must come to an agreement on which documents to exchange, how to contribute to the expense of setting up and maintaining the network, and how to handle access control to realize this desired vision for record keeping [38].

Due to its immutability feature and consensus procedures, blockchain technology is well-positioned to be the source of truth, the creator of trustworthy records, and ultimately the platform for trust and record keeping. A blockchain ledger record of information becomes more trustworthy with time [37]. Therefore, blockchain technology may naturally, easily, and more transparently provide a full audit trail of records of dividend payments, ownership data, stock split terms, stock transaction timestamps, tax filings, and compliance reporting obligations [29].

Because blockchain technology offers an accessible reporting infrastructure, financial institutions and regulatory bodies prefer the auditing and monitoring [25] of norms and practices that it affects [26]. It would be necessary to provide the relevant tools and practices to implement this collaborative record-keeping interface. Furthermore, as blockchain data cannot be changed or reversed, the sector needs to develop novel solutions to problems that may result from inaccurate human or platform record inputs. A blockchain's growing ledger, which is redundantly maintained on multiple nodes, requires computational resources, which must also be taken into account [26].

In this scenario, Moore's Law allows for less expensive record keeping and speedier record retrieval. Moore's Law states that computational storage and central processing units (CPUs) tend to get faster and less expensive. Furthermore, current blockchain solutions are often inapplicable when utilized on the Internet of Things (IoT) periphery because IoT devices only have very limited computational capabilities and are only able to use very little amounts of energy, even if machine-to-machine transactions are widely employed [34]. Late in 2015, Nasdaq used its blockchain to effectively deploy the first private security record keeping, drastically cutting settlement times and getting rid of the need for paper stock certification documentation [39]. A number of financial sectors may look to adopt blockchain technology to improve their record-keeping procedures, such as (a) equity markets, where the current process requires a slow and manual tracking of records of share ownership; (b) debt markets, where the current settlement time is lengthy and involves multiple parties; (c) repurchase agreements, where there is currently a risk of settlement failures and a lengthy settlement time; and (d) corporate bonds, where the current process requires a lengthy settlement time and involves multiple parties [26].

In terms of record keeping, a blockchain-based solution must once again adhere to legal requirements. Broker-dealers, for instance, are subject to the Exchange Act and FINRA rules that specify the required data types, the minimum record retention period, and the availability of attestations [40].

9.1.5.3 Data Privacy

Businesses must be concerned about protecting the privacy of client data because doing so is highly profitable. Data privacy is a crucial component of financial operations. Regulations about privacy also apply to financial firms. The term "data" in this context can be used to describe two separate types of information: content data, which deals with transactions and associated themes, and identification data, which contains details about users on a blockchain network. Furthermore, while transparency and privacy are both admirable objectives, they could be incompatible. The collective values transparency more than privacy, although individuals often care more about it.

Members of these blockchains can stay anonymous because of the built-in cryptography of Bitcoin and comparable blockchains and the lack of a central body that controls network users. While decentralization of a public blockchain ledger improves data accessibility, blockchain technology paradoxically and flexibly swings between a continuum of a high degree of openness and a high level of privacy [33, 40]. The degree of data privacy and transparency is dependent on the blockchain network's operational design, including whether it is public, private, or hybrid. How data is kept on a network also affects how transparent a system is since data may be encrypted before being sent across it. However, poor access control management might have negative effects [29]. Furthermore, even while the blockchain network's decentralized structure may lessen security and privacy risks, it could also result in new problems as a result of this [26]. In a public blockchain network, for instance, private key protection is essential. While stealing a user's private keys from a blockchain network is comparable to stealing a user's password from a non-blockchain network, there is a slight difference in that in a decentralized blockchain network, private keys cannot be recovered because there is no central authority, as opposed to centralized networks where it is possible to retrieve passwords. Because users of Bitcoin and comparable blockchains can stay anonymous, some people are concerned that they could be used for illegal activities. However, despite the fact that the Bitcoin blockchain uses pseudonyms, the research of Narayanan *et al.* (2016) demonstrates that network identities can be connected to real-world identities. Furthermore, the risk that cryptocurrencies may be used for unlawful activity is no greater than the risk that currency poses. Furthermore, given that blockchain data cannot be changed, knowing that their actions will be permanently recorded on the ledger may deter thieves [28, 29].

Workie and Jain [26] asserted that modern technologies have the potential to improve accessibility, efficiency, and transparency when used in a way that promotes market integrity and protects investors. They continued by stating that blockchain technology must be supplemented with legislation that promotes privacy goals, such as securing "personally identifiable information and trade procedures." Furthermore, they claimed that private blockchain networks can reduce the level of openness by limiting access to data for people outside the network.

According to Guo and Liang [23], one of the issues the financial sector faces is the absence of definitions for concepts like privacy and security about who owns user data. It is questionable whether the blockchain technology's design ethos is to offer users control over their transactions and data. As a result, some proponents of blockchain technology, including

Tapscott and Tapscott [28], urged for a change in society so that people have complete ownership over their data.

The unknown is whether financial institutions will move toward a less focused approach to maintaining user data. Laws like KYC, AML, and consumer data protection further complicate the field of user data [40]. The complexity of legal and regulatory regulations, on the other hand, makes it difficult for financial institutions to assess blockchain technology in light of privacy and transparency standards. Because a blockchain network may cross international borders, financial institutions need to consider how to adhere to the privacy and transparency regulatory obligations in these many jurisdictions. Financial authorities are also still investigating the effects of blockchain technology [25]. For instance, blockchain networks define finality very differently from traditional settlements because they employ a protocol-based consensus approach [28].

9.1.5.4 Transaction Costs

Prior technological developments sparked the creation of substitutes, increasing the degree of competition. For instance, the market share of conventional financial institutions has declined as a result of Internet financial goods [23]. The financial industry needs to constantly innovate [23] and employ new technologies to reduce transaction costs [34] to thrive and fulfill rising client demands. Due to its applicability in operational risks, payment methods, clearing and settlement, and insurance, among others, blockchain technology has been hailed as the driving force behind financial innovation [2, 26].

Interbank payments are currently routinely processed through intermediary clearing houses, where they are subject to strict, costly, and time-consuming examination processes [23].

In the peer-to-peer and business-to-business payment marketplaces, the technology may lead to cheaper transaction costs and quicker transaction times, according to Meijer [24]. Furthermore, it might assist in lowering the cost of the securities market, which includes conventional banks and exchanges. According to Workie and Jain [26], blockchain technology players focus on specialized applications that tackle urgent problems with significant inefficiency rather than adopting radical changes. From the standpoint of implementation, Mougayar [35] asserted something similar, saying that implementing decentralization from scratch is simpler than doing so within centralized systems.

Although initially pricey, creating a blockchain-based infrastructure may allow for long-term cost reductions. FinTech innovation received investments of US$5.4 billion in 2013 and 2014, with the payments industry as the top candidate for blockchain innovation [25], in the hopes that the infrastructure will be revolutionized by blockchain technology, spawning fresh business models that would raise value and drive down costs. According to a 2016 World Economic Forum report, more than US$1 billion has been spent on research into the financial applications of blockchain technology [26].

The system may also significantly shorten settlement times and lower transaction costs associated with credit information in addition to the payment and clearing sectors [23]. This is made feasible by the technology's network-based consensus procedure, which enables close to real-time settlement and prevents days of delay. However, the adoption of blockchain real-time settlement would necessitate a shift away from conventional procedures for lending and borrowing securities, as well as the conventional belief that contracts should only be entered into during market open hours [30]. Blockchain technology provides the ability to automate back-office tasks in the areas of clearing and settlement and minimize transaction costs associated with trade record verification by making trading records transparent to all parties involved [24]. Trading private equity is another sector where using blockchain technology might reduce transaction costs. For instance, Nasdaq established chain.com as a company to offer a blockchain-based platform for private equity markets [23, 29]. IBM intends to leverage blockchain technology to streamline capital market coordination and expedite futures market settlements [28]. Blockchain technology can reduce financial costs in the supply chain by automating repetitive tasks and reducing legal risks with smart contracts [23]. According to McKinsey, blockchain technology has the potential to (a) lower risk costs by up to US$1.6 billion annually, (b) reduce operating expenditures by up to US$15 billion, and (c) reduce the cost of a cross-border transaction fee from US$26 to US$15 [23]. According to a FinTech analysis, using blockchain technology for international payments, securities trading, and regulatory compliance will allow banks to save up to US$20 billion [37].

Some analysts assert that using blockchain technology alone would not significantly lower transaction costs. For instance, Mori [30] claimed that just 20% of the problems affecting the banking industry may be due to technology constraints, with the remaining 80% being brought on by business operations and organizational structures. That implies that simply introducing blockchain technology is insufficient. Such projects require major changes to current company practices and processes to be effective [2].

Each component of the financial system could be impacted by blockchain technology. Private securities, insurance, Internet finance, and other financial industries might be impacted [2]. According to Zhu *et al.* [32], the implementation of blockchain functionalities should be done in a modular and segregated manner, with each module focusing on a particular functionality, such as trading or accounting but not both. This is following the acknowledged standards for system development. It is advised to carefully consider the value of centralization and to avoid using blockchain technology for issues that conventional decentralized databases can adequately address.

9.2 Discussion and Conclusion

Due to its ability to provide asset verification, record keeping, data privacy, and transfer costs, blockchain technology is crucial in the field of FinTech. One of the most active areas of blockchain technology development right now is smart contracts. The current study focuses on the technical aspects of smart contracts, including their traits, automation strategies, and associated carrier forms. However, there is surprisingly little research on smart contract law in this area. This paper examines the legal framework surrounding smart contracts. This article investigates the use of blockchain technology in FinTech, explains how to develop smart contracts legally, presents the author's thoughts and proposals, and looks at the legal implications of smart contracts through the use of blockchain technology and smart contracts.

References

1. Cai, C.W., Disruption of financial intermediation by FinTech: a review on crowdfunding and blockchain. *Account. Finance*, 58, 965–992, 2018.
2. Mattila, J. and Seppälä, T., Blockchains as a Path to a Network of Systems-An Emerging New Trend of the Digital Platforms in Industry and Society, in: ETLA Report, 2015.

3. Carruthers, P., The case for massively modular models of mind, in: *Contemporary debates in cognitive science*, R. Stainton (Ed.), pp. 205–225, Wiley, Hoboken, NJ, 2005.
4. Schellekens, E., Blockchain technology and its possibilities: A qualitative study of the connections between blockchain technology, the banking sector, and (self-) regulation, 2017.
5. Huckle, S., Bhattacharya, R., White, M., Beloff, N., Internet of things, blockchain and shared economy applications. *Proc. Comput. Sci.*, 98, 461–466, 2016.
6. Lee, and Shin, Y.J., Fintech Ecosystem, Business Models, Investment Decisions, and Challenges. *Bus. Horiz.*, 61, 35–46, 2018.
7. Zavolokina, L., Dolata, M., Schwabe, G., The FinTech phenomenon: antecedents of financial innovation perceived by the popular press. *Financ. Innov.*, 2, 1, Dec. 2016, doi: 10.1186/ s40854-016-0036-7.
8. Zhu, H. and Zhou, Z.Z., Analysis and outlook of applications of blockchain technology to equity crowdfunding in China. *Financ. Innov.*, 2, 1–11, 2016.
9. Carson, B., Romanelli, G., Walsh, P., Zhumae, A., Blockchain beyond the hype: What is the strategic business value? *McKinsey Company*, 2018.
10. Yeboah-Boateng, Ezer Osei, *et al.* Developing Use Cases of Blockchain Technology: Value Creation Perspectives. In: *Cross-Industry Use of Blockchain Technology and Opportunities for the Future.* IGI Global, 2020. p. 131–140.
11. Lin, F., Chung, D., Shayo, C., Beer, F., A Framework of Blockchain Technology. *Commun. IIMA*, 17, 6, 2019.
12. Karamitsos, I., Papadaki, M., Barghuthi, N.B.A., Design of the Blockchain Smart Contract: A Use Case for Real Estate. *J. Inf. Secur.*, 09, 03, 177–190, 2018, doi: 10.4236/jis.2018.93013.
13. Liu, Y. and Huang, J., Legal creation of smart contracts and the legal effects. *J. Phys. Conf. Ser.*, 1226, 4, 042033, IOP Publishing, 2019.
14. Mezquita, Y., Valdeolmillos, D., González-Briones, A., Prieto, J., Corchado, J.M., Legal aspects and emerging risks in the use of smart contracts based on blockchain, in: *International Conference on Knowledge Management in Organizations*, Springer, pp. 525–535, 2019.
15. Governatori, G., Idelberger, F., Milosevic, Z., Riveret, R., Sartor, G., Xu, X., On legal contracts, imperative and declarative smart contracts, and blockchain systems. *Artif. Intell. Law*, 26, 377–409, 2018.
16. Bobkov, K.A., Smart contracts in OTC derivatives trading: Legal aspects. *Digit. Law J.*, 1, 51–64, 2020.
17. Ante, L., Smart contracts on the blockchain – A bibliometric analysis and review. *Telemat. Inform.*, 57, 101519, Mar. 2021, doi: 10.1016/j.tele.2020.101519.
18. Gilcrest, J. and Carvalho, A., Smart contracts: Legal considerations, in: *2018 IEEE International Conference on Big Data (Big Data)*, pp. 3277–3281, Dec. 2018.

19. Giancaspro, M., Is a 'smart contract' really a smart idea? Insights from a legal perspective. *Comput. Law Secur. Rev.*, 33, 6, 825–835, Dec. 2017, doi: 10.1016/j.clsr.2017.05.007.
20. Tjong Tjin Tai, E., Formalizing Contract Law for Smart Contracts. *SSRN Electron. J.*, 2017, doi: 10.2139/ssrn.3038800.
21. Jaccard, G., Smart contracts and the role of law, 2018, SSRN 3099885.
22. Amato, F., Cozzolino, G., Moscato, F., Moscato, V., Xhafa, F., A model for verification and validation of law compliance of smart contracts in an IoT environment. *IEEE Trans. Ind. Inf.*, 17, 7752–7759, 2021.
23. Guo, Y. and Liang, C., Blockchain application and outlook in the banking industry. *Financ. Innov.*, 2, 1–12, 2016.
24. Meijer, A., E-governance innovation: Barriers and strategies, in: *Government Information Quarterly*, vol. 32, no. 2, pp. 198–206, Apr. 2015.
25. Kiviat, T., II, Beyond bitcoin: Issues in regulating blockchain transactions. *Duke Law J.*, 65, 569, 2015.
26. Workie, H. and Jain, K., Distributed ledger technology: Implications of blockchain for the securities industry. *J. Secur. Oper. Custody*, 9, 347–355, 2017.
27. Geyskens, I., Steenkamp, J.-B.E., Kumar, N., Make, buy, or ally: A transaction cost theory meta-analysis. *Acad. Manage. J.*, 49, 519–543, 2006.
28. Tapscott, D. and Tapscott, A., Blockchain revolution: how the technology behind bitcoin is changing money, business, and the world. *Penguin*, 2016.
29. Rechtman, Y., Blockchain: The making of a simple, secure recording concept. *CPA J.*, 87, 15–17, 2017.
30. Mori, T., Financial technology: blockchain and securities settlement. *J. Secur. Oper. Custody*, 208–227, 2016.
31. Crosby, M., Pattanayak, P., Verma, S., Kalyanaraman, V., Blockchain technology: Beyond bitcoin. *Appl. Innov.*, 2, 6-10, 71, 2016.
32. Zhu, Y., Guo, R., Gan, G., Tsai, W.T., Interactive incontestable signature for transactions confirmation in bitcoin blockchain, in: *2016 IEEE 40th Annual Computer Software and Applications Conference (COMPSAC)*, vol. 1, pp. 443–448, June 2016.
33. Yli-Huumo, J., Ko, D., Choi, S., Park, S., Smolander, K., Where is current research on blockchain technology?—a systematic review. *PloS One*, 11, e0163477, 2016.
34. Zhao, J.L., Fan, S., Yan, J., Overview of business innovations and research opportunities in blockchain and introduction to the special issue. *Financ. Innov.*, 2, 1–7, 2016.
35. Mougayar, W., *The business blockchain: Promise, practice, and application of the next internet technology*, John Wiley & Sons, 2016.
36. Witte, J. (2016). The blockchain: a gentle introduction. Available at SSRN 2887567.
37. Dupont, Q. and Maurer, B., Ledgers and Law in the Blockchain. *Kings Rev.*, 23, 2015.

38. Nasdaq, O., Nasdaq OMX Contract Specifications of German Wind Index Futures, 2015.
39. FINRA (Financial Industry Regulatory Authority), Code of Arbitration Procedure for Customer Disputes, 2017.
40. Puschmann, T., Fintech. *Bus. Inf. Syst. Eng.*, 59, 69–76, 2017.

10

ESG Excellence in the Digital World: Circular Economy E-Business Solutions

Rubee Singh[1,2]*, Akash Gupta[3] and Vinay Kandpal[4]

[1]*Institute of Business Management, GLA University, Mathura, Uttar Pradesh, India*
[2]*Department of Management Studies, Kumaun University, Nainital, Uttarakhand, India*
[3]*Jindal Global Law School, Jindal Global University, Sonipat, Haryana, India*
[4]*Department of Management Studies, Graphic Era Deemed to be University, Dehradun, India*

Abstract

Circular economies are emerging as one of the most vital forces for advancing sustainability in the digital age because of their ability to leverage the power of data for different sectors. Governments and consumers alike have been increasingly concerned about the environmental damages caused by the production cycle, which is pushing firms toward a sustainable environment and circular economy. Businesses operating in the circular economy have significantly boosted the GDP, and there is potential for more evolution in the digital field. E-businesses in the era of digitalization should also focus on the sustainable growth of the circular economy instead of only being bothered by environmental concerns. Sustainability has become one of the top priorities of any country's current business economy. Working under the framework of circular economy, an electronic business approach is put forward in the current study, which is feature-based on environmental sustainability and has the goal of upgrading sustainable companies' performance in the context of ESG. Various indicators have been used to monitor the circular economy process, the reduction of operating costs, and the resource demand through pre-existing studies–the development of sustainable business applications for circular economies, an evaluation of performance, and a model of e-commerce for the circular economy in the digital world.

***Keywords*:** Circular economy, environmental performance, e-business, sustainability, ESG excellence

**Corresponding author*: dr.rubeerajput@gmail.com

Ernesto D.R. Santibanez Gonzalez, Vinay Kandpal, Peterson K. Ozili and Prasenjit Chatterjee (eds.) Fintech for ESG and the Circular Economy, (193–204) © 2024 Scrivener Publishing LLC

10.1 Introduction

The concept of environmental, social, and governance, or ESG, is a concept in which the financial performance of an organization is analyzed through the lens of the three factors that contribute to its performance. The stakeholder theory explains that ESG is based on the idea that companies should be attentive to the interests of all stakeholder groups, including employees, and is therefore grounded in stakeholder theory. ESG ratings have become an integral part of many companies' strategies for identifying long-term goals and objectives. The concept can also be used as a basis for the prediction of future threats and risks that may appear for the company in the future.

There are many examples of resource depletion and rising environmental catastrophes as a result of inefficient production and consumption practices. These issues have become especially concerning in recent years worldwide. Many countries have strategically planned initiatives to solve this problem, such as "sustainable development," "climate action plans," and "goals." These tactics recognize a boost to ESG's influence and awareness measurements and indications that aid in the performance of the company with respect to governance. It is not surprising that many countries around the world are looking at efficient methodologies and methods in order to complete these strategic objectives. In order to continuously reduce the damaging effects of wasteful production and consumption on the environment, a circular economy (CE) is a vital strategy to reduce environmental pollution. In addition, it supports the organization in moving toward ESG indicators that are of a higher level of reliability (Dragomir and Dumitru, 2022).

Basically, it can be seen as a production and consumption model that is incredibly effective in order to achieve sustainability (Singh *et al.*, 2023). From 2012 to 2021, Babkin *et al.*, 2023 saw both favorable and unfavorable patterns in the progress of the CE in the Russian Federation. The upward trajectory of air emissions of pollutants originating from stationary sources is exhibiting a positive trend. Conversely, the downward trajectory is characterized by a rapid surge in the production and consumption of waste, inadequate rates of waste recycling and disposal, and a rise in domestic material use. Presently, numerous endeavors are being undertaken to execute the CE. The primary catalysts behind this progress are the legislative and governmental entities, non-governmental organizations (NGOs), and consultant firms. Simultaneously, a consensus has not been reached on the diverse range of available techniques (Kalmykova *et al.*, 2018).

A CE is "A business model in which the conceptual logic for value creation is based on utilizing the economic value retained in products after use in the production of new offerings" (Linder and Williander, 2017). Another definition is the "reasoning behind how an organization creates, delivers, and captures value with closed material loops and inside them" (Mentink, 2014). A linear system becomes circular due to many CE practices. The alignment of future research in supply chain (SC) visibility with socially, economically, and environmentally sustainable aims is crucial for the realization of the goals of Industry 5.0 (I5.0), which places significant emphasis on data interoperability as a fundamental premise. Enhanced openness within SCs facilitates improved inventory accuracy, enhanced management practices, the adoption of a just-in-time mindset, and cost savings in freight expenses. It aids in reducing waste, assessing productivity and performance, and facilitating potential automation in SC management processes. The enhanced visibility and traceability offer potential decision-makers in the CE field the necessary tools to develop and execute sustainable policies and procedures in SC management (Khan and Abonyi, 2022).

A CE is defined as a theoretical framework that indicates a movement toward recycling and reusing energy as well as material resources. The goal of this paper is to decrease and lower the amount of environmental pollution, improve manufacturing process feasibility, clean up ecosystems, and create more social, environmental, and economic value (Shkarupeta and Ilyina, 2022). As a contextualization for this study, a circular industrial system is viewed as a web of establishments that collaborate to interact and foster an environment that is favorable for collective changes that allow the whole value chain system (or particular sectors or regions) to adopt practices that are environment-friendly in nature (Babkin *et al.*, 2021). Since the beginning of the 20th century, companies have witnessed a period of significant transformation in terms of how they approach their core manufacturing activities, including product planning, product development, SC management, procurement, and marketing, all of which have witnessed significant changes in their approach to core manufacturing activities. Investments in India have contributed to these transformations toward companies' sustainability and ESG performance.

The development of Industry 4.0 (I4.0) mechanisms is a result of a number of studies that have been carried out recently (Chen *et al.*, 2020; Jabbour *et al.*, 2019). There has been a great deal of research (Lopes *et al.*, 2018) that has incorporated I4.0 mechanisms, as well as circular economies, into a conceptual framework designed to demonstrate the sustainability of a society. A broader range of stakeholders is taking an interest in both paradigms in addition to communities, scholars, governments, decision-makers, practitioners, regulatory bodies, and standard setters around the world. These two paradigms have gained attention from a broader range of stakeholders. Awan *et al.* (2021), however, pointed out that despite the evolution of conceptual frameworks explaining the relationship between the two perspectives, their confluence remains one of the most critical factors contributing to their relevance in driving academia and industry in recent years. Despite the fact that the evidence gathered from the available research at this time does appear to suggest that I4.0 has had a tremendous impact at the discursive level, the evidence gathered from the current research is less clear about what type of impact I4.0 has had on industries to date (Madsen, 2019). According to Buer *et al.*, (2018), a research agenda for I4.0 research has been established, which is intended to guide future research on I4.0 and to encourage researchers further to examine the operations of companies aiming to transform their business through emerging I4.0 mechanisms to achieve their goals. Furthermore, researchers have emphasized the potential of I4.0 for innovation to be a sustainable paradigm, and they have called for additional research to investigate how these two paradigms or paradigms of innovation can be integrated and explored comprehensively in conjunction (Machado *et al.*, 2019; Okorie *et al.*, 2018). With a thorough understanding of the connections between sustainability and the Internet of Things (I4.0), sustainable manufacturing research contributes to the development of the I4.0 agenda. This is a result of a systematic review conducted by Machado *et al.* (2019). In the past few years, a key objective of I4.0 has been noted to increase the profitability of the manufacturing sector through enhanced efficiency (Fuchs, 2018). There is, however, very little research available on the impact of I4.0-related information on the financial performance of companies and on the impact of this information on annual reports as a whole.

10.2 Literature and Theoretical Background

10.2.1 Connecting ESG and CE

A clear definition of both CE and ESG (environmental, social, and governance) has already been provided in the previous sections of this report. As you know, ESG, or environmental, social, and governance, is a standard or rating used to evaluate the performance of a company in terms of its green, social, and governance policies. An economy that uses a circular model is one in which products and materials are recycled and refurbished into reusable objects, increasing the recovery of materials and minimizing waste. It may be argued that CE practices have an essential role to play in determining the environmental performance of an organization as a whole.

10.2.2 I4.0 (Digitalization), CE, and ESG

Information and communication technologies are being used in conjunction with digital manufacturing technologies in the I4.0 concept, which is a relatively new concept. It was at the 2011 Hannover Fair event in Germany that the revolution of the I4.0 concept was introduced as a product of a working group formed by the Research Union Economy-Science of the German Federal Ministry of Education and Research. It is essential to make the point that this marks the beginning of the implementation of Internet I4.0, which has enjoyed a rapid rise in popularity and is currently a topic of interest to researchers, businesses, and governments. The primary purpose of I4.0 is to improve the profitability of the manufacturing sector (Fuchs, 2018) and the other goal is to increase productivity. There are many interchangeable concepts used to describe I4.0, such as smart manufacturing industries, digital transformation, emerging technologies of I4.0, and a multitude of other concepts. The current confusion surrounding the concept of I4.0 has been continuing. It will continue to be a significant barrier to academic investigations, as it negatively impacts the scope, theoretical foundation, and effectiveness of the research (Osterrieder *et al.*, 2020). It has been demonstrated that this concept can be applied to many settings and using many different research paradigms in different contexts (Culot *et al.*, 2020). Essentially, I4.0 is all about connecting machines, orders, customers, employees, suppliers, and suppliers in order to get the maximum value out of I4.0. Industrie 4.0, in its simplest form, enables sustainable manufacturing processes, bringing high ESG performance to the design, production, and logistics of products through the communication between human machines and digital devices through connectivity between the machine and the user's device. I4.0 is an umbrella term that describes four fundamental mechanisms that have been set in motion in order to support several aspects of new technology that are influencing the digital transformation of industries, including the Internet of Things, cloud computing, big data, and artificial intelligence (Benitez *et al.*, 2020; Meindl *et al.*, 2021).

10.2.3 Circular Economy Practices and ESG

It is essential to assess and implement a comprehensive waste management program that takes trash reduction, recycling, and proper disposal to the forefront when implementing this NRM option. This report includes a number of initiatives, including waste segregation, recycling facilities, composting facilities, and waste-to-energy projects (Li, 2018). In addition, as part of its mission, it attempts to promote the development of products that are both environmentally friendly and have a low environmental impact during their entire lifetime. As part of that approach, we promote eco-design principles and use recyclable materials, reduce packaging waste, and maximize the product's longevity and recyclable capabilities. This term describes a transformation that involves utilizing new digital technologies, such as cyber-physical systems, mobile technology, artificial intelligence, cloud computing, blockchain technology, and the Internet of Things (a computer-based approach to collecting and transferring data that is acquired from electronic devices) to transform organizations into digital businesses. Using these I4.0 mechanisms, businesses are able to improve customer experiences, streamline operations, and stimulate the creation of new business models. In a study published by Zhong *et al.* (2017), researchers identified four fundamental mechanisms responsible for I4.0: cyber-physical systems, the Internet of Things, big data, and cloud manufacturing. This is because additive manufacturing, such as 3D printing, enables the rapid prototyping of components on a large scale and allows the customization of the product (Awan *et al.*, 2018).

A number of technologies have been invented over the past few decades that have made it possible for us to automate, monitor, and control processes and objects in real-time (Wang *et al.*, 2015). In its many forms, I4.0 can be described as a collection of processes that can be integrated, adapted, optimized, and interoperable to achieve manufacturing success and efficiency. Several I4.0 applications have been developed in recent years that enable us to monitor and control processes in real-time, including the status of production, the use of energy, the flow of materials, customer orders, and supplier information, all of which can be controlled in real-time. Using that business model, Rosa *et al.* (2020) stated that the model could provide value to customers, generate revenue for the organization, and reduce costs for the organization by creating value for customers. A great deal of potential exists for I4.0 mechanisms to positively impact the environment, reduce risk, and improve productivity by reducing its impact on the environment and minimizing risks. A number of mechanisms that are part of I4.0 are capable of having a positive impact on the environment and also on people as a powerful tool for reducing risk and improving productivity on a global scale. In order for the transition to a CE to be successful, I4.0 mechanisms are necessary. There are a number of companies today that use the Internet of Things to reuse, recycle, and repair items, for example.

It is important to note that social sustainability issues have been integrated into the United Nations Sustainable Development Agenda (Awan *et al.*, 2018).

10.3 Research Methodology

From a methodological standpoint, the research will be conducted by utilizing a literature review approach instead. As a part of a literature review, the researcher evaluates and discusses the pre-existing research and offers an unbiased and holistic interpretation of the work conducted in the past. This review was performed using a combination of databases, including Google Scholar, Research Gate, and Science Direct, to conduct its research and to access the results throughout the process of writing the chapter. This literature review aims to examine and provide an analysis of the concepts of ESG and CE for e-business in the digital world, as well as how they relate to one another—analyzing how the principles of CE, especially the environmental dimension, affect a company's overall performance when it comes to ESG, in particular, its environmental impact. As a result, we plan to utilize and include throughout the chapter research papers that contribute and evolve around the research question, "How do circular economy business practices impact the ESG Excellence/performance of businesses in the Digital World?". A keyword search was performed on databases using the following combinations of terms that were used in the search string: (ESG OR Sustainability OR Environment*) AND (CE OR Business Model OR Recycling).

10.4 Discussion and Recommendations

Based on the literature review, it is apparent that the CE contributes to and impacts the ESG performance of businesses to some extent. It is widely recognized in a number of articles and research papers that the CE has a significant impact on the environmental factor of ESG performance and is strongly influenced by it. It is widely accepted that a CE is a method of reusing and recycling materials in a circular loop in order to foster a more responsible production of products and a more responsible consumption of materials. The CE plays a vital role in enhancing the environmental aspect of ESG by supporting sustainable development practices and fostering the idea of sustainability within organizations and business sectors.

ESG ratings are based on the concept of sustainability in order to assess the environmental impact they have.

In order to use resources efficiently and to produce at their maximum capacity, one of the principles of CE consists of ensuring that no additional materials are wasted, in addition to using resources efficiently. The CE emphasizes the idea of a circular loop as opposed to a linear one, as well as an eco-friendly method for actually reusing waste and materials for the purpose of creating a new one. A CE is aimed at promoting sustainability, and it also enhances the environmental factor of ESG, a factor that complements ratings in this regard. In general, the existing research indicates that the CE and ESG can be seamlessly integrated with the theoretical framework of the CE. Several theoretical frameworks support the CE's positive impact on ESG. Despite contrasting evidence, most research indicates that a CE business model can improve ESG ratings, especially the "e" dimension. In order to improve their sustainability and environmental aspects, companies can implement CE practices.

ESG ratings have a significant social factor, which in turn is primarily attributed to the supportive environment that circular economies can create and the supportive health systems that they foster. Although some aspects of the social dimension have been explored in the literature review, it appears there is a lack of attention to other dimensions of social dimensions as well as governance aspects that also need to be addressed. Despite the fact that many social aspects were not touched upon with the CE, there is evidence to suggest that CE practices contribute to the social dimension of environmental, social, and governance.

There has been some discussion regarding the relationship between CE and ESG, the lack of resonance between the two, and the need for further research to establish that relationship. However, what is interesting to note is that the CE has shown a closer relationship than expected with the social aspect. There is no doubt that CE practices have some effect on social factors. At the same time, they are considered to be part of integrating the economy, but further investigation is needed in order to prove this. The implementation of a CE model within the scope of a company does not seem to have a clear connection to improvements in the governance structure of a company from the perspective of governance. The problem is that there is little research that explores how CE practices can have a positive impact on the governance structure and stability of a business. This potential mismatch between the CE and ESG ratings, especially when it comes to the social and governance aspects, suggests the need for further research and literature reviews so that a more comprehensive understanding of these topics can be developed. Future studies should focus on narrowing these potential gaps one by one by investigating and examining them individually. Even if existing reviews suggest a positive correlation between these two concepts, further research is necessary in order to confirm the existence of this relationship conclusively.

10.5 Conclusion

According to a review and examination of various streams of literature on the concepts of CE and ESG, researchers have taken a wide range of approaches to address this core question by using different methodologies. It has used quantitative and qualitative research methods, as well as case studies and literature reviews, in order to conduct the research and draw conclusions from it. In order to grasp the interplay between ESG and CE, different approaches will be taken that will lead to different results, thus resulting in a more comprehensive understanding of their interaction. It is worth noting, however, that each review cuts into the concepts of ESG and CE differently, with some of them focusing on the environmental indicator, the social indicator, sustainable development, and more. This variability between each study ensures that the findings regarding the influences of CE practices on ESG performance are more thorough and diverse since the variables differ between each study. Based on the case study of the current CE e-business model, it is apparent that there are sectors with e-commerce businesses that are currently dependent on a relatively small number of essential apps in order to maintain the performance of their online service businesses. It has been concluded that the CE e-business framework offers a number of possible methods and uses that may assist industries in the development of long-term e-business models using four essential processes in the assessment and evaluation. The purpose of this chapter is first to provide detailed and fundamental digital strategies and applications for a CE enterprise within an innovative and sustainable environment in which ESG dimensions are taken into account in the course of the scientific examination. As a second benefit, it offers a number of exciting examples of the CE in action. Using the circularity indicator of cluster-type industrial ecosystems as an indicator of sustainability ESG initiatives, we developed a methodology and application to support the development of a multilayer cyber social industrial ecosystem based on the concept of I5.0, involving the development of a multilayer cyber social, industrial ecosystem that is a cluster type in the CE.

References

Awan, U., Kraslawski, A., Huiskonen, J., Governing Interfirm Relationships for Social Sustainability: The Relationship between Governance Mechanisms, Sustainable Collaboration, and Cultural Intelligence. *Sustainability*, 10, 12, 1, 2018, https://doi.org/10.3390/su10124473.

Awan, U., Nauman, S., Sroufe, R., Exploring the effect of buyer engagement on green product innovation: Empirical evidence from manufacturers. *Bus. Strateg. Environ.*, *30*, 1, 463–477, 2021, https://doi.org/10.1002/bse.2631.

Babkin, A., Glukhov, V., Shkarupeta, E., Kharitonova, N., Barabaner, H., Methodology for Assessing Industrial Ecosystem Maturity in the Framework of Digital Technology Implementation. *Int. J. Technol.*, *12*, 7, 1397–1406, 2021, https://doi.org/10.14716/IJTECH.V12I7.5390.

Babkin, A., Shkarupeta, E., Tashenova, L., Malevskaia-Malevich, E., Shchegoleva, T., Framework for assessing the sustainability of ESG performance in industrial cluster ecosystems in a circular economy. *J. Open Innov. Technol. Market Complexity*, *9*, 2, 100071, 2023, https://doi.org/10.1016/j.joitmc.2023.100071.

Benitez, G.B., Ayala, N.F., Frank, A.G., Industry 4.0 innovation ecosystems: An evolutionary perspective on value cocreation. *Int. J. Prod. Econ.*, *228*, 107735, 2020, https://doi.org/10.1016/j.ijpe.2020.107735.

Buer, S.-V., Strandhagen, J.O., Chan, F.T.S., The link between Industry 4.0 and lean manufacturing: mapping current research and establishing a research agenda. *Int. J. Prod. Res.*, *56*, 8, 2924–2940, 2018, https://doi.org/10.1080/00207543.2018.1442945.

Chen, J., Gao, M., Mangla, S.K., Song, M., Wen, J., Effects of technological changes on China's carbon emissions. *Technol. Forecast. Soc. Change*, *153*, 119938, 2020, https://doi.org/10.1016/j.techfore.2020.119938.

Culot, G., Nassimbeni, G., Orzes, G., Sartor, M., Behind the definition of Industry 4.0: Analysis and open questions. *Int. J. Prod. Econ.*, *226*, 107617, 2020, https://doi.org/10.1016/j.ijpe.2020.107617.

Dragomir, V.D. and Dumitru, M., Practical solutions for circular business models in the fashion industry. *Clean. Logist. Supply Chain*, *4*, 100040, 2022, https://doi.org/10.1016/j.clscn.2022.100040.

Fuchs, C., Monitoring progress in national initiatives on digitising industry - Country report Finland. *TripleC*, *16*, 1, 36, 2018.

Jabbour, C.J.C., Jabbour, A.B.L., de, S., Sarkis, J., Filho, M.G., Unlocking the circular economy through new business models based on large-scale data: An integrative framework and research agenda. *Technol. Forecast. Soc. Change*, *144*, 546–552, 2019, https://doi.org/10.1016/j.techfore.2017.09.010.

Kalmykova, Y., Sadagopan, M., Rosado, L., Circular economy – From review of theories and practices to development of implementation tools. *Resour. Conserv. Recycl.*, *135*, 190–201, 2018, https://doi.org/10.1016/j.resconrec.2017.10.034.

Khan, A.A. and Abonyi, J., Information sharing in supply chains – Interoperability in an era of circular economy. *Clean. Logist. Supply Chain*, *5*, 100074, 2022, https://doi.org/10.1016/j.clscn.2022.100074.

Li, L., China's manufacturing locus in 2025: With a comparison of "Made-in-China 2025" and "Industry 4.0.". *Technol. Forecast. Soc. Change*, *135*, 66–74, 2018, https://doi.org/10.1016/j.techfore.2017.05.028.

Linder, M. and Williander, M., Circular Business Model Innovation: Inherent Uncertainties. *Bus. Strateg. Environ.*, *26*, 2, 182–196, 2017, https://doi.org/10.1002/bse.1906.

Lopes de Sousa Jabbour, A.B., Jabbour, C.J.C., Godinho Filho, M., Roubaud, D., Industry 4.0 and the circular economy: a proposed research agenda and original roadmap for sustainable operations. *Ann. Oper. Res.*, *270*, 1, 273–286, 2018, https://doi.org/10.1007/s10479-018-2772-8.

Machado, C.G., Winroth, M.P., Ribeiro da Silva, E.H.D., Sustainable manufacturing in Industry 4.0: an emerging research agenda. *Int. J. Prod. Res.*, *58*, 5, 1462–1484, 2019, https://doi.org/10.1080/00207543.2019.1652777.

Madsen, D. Ø., The Emergence and Rise of Industry 4.0 Viewed through the Lens of Management Fashion Theory. *Adm. Sci.*, 9, 3, 1, 2019, https://doi.org/10.3390/admsci9030071.

Meindl, B., Ayala, N.F., Mendonça, J., Frank, A.G., The four smarts of Industry 4.0: Evolution of ten years of research and future perspectives. *Technol. Forecast. Soc. Change*, *168*, 120784, 2021, https://doi.org/10.1016/j.techfore.2021.120784.

Mentink, B.A.S., Circular Business Model Innovation, in: *Delft University of Technology*, 2014, https://doi.org/10.5771/9783957104311-105.

Okorie, O., Salonitis, K., Charnley, F., Moreno, M., Turner, C., Tiwari, A., Digitisation and the Circular Economy: A Review of Current Research and Future Trends. *Energies*, 11, 11, 1, 2018, https://doi.org/10.3390/en11113009.

Osterrieder, P., Budde, L., Friedli, T., The smart factory as a key construct of industry 4.0: A systematic literature review. *Int. J. Prod. Econ.*, *221*, 107476, 2020, https://doi.org/10.1016/j.ijpe.2019.08.011.

Rosa, P., Sassanelli, C., Urbinati, A., Chiaroni, D., Terzi, S., Assessing relations between Circular Economy and Industry 4.0: a systematic literature review. *Int. J. Prod. Res.*, *58*, 6, 1662–1687, 2020, https://doi.org/10.1080/00207543.2019.1680896.

Shkarupeta, E.V. and Ilyina, E. A., Digital Circular Economy: Concept, Model, Strategies, Framework, Technologies. *Organ. Prod.*, *30*, 4, 9–17, 2022, https://doi.org/10.36622/vstu.2022.30.4.001.

Singh, R., Khan, S., Dsilva, J., A framework for assessment of critical factor for circular economy practice implementation. *J. Model. Manage.*, *18*, 5, 1476–1497, 2023, https://doi.org/10.1108/JM2-06-2021-0145.

Wang, L., Törngren, M., Onori, M., Current status and advancement of cyber-physical systems in manufacturing. *J. Manuf. Syst.*, *37*, 517–527, 2015, https://doi.org/10.1016/j.jmsy.2015.04.008.

Zhong, R.Y., Xu, X., Klotz, E., Newman, S.T., Intelligent Manufacturing in the Context of Industry 4.0: A Review. *Engineering*, 3, 5, 616–630, 2017, https://doi.org/10.1016/J.ENG.2017.05.015.

11

Role of FinTech in Fueling Social Change: A Field Study

Sai Aanchal

PG Department of Sociology, SGGS College, Sector-26, Chandigarh, India

Abstract
FinTech has brought about a social change in India, which is often underrated in terms of economic development. Information technology and FinTech have now given online visibility to villages like Taksal and Pabri, which have been disconnected from the luster of city life and urbanity. The present study looks at how FinTechs like Paytm are being effectively used by respondents of the villages Taksal and Pabri. The study also examines the process of social change in the lives of respondents, especially the extent of women's empowerment in terms of financial inclusion through FinTech accessibility. Based on extensive fieldwork, the research paper seeks to understand the thought process of the respondents and the rural societies, which they represent in terms of FinTech accessibility. Further, the case studies have been used to explore how patriarchal ideologues pose obstacles for young rural women in the context of FinTech usage.

***Keywords*:** FinTech, financial inclusion, social change, women empowerment, Paytm, theory of gendered money, theory of gender oppression, patriarchy, gender inequality, gender difference

11.1 Introduction

Social change is a dynamic process and a multifaceted concept that entails varied perspectives and definitions. In simple words, it can be explained as the modification and transformation of varied aspects of society over

Email: saiaanchal99@gmail.com; ORCID: https://orcid.org/0000-0002-1907-2069

Ernesto D.R. Santibanez Gonzalez, Vinay Kandpal, Peterson K. Ozili and Prasenjit Chatterjee (eds.) Fintech for ESG and the Circular Economy, (205–224) © 2024 Scrivener Publishing LLC

a period of time. It can be defined as significant changes or alternations in the economy, culture, technology, politics, demographics, and environment. Sociologists like William F. Ogburn and Gerhard Lenski, who were known for being technological determinists, have substantiated through their research studies that technology is a significant factor behind the occurrence of social and cultural change [1, 2]. Economic growth can only be possible if societies are supported by advanced tools and technology, and economically developed countries backed by the power of technology have immense potential to globally connect with the rest of the world [3]. The generation of the '80s can relate to those days of shopping in their lives when they visited a shop to buy chocolate only to come back home with additional chocolate in hand because the shopkeeper denied returning the balance amount in cash. This exchange in kind against the balance was not always taken positively by the elders of the family. However, today's generation has found FinTech, i.e., financial technology, as a solution to the problem that their predecessors faced. So, no more paying in cash to the shopkeepers and no more extra chocolates or candies—not only saves money for the customer but also saves customers from excessive or undesired consumption. Globally, FinTech has played a significant role in fueling social change by leveraging technological innovations to combat financial and social challenges. FinTech has an immense potential to drive positive social change by promoting financial inclusion, democratizing financial services, improving financial literacy, facilitating charitable giving, promoting responsible peer-to-peer lending, and supporting various social and environmental initiatives [4–8]. However, it is essential to address regulatory and ethical considerations to ensure that FinTech developments align with the goals of inclusivity, fairness, and sustainability in promoting social change [7].

11.1.1 FinTech Usage in India

Netherlands Prime Minister Mark Rutte on his recent visit to Church Street in Bengaluru praised India's UPI. He said that making payments via UPI was "*simple and easy*" [9]. This is not the first instance when FinTech in India has been appreciated or discussed by someone. Mauritius Prime Minister Pravind Jugnauth on his visit to India for the G20 Summit expressed his interest in holding discussions with Indian Prime Minister Narendra Modi on cooperation in sectors like FinTech, infrastructure, and culture. Athique [10] studied the rationale behind the November 2016 demonetization in India. He emphasized that demonetization was a result of the *international monetary experiment*. Through constructive and objective analysis, one can observe a direct correlation between demonetization and the advancement of the global *cashless agenda*. Forbes gave its Business of the Year Award in 2016 to FinTech company Paytm, the leading digital payments business in India. Paytm directly benefitted from demonetization because many people switched to cashless transactions in India.

Pant [11] highlighted the emerging trends associated with FinTech in India while advocating for innovation in research for the growth of Indian FinTech. India is one of the significant emerging markets for FinTech. Previous studies have examined how FinTech is being successfully and extensively used in India for mobile payments [12–15]. FinTech-led mobile payments are estimated to see a rise of US$1.3 trillion by 2025. Jaiswal *et al.* [16] and Singh and Sharma [17] found that usage of FinTech payment services increased during the COVID-19 pandemic among consumers identifying themselves as Gen X and Millennials. According to Invest India [18], "A pan-India digital payments survey (covering 90,000 respondents) revealed that 42% of respondents have used digital payments. UPI recorded the highest ever volume of transactions in April 2023—8.8 Bn." A few credible studies have previously examined financial inclusion through FinTech accessibility in rural areas [19–22]. However, many of these studies are not specific to India and are disconnected from the sociological perspectives [23–26].

Thus, considering the research gaps, it is imperative to study the impact of FinTech with an emphasis on the rural areas in India.

11.1.2 Rationale of the Study

With the enormous use of FinTech globally, it has been a subject matter of study for economists and information technology scientists. Previous studies have highlighted the impact of FinTech in the context of economics and financial inclusion in urban areas. However, not much has been explored by sociologists in the realm of FinTech and its usage. Furthermore, the sociocultural impact of FinTech has not been examined much in rural areas, especially small and less-known villages with peculiar geographical locations, which disconnects them from the luster of city life and urbanity. Thus, the present study was conducted in the two such villages of Himachal Pradesh and Punjab in India.

11.1.3 Objectives of the Study

- To examine the FinTech usage in the Taksal village located in the state of Himachal Pradesh.

- To examine the FinTech usage in the village of Pabri located in the state of Punjab.
- To investigate the factors behind the FinTech usage in the Taksal and Pabri.
- To study the impact of FinTech on the lives of respondents from Taksal and Pabri.

11.1.4 Research Methodology

For achieving the abovementioned objectives, qualitative tools of data collection, such as in-depth interviews and oral narratives, were used to gather data about the usage of FinTech and its impact on rural men and women. A case study method was also used to study the impact of FinTech like Paytm on the lives of rural women in the context of women empowerment through financial inclusion and FinTech accessibility.

11.1.5 Area of Study

Taksal and Pabri were purposively selected as villages for the area of study because both the villages are less known and meet the criteria of a peculiar geographical location, which disconnects the population of these villages from the luster of city life and urbanity. Taksal is a small Himachali village that lies in the foothills of the Himalayas. Taksal derived its name from "*takka*," which means coins because it used to be a place where coins were made in the time of Kings. In the year 2006, not many knew about the Taksal village. Today, one can find Taksal on Google Maps. Though, it has become somewhat easy to trace the route, but difficult geographical terrain is a major factor that prevents tourists from visiting Taksal. Anyone aiming to reach Taksal has to pass through Kalka town in the Panchkula district of Haryana. Taksal is approximately 6.4 km away from Kalka and it takes around 25 minutes to reach Taksal via Taksal road. This connection often deprived Taksal of its identity of being a village located in the Solan district of Himachal Pradesh, and Taksal was often mistaken to be part of the Panchkula district of Haryana, irrespective of it being located just above the Parwanoo, which is a town of Solan district.

Pabri is a small and less-known village in Rajpura Tehsil of Patiala District. It is approximately 24 km away from Patiala. Villagers usually visit the nearest town Rajpura for all economic activities.

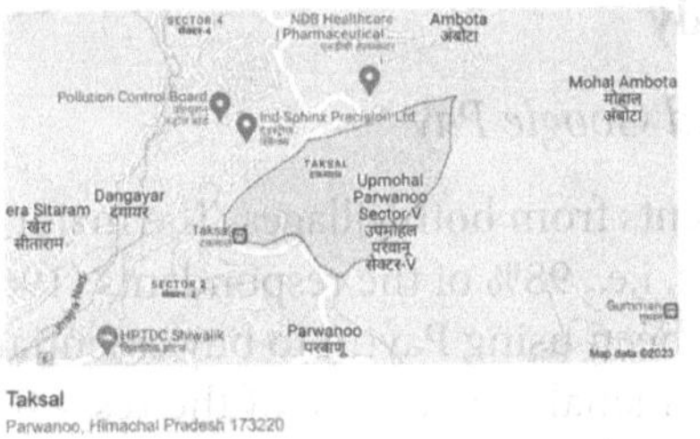

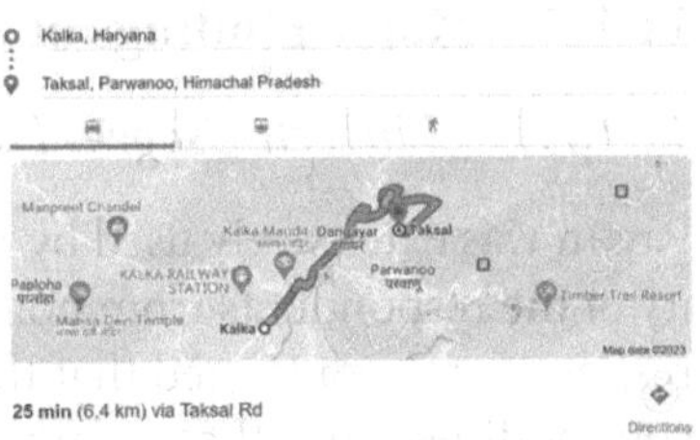

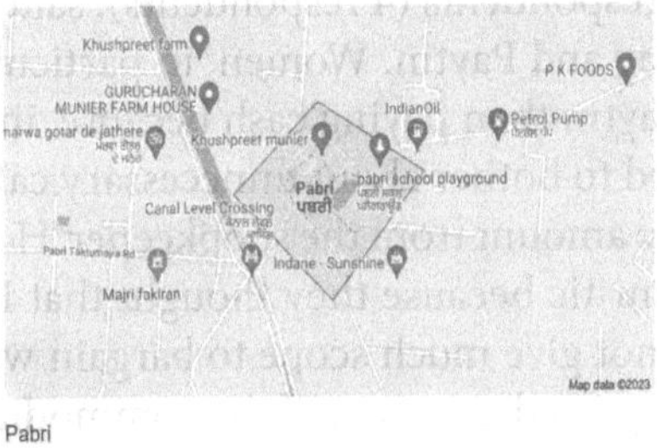

11.1.6 Sampling Frame and Sample of Respondents

The convenience sampling method was used for selecting the sample of respondents. Overall, 200 respondents were interviewed from both the Taksal and Pabri villages. Equal numbers of male and female respondents, i.e., 50 respondents each from both genders were interviewed, and in total 100 respondents were interviewed from each village. No respondent was available to act as a respondent and representative of the transgender community from either of the villages.

Sample of respondents from Taksal		Sample of respondents from Pabri	
Gender	**Number of respondents**	**Gender**	**Number of respondents**
Male	50	Male	50
Female	50	Female	50
Total	**100**	**Total**	**100**
Total number of respondents from villages Taksal and Pabri – 200			

11.1.7 Major Findings of the Study

11.1.7.1 FinTech Usage—Paytm and Google Pay

Paytm was extensively used by respondents from both villages. The majority of the respondents from both villages, i.e., 98% of the respondents (196 respondents), confirmed that they have been using Paytm to buy essential commodities from their nearby shops. A small percentage of the respondents, i.e., 2% of the respondents (4 respondents), said that they have been using both Google Pay and Paytm. Women, in particular, were more optimistic about using Paytm than paying cash because, in their opinion, they no longer are required to bother about unnecessary calculations or wait in queue to avail balance amount from the shopkeeper. However, respondents seemed a little pessimistic because they thought that FinTechs like Paytm and Google Pay did not give much scope to bargain with the shopkeepers who started displaying fixed amounts of the commodities at their shops.

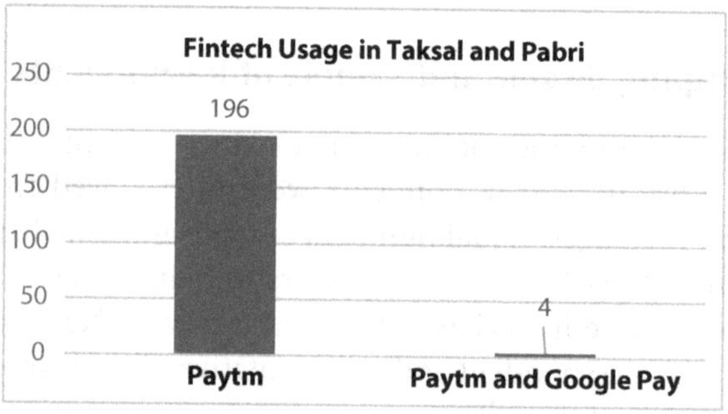

11.1.7.2 FinTech Usage in Taksal

In Taksal village, Paytm was more popular among the female respondents, with 100% of them confirming their frequent use of Paytm for shopping. On the other hand, 92% of the male respondents in Taksal said that they used Paytm more frequently, whereas 8% of the male respondents said that they used both Paytm and Google Pay for shopping grocery and other essential commodities.

FinTech usage in Taksal		Gender wise usage	
		Male	Female
Paytm	96 (96%)	46 (92%)	50 (100%)
Paytm and google pay	4 (4%)	4 (8%)	0
Total	100	50	50

11.1.7.3 FinTech Usage in Pabri

In Pabri village, Paytm was used frequently by both men and women. As per the narratives of the respondents, Paytm had a monopoly in Pabri village. Paytm was quite popular FinTech among the respondents, with 100% of the respondents confirming their preference for Paytm. All the respondents interviewed in the village found Paytm easy to use. Agrawal [27] also found that ease of access was a major factor behind the popular usage of Paytm in rural areas.

FinTech usage in Pabri		Gender wise usage	
		Male	Female
Paytm	100 (100%)	50 (100%)	50 (100%)
Total	100	50	50

The availability of Paytm in the small shops located near the homes of these respondents also aided in the popularity of Paytm. Thus, the popularity of Paytm can be seen in the context of its easy accessibility, which made it a preferred mode of digital payment. The findings of the present study are consistent with the previous studies, which found Paytm to be a popular FinTech in rural areas [27, 28].

11.2 Factors Behind the FinTech Usage in Taksal and Pabri

The following factors were found to be significant behind the FinTech usage in Taksal and Pabri.

11.2.1 No Need for the Bank Account Information to Send Money to One's Relatives

Users of Paytm wallet can receive money from their Paytm wallet from their friends and families. This money/wallet balance can be used for making payments at stores, merchants, etc. To open a Paytm wallet account, the user only needs a working phone number, a mobile phone, and a stable internet connection. Users need not have a bank account to use the Paytm wallet. However, the user who is sending money to the Paytm wallet of the recipient user must have their Paytm linked with the bank, i.e., the bank account from which they will be sending money via Paytm. This was indicated in the responses given by the respondents from both villages. A woman from Pabri said, "I do not have a bank account. My husband works in the army. I receive money in my Paytm wallet from my husband. So, whenever I have to buy something, I make use of the same."

11.2.2 Perceived Ease of Access and Safety

The Paytm wallet was easy to use because of its user-friendly interface. It saved respondents from the hassle of carrying cash. Respondents, especially female respondents, said that they were no longer worried about hiding cash. A middle-aged woman from Taksal said, "When I was young, I often had to worry about carrying money safely. Today, my children don't have similar concerns." This finding is consistent with the previous studies that found technologies could gain more popularity among users when there was a significant ease of access coupled with a user-friendly interface [29, 30].

11.2.3 Aided in Keeping a Stringent Check on the Expenses of One's Spouse

It was found that often husbands transferred only the required amount to the Paytm wallet of their wives, which was a deliberate attempt on their part to keep a stringent check on the expenses of their wives. This was true, especially in cases where husbands were working in cities or abroad. A man from Taksal narrated the following account:

Earlier whenever I would give cash to my wife, she would often run out of cash. She would come back home telling me that she had bought some additional items for which she had asked the shopkeeper to maintain a record. I had to always oblige to pay for those additional items which we essentially did not require as she would bring them home by incurring debt. Paytm has saved me from paying for the debts incurred by my wife. I told her that she has to manage the expenditure as per the money transferred to her Paytm wallet. I only transferred the amount once to her wallet. Though she might gossip at my back, I am not bothered much.

The above narrative resonates with the experiences narrated by a few other men from Taksal and Pabri. Such narratives opened up the scope for a question on the impact that FinTech usage was having on the lives of women. A woman from Taksal answered the same and said, "Incurring debt was easier in terms of paying cash, especially when kids demanded something unexpectedly. Our husbands have found new ways of controlling money." However, there were a few witty women who boldly expressed dissent and did not shy away from admitting that they do not mind incurring debt if their husbands do not transfer the desired amount to their Paytm wallet. These findings substantiate the "theory of gendered money," wherein a substantial value and visibility are attached to the money earned by men, giving rise to their superior image as primary breadwinners of the family [31]. In the context of these findings, money can be viewed as symbolic of a husband's power and authority in a way that a wife's role in running the household becomes secondary to that of her husband—this clearly gives the upper hand to the husband in a relationship [31–33].

11.2.4 Easy to Receive Money in Times of Emergency

Both male and female respondents said that it became easy for them to receive money from their family and relatives in times of emergency, especially when the person transferring the amount was unable to see them in person. This finding is in agreement with the previous studies [34, 35].

11.2.5 Fear of Demonetization

Female respondents in both villages feared demonetization more than men, especially working women and those women who saved money from what they received from their relatives as gifts on festivals. These women used Paytm due to the fear of demonetization. Men also admitted to using Paytm after demonetization to avoid incidents of bringing cash from their bank account at home with the intention to pay for any expenses incurred. Previous studies also found that demonetization increased the use of FinTech like Paytm for making digital payments [10, 28, 36–38].

11.2.6 Influence of Peers

There were many respondents who said that they started using Paytm and Google Pay under the influence of their peers. Some even admitted to using Paytm to make small donations in the temples as per the insistence of their elders. Peers exerted greater influence over both men and women, but mostly men were the first to follow their peers because men exercised more control and authority over their family income. The notion of being looked down upon by peers and being judged as technologically incompetent also influenced respondents to use FinTech like Paytm and Google Pay. The peer influence was indicated in the responses of the respondents. A man from Pabri said, "My friends often ridiculed me over tea. They would gossip that I, being educated, have not yet learned to use Paytm. They would pay for tea every time we would get together. I started using Paytm just to avoid listening to their jokes." This finding is consistent with the previous studies that found peer influence to be a significant factor in changing the mindset of individuals by accentuating their intention to adopt FinTech for digital payments [39, 40].

11.3 Impact of FinTech on the Lives of Respondents of Taksal and Pabri

The impact of FinTech on the lives of respondents was studied in the following two contexts:

1. In the context of the sociocultural change with an emphasis on the thought process of the respondents and the rural societies that they represent in terms of access to FinTech.
2. In the context of the extent of women empowerment that FinTech like Paytm brought about in the villages.

11.3.1 Socio-Cultural Change

When it came to socio-cultural change, it was observed that many socio-cultural processes like exchange during the celebrations and observations of festivals had undergone change in some cases. Many times, Paytm was being used by women to receive money as gifts from their brothers and parents during festivals like *Raksha Bandhan, Diwali,* or *Navami.* So, while in cases of husbands who were in long-distance relationships with their wives, Paytm was found to be operating as a FinTech, strengthening the emotional bond between husband and wife, whereas, in the case of sisters living at a long distance from their brothers, Paytm was found to be exacerbating emotional disconnect between sisters and brothers. Women did not like receiving money from their brothers or parents unless they desired it. They wished to see their brothers and parents in person, but the traditional bonds and relationships were reduced to mere transactions in many cases.

A woman from Pabri narrated the following account:

> Once I planned to visit my parents in person for the *Diwali* festival. Surprisingly, shortly after I discussed it with my parents, I received some money in my Paytm wallet with a request from my brother and his wife that they would be unable to host me due to unforeseen circumstances. It took me a year to understand that it was a deliberate move on their part to prevent me from visiting them. They repeated the same behavior in other instances, forcing me to rationally reflect on the consequences of their absurd behavior. My husband, too, retaliated on one occasion and asked me to return the Paytm amount that they sent to me, and right from that day, I am not in talking terms with anyone from my parent's side.

The above account could have occurred differently in the absence of FinTech like Paytm. The instant sending of money when one should be meeting in person to express their love and warmth can be detrimental to any relationship. Money as such cannot completely replace the physical proximity or warmth that one gets to exchange in person. This sentiment was also reflected in the narrative of another elderly woman who said, "My son has not met me in person for the past 2 years, but he has been sending money to my Paytm wallet. He works in the city." One can argue how much it takes for someone to visit their mother in person, but the convenience with which one gets to compensate for a maternal relationship is something beyond debate. These findings are consistent with the studies that have significantly contributed to the Sociology of Internet and Digital Sociology, especially studies that highlighted the repercussions of Internet and social media usage in terms of negatively impacting parent-child relationships [41–44]. With this, we can state that, while FinTech can be seen as promoting a cashless economy, its usage was found to be accompanied by varied sociocultural repercussions, much of which were viewed as detrimental to the existence of social relationships. It was a common practice in the village of Taksal to receive services by offering something tangible in kind; this practice of exchange declined largely after the service providers started using Paytm to receive money from the recipients of their services. This is evident from the following case, which highlights the social change in terms of exchange.

Case 1

A woman from Taksal recalled about legacy of her father who served as a village carpenter with a specialization in making bamboo and wooden products. Her father often offered his services in lieu of grains and other agricultural products. He rarely received cash for the services that he offered, and this went on till his death. Today, her family members, who are pursuing the same vocation, are skilled in seeking cash in exchange for the handmade products that they sell. Paytm is being used by her family to receive money from their loyal customers who have been buying their products for generations. In her opinion, this transition has brought a significant socio-economic change for them. Their labor is paid for, and they have started selling products at fixed but reasonable prices, leaving less scope for bargaining by the customers. Their service recipients are also content with this new method of transaction because for them, too, paying in kind came with additional responsibilities. According to one of their service recipients, it was difficult for them also to assess the worth of the products that they bought from them. The Himachali culture of the recipients bound them to their village fraternity and made them oblige to their service providers in kind on social occasions like weddings and birthdays. This traditional exchange was taking a financial toll on both the service providers and the service recipients. It also resulted in a lack of accountability on both sides. Sometimes, service recipients ended up paying more in kind and, sometimes, they ended up paying less, whereas service providers could not themselves decisively ascertain the worth of the products that they made for consumption by the service recipients. The perceived change in the transactional system did not occur in a day or a year, but it occurred gradually. It was apparent from the responses of the respondents that small business owners in Taksal, especially service providers and shopkeepers, decided to use Paytm after seeing advertisements. Many responses also confirmed that Paytm transactional exchange in the village of Taksal resulted from consistent observation followed by imitation of the prevalent use of FinTech in the adjoining towns of Kalka and Parwanoo.

11.3.2 Extent of Women's Empowerment

It was found that, in some cases, FinTech promoted women's empowerment. However, that was not true for other cases, wherein FinTech offered only digital financial accessibility, and the financial inclusion was not visible enough to promote women's empowerment. FinTech usage did not bring much change in terms of social development or improvement in the status of women. It was found that the financial inclusion and accessibility to financial services were thwarted by the patriarchal ideologues as is evident from the following case studies.

Case 2

A case of women empowerment explored during the fieldwork was of a woman who strongly asserted that FinTech like Paytm saves her from the risk of cash theft. She narrated her experience and shared how, on a bus route from Patiala to Pabri, she was robbed of her cash by two unidentified strange women on the bus. Firstly, those two women offered her a biscuit, and she denied their offering as she was with her kids. After some time, those two women again persuaded her to eat a cut fruit and, unfortunately, this time guava with black salt tempted her. Shortly after consumption of the fruit, this woman felt dizzy and dozed off to sleep, only to be woken up by her kids. As per what she recalled, her kids had not consumed the fruit. When she woke up, she realized that she had missed her destination and the cash that she was carrying in her handbag was stolen. When she inquired to the bus conductor, he said that he felt the two strange women were known to her, which is why he did not object when they took out money from her purse. For the record, she knew that she was scammed by those two women and her money was stolen by them, but she did not register any complaint with the local police. According to her, Paytm saves her from the risk of cash theft while traveling. She does not have to carry any big amount while traveling. She asserted that, with a Paytm wallet, she could travel safely and shop safely. However, her husband was not on the same page as her. He asserted that if she travels alone for long distances, then she might be at another risk of losing her smartphone. Therefore, whenever he realizes that she has to travel alone, he avoids transferring a big amount to her Paytm wallet. In this case, even though a woman had access to FinTech, one cannot observe the FinTech accessibility translating into financial inclusion in her case. This is because her husband eventually controlled her access to money and made major decisions regarding the amount meant to be transferred to her Paytm wallet.

Case 3

During the fieldwork, respondents of the Taksal village referred to an unreported case of a girl who used Paytm wallet money to escape from her home. According to the respondents, she was in depression after the death of her mother. The girl's relatives were residing in Taksal and Parwanoo. Shortly after her elopement, the girl in question returned to her father's home but her marriage was arranged in haste by her father and uncle to suppress the suspected rumors floating in their village. According to the respondents, all those rumors were baseless and had less merit. These respondents remarked that the girl had a good character. The girl's family left Taksal shortly after her marriage, but the case of elopement though holding less substance impacted the thought process of the elders of the village in terms of FinTech usage by the young girls and women. A few of the male respondents came across as conservatively orthodox in opining that, while digital literacy was important for men, the same was irrelevant for unmarried and single women. They asserted that their daughters and sisters are carriers of their family honor/*ghar ki izzat*. They felt that it was pertinent for them to ensure that young women of their family were not given access to anything detrimental, which in the long run could pose a grave threat to their family honor.

Case 4

A peculiar case was also found in which a woman running a small shop from her home could challenge domestic violence through financial inclusion and overcome other ordeals faced. According to her, it was difficult for her to hide the money that she earned from her husband. Whenever any customer would visit her shop to buy goods, they would pay in cash for the same. Her husband's room is adjoining to the shop that she has been running. He would often get to know about the customers who visited her shop and quietly steal from her every single penny that she earned. If she resisted, then he would forcibly snatch the money from her or violently threaten her to share the whereabouts of the cash that she was hiding in their home. She said, "He would not do anything with the money or waste money on buying liquor like other men do, but he often expressed insecurity in terms of my control over the money that I was earning." The equation between husband and wife in this case eventually changed after the announcement of demonetization. The woman in question found that IN₹10,000 was securely lying with her husband. Her husband did not tell her anything about the amount he had saved from the money that he took from her. She started using Paytm in 2017, which further meant her husband not rushing to the shop to snatch money from her. In the absence of cash visibility, he also failed to use violence to prevent her from controlling the amount that she earned from her daily labor. His impulsive behavior underwent a drastic transformation because he knew he could not get immediate control over cash.

The above **cases 2, 3, and 4** highlight the patriarchal subjugation of women through male dominance, which perpetuates the sustenance and reinforcement of male hegemony in the lives of women. Thus, the findings of the present study support the "theory of gender oppression" and the concept of "patriarchy" [45–47].

Case 2 brought to light the plight of a subjugated wife oppressed by her dominating husband who controlled her access to money by making major decisions regarding the amount meant to be transferred to her Paytm wallet. Case 3 also reeks of patriarchy, which entails gender inequality and gender difference, impacting the freedom and rights of young single and unmarried women in terms of digital literacy. The question that emerges in this context is: What if a young man would have eloped? The obvious answer to the same is that not much would have been done to reflect on the elopement of a man, and the elopement would have been reported to the police in the case of a man. Furthermore, we do not know any definite reasons behind the girl's elopement, considering that the respondents said the girl had a good character. We can only assume that perhaps, after the death of her mother, her father's family imposed several restrictions on her, which suffocated her individuality to the extent that the girl decided to elope only to return back to her father. Gender oppression is evident in Case 4 in terms of male dominance that resulted from the husband's insecurity of his wife's status as a working woman. The statement given by a woman in Case 4 has to be taken with a grain of salt. Her statement about her husband not wasting money that he stole from her could most certainly have been the result of the fear of her husband's continued presence in her life. Hart [48], too, found that husbands having working wives often expect them to be submissive.

In the context of Case 4, demonetization and going cashless by switching to Paytm for accepting money helped the concerned woman experience financial inclusion through FinTech. In this context, much of the money that she was earning was being digitally and safely transferred to her account via Paytm.

11.4 Conclusion

Constructive socio-cultural change in terms of advancement in technology and modernization of social institutions, economy, education, and polity demands acceptance from the masses. In every society, social change is met with resistance whenever there is any kind of transition from the traditional to a modern setup. This resistance comes to the fore as obstacles that pose a threat to that change. With regards to FinTech usage, we can observe the same resistance in terms of patriarchal ideologues that posed obstacles for some young women in terms of depriving them of financial inclusion by controlling their FinTech accessibility. It would not be wrong to state that this patriarchal resistance reflects one's disinterest in embracing modernization. Gradually, with time, people adapt to new ways of living and working and adapt to new forms of technology [49–51]. The findings of the present study substantiate the theory of gendered money and the theory of gender oppression by supporting the concept of patriarchy, which entails gender inequality and gender difference. Good or bad, the social change ushered in by FinTech like Paytm is here to stay for us to see, and it comes with a strong probability to remain consistently popular for the years to come.

References

1. Volti, R., William F. Ogburn 'Social Change with Respect to Culture and Original Nature. *Technol. Cult.*, 45, 2, 396–405, Feb. 2004, [Online]. Available: http://www.jstor.org/stable/40060750.
2. DeFleur, L.B., Technology, Social Change, and the Future of Sociology. *Pac. Sociol. Rev.*, 25, 4, 403–417, Oct. 1982, doi: 10.2307/1388922.
3. Kuznets, S., Modern Economic Growth: Findings and Reflections. *Am. Econ. Rev.*, 63, 3, 247–258, 1973.
4. Kandpal, V. and Mehrotra, R., Financial inclusion: The role of fintech and digital financial services in India. *Indian J. Econ. Bus.*, 19, 1, 85–93, 2019.
5. Arner, D.W., Buckley, R.P., Zetzsche, D.A., Veidt, R., Sustainability, FinTech and Financial Inclusion. *Eur. Bus. Organ. Law Rev.*, 21, 1, 7–35, 2020, doi: 10.1007/s40804-020-00183-y.
6. Kukreja, G., FinTech Adoption in China: Challenges, Regulations, and Opportunities, in: *Innovative Strategies for Implementing FinTech in Banking*, pp. 166–173, 2021.
7. Baporikar, N., Fintech Challenges and Outlook in India, in: *Innovative Strategies for Implementing FinTech in Banking*, pp. 136–153, 2021.
8. Gengler, E.B., Leveraging Blockchain Technology for Corporate Social Responsibility. *Payments J.*, 2017, [Online]. Available: https://www.payments-journal.com/author/emmy-b-gengler/.
9. ANI, Netherlands PM Mark Rutte fascinated by India's UPI, calls it 'simple and easy, in: *Economic Times*, Accessed: Sep. 20, 2023. [Online]. Available: https://economictimes.indiatimes.com/news/india/netherlands-pm-mark-rutte-fascinated-by-indias-upi-calls-it-simple-and-easy/videoshow/103586824.cms.

10. Athique, A., A great leap of faith: The cashless agenda in Digital India. *New Media Soc.*, 21, 8, 1697–1713, Feb. 2019, doi: 10.1177/1461444819831324.
11. Pant, S., Fintech: Emerging Trends. *Telecom. Bus. Rev.*, 13, 1, 47–52, Jan. 2021.
12. Morgan, P.J., Fintech and Financial Inclusion in Southeast Asia and India. *Asian Econ. Policy Rev.*, 17, 2, 183–208, Jul. 2022, doi: https://doi.org/10.1111/aepr.12379.
13. Kukreja, G., Bahl, D., Gupta, R., The Impact of FinTech on Financial Services in India: Past, Present, and Future Trends, in: *Innovative Strategies for Implementing FinTech in Banking*, pp. 191–200, 2021.
14. Jacopin, T., Fintech, Bigtech and Banks in India and Africa, in: *The Palgrave Handbook of FinTech and Blockchain*, pp. 171–185, Springer, Cham, Switzerland, 2021, [Online]. Available: https://econpapers.repec.org/RePEc:spr:sprchp:978-3-030-66433-6_7.
15. Goel, P., Kulsrestha, S., Maurya, S.K., Fintech Unfolding: Financial Revolution in India. *Thail. World Econ.*, 40, 2, 41–51, 2022.
16. Jaiswal, D., Mohan, A., Deshmukh, A.K., Cash rich to cashless market: Segmentation and profiling of Fintech-led-Mobile payment users. *Technol. Forecast. Soc. Change*, 193, 122627, 2023, doi: https://doi.org/10.1016/j.techfore.2023.122627.
17. Singh, A.K. and Sharma, P., A study of Indian Gen X and Millennials consumers' intention to use FinTech payment services during COVID-19 pandemic. *J. Model. Manage.*, 18, 4, 1177–1203, Jan. 2023, doi: 10.1108/JM2-02-2022-0059.
18. Invest India, Industry Scenario: Fintech Funding & Valuation and Digital Payments, in: *Invest India*, [Online]. Available: https://www.investindia.gov.in/sector/bfsi-fintech-financial-services.
19. Asif, M., Khan, M.N., Tiwari, S., Wani, S.K., Alam, F., The Impact of Fintech and Digital Financial Services on Financial Inclusion in India. *J. Risk Financ. Manag.*, 16, 2, 1–12, 2023, doi: 10.3390/jrfm16020122.
20. Goswami, S., Sharma, R., Chouhan, V., Impact of Financial Technology (Fintech) on Financial Inclusion(FI) in Rural India. *Univers. J. Account. Financ.*, 10, 483–497, Mar. 2022, doi: 10.13189/ujaf.2022.100213.
21. Siddiqui, T.A. and Siddiqui, K., II, FinTech in India: An analysis on impact of telecommunication on financial inclusion. *Strateg. Change*, 29, 3, 321–330, May 2020, doi: 10.1002/jsc.2331.
22. Ranade, A., Role of 'Fintech' in Financial inclusion and new business models. *Money, Bank. Financ.*, 52, 125–128, 2017.
23. Odei-Appiah, S., Wiredu, G., Adjei, J.K., Fintech use, digital divide and financial inclusion. *Digit. Policy, Regul. Gov.*, 24, 5, 435–448, Jan. 2022, doi: 10.1108/DPRG-09-2021-0111.
24. Setiawan, B., Nugraha, D.P., Irawan, A., Nathan, R.J., Zoltan, Z., User Innovativeness and Fintech Adoption in Indonesia. *J. Open Innov. Technol. Mark. Complex.*, 7, 3, 2021, doi: 10.3390/joitmc7030188.

25. Kong, S.T. and Loubere, N., Digitally Down to the Countryside: Fintech and Rural Development in China. *J. Dev. Stud.*, 57, 10, 1739–1754, Oct. 2021, doi: 10.1080/00220388.2021.1919631.
26. Buckley, R. and Webster, S., FinTech in Developing Countries: Charting New Customer Journeys. *J. Financ. Transform.*, 44, 151–159, Jan. 2016.
27. Agrawal, R., *India Connected: How the Smartphone Is Transforming the World's Largest Democracy*, Oxford University Press, New York, 2018.
28. Kalluri, A.B. and Caraway, B.R., Transformation of the Digital Payment Ecosystem in India : A Case Study of Paytm. *Soc. Incl.*, 11, 3, 320–331, 2023.
29. Mehta, P., Singla, H., Saha, R., Tyagi, S., A Pathway to Technology Integration: Eliciting Consumer's Behavioural Intention to Use Paytm Services. *Paradigm*, 25, 1, 7–24, Apr. 2021, doi: 10.1177/09718907211003712.
30. Singh, S. and Srivastava, R.K., Predicting the intention to use mobile banking in India. *Int. J. Bank Mark.*, 36, 2, 357–378, Jan. 2018, doi: 10.1108/IJBM-12-2016-0186.
31. Anderson, N., To Provide and Protect: Gendering Money in Ukrainian Households. *Gend. Soc.*, 31, 359–382, Jun. 2017, doi: 10.1177/0891243217705875.
32. Hochschild, A. and Machung, A., *The Second Shift: Working Parents and the Revolution at Home*, Penguin Publishing Group, New York, 2012.
33. Parsons, T., The Social System. 56, 3, 1951, doi: 10.1525/aa.1954.56.3.02a00240.
34. Mhlanga, D., FinTech for Sustainable Development in Emerging Markets with Case Studies, in: *FinTech and Artificial Intelligence for Sustainable Development*, pp. 337–363, 2023.
35. Ghaith, M.M. and Ghaith, Y.M., Impact Of E-Payment System On Consumer Buying Behavior: A Study In Jordan. *J. Posit. Sch. Psychol.*, 2022, 6, 8, 3813–3824, 2022, [Online]. Available: http://journalppw.com.
36. Balaji, K.C., A study on demonetisation and its impact on cashless transactions. *Int. J. Adv. Sci. Res. Dev.*, 4, 3, 58–64, 2017.
37. Fouillet, C., Guérin, I., Servet, J.-M., Demonetization and digitalization: The Indian government's hidden agenda. *Telecomm. Policy*, 45, 2, 102079, 2021, doi: https://doi.org/10.1016/j.telpol.2020.102079.
38. Singh, A. and Tiwari, P., Effect of Demonetization on E-Payment: With Special Reference to PayTM. *SEMCOM Manage. Technol. Rev.*, 6, 1, 94–123, 2018.
39. Chopra, A. and Ranjani, K., Adoption of digital transaction model by micro enterprises to target millennials in India: An exploratory study. *Soc. Bus.*, 10, 4, 411–434, Dec. 2020, doi: 10.1362/204440820X15813359568318.
40. Ravikumar, T., Rajesh, R., Krishna, T.A., Haresh, R., Arjun, B.S., Changing customer mindset in adopting digital financial services during the COVID-19 pandemic: Evidence from India. *Banks Bank Syst.*, 17, 3, 58–71, 2022, doi: 10.21511/bbs.17(3).2022.06.

41. Aanchal, S., *Social media and its impact a study on parent child peer group and teacher taught relationships*, Panjab University, Chandigarh, 2021, [Online]. Available: http://hdl.handle.net/10603/446706.
42. Aanchal, S.A., II, Social Media Addiction and Its Impact on the Parent-Child and Romantic Relationships. *Int. J. Innov. Stud. Sociol. Humanit.*, 4, 5, 143–154, 2019.
43. Turkle, S., Alone Together: Why We Expect More from Technology and Less from Each Other., 1, 2011.
44. Arora, N.K., *Adolescent computer users in Chandigarh a study into Social effect of computer use*, Panjab University, 2005, [Online]. Available: http://hdl.handle.net/10603/79714.
45. Lengermann, P.M. and Niebrugge, J., Intersubjectivity and Domination: A Feminist Investigation of the Sociology of Alfred Schutz. *Sociol. Theory*, 13, 1, 25–36, Feb. 1995, doi: 10.2307/202003.
46. Rowland, R. and Klein, R.D., Radical feminism: History, politics, action, in: *Radically Speaking: Feminism Reclaimed*, pp. 9–36, 1996, [Online]. Available: https://api.semanticscholar.org/CorpusID:152542718.
47. Ritzer, G., *Sociological Theory*, McGraw-Hill, New Delhi, 2012.
48. Hart, N., *When Marriage Ends: Study in Status Passage*, Routledge, London, 1976.
49. Shankar, A. and Datta, B., Factors Affecting Mobile Payment Adoption Intention: An Indian Perspective. *Glob. Bus. Rev.*, 19, 3, S72–S89, Feb. 2018, doi: 10.1177/0972150918757870.
50. Singh, N. and Sinha, N., How perceived trust mediates merchant's intention to use a mobile wallet technology. *J. Retail. Consum. Serv.*, 52, 101894, 2020, doi: 10.1016/j.jretconser.2019.101894.
51. Singh, S., Sahni, M.M., Kovid, R.K., What drives FinTech adoption? A multi-method evaluation using an adapted technology acceptance model. *Manage. Decis.*, 58, 8, 1675–1697, Jan. 2020, doi: 10.1108/MD-09-2019-1318.

12

Significance of Digital Currencies in Sustainable Finance and Investment—An Indian Perspective

Sulagna Das

School of Management Studies, JIS University, Kolkata, India

Abstract
Digital currencies, including cryptocurrencies and central bank digital currencies (CBDCs), have the potential to revolutionize the financial system and economy. The Indian FinTech sector is expected to dominate the global market by 2030. The Jan Dhan Yojana, Aadhar biometric identity system, and mobile connectivity have significantly boosted financial inclusion and digitization. Central Banks are exploring CBDCs to enhance their economies and payment systems, with 86% researching and 60% experimenting. India is experimenting with the e-Rupee, aiming to reduce cash reliance and strengthen its position as the fifth largest economy and e-commerce market globally. Cryptocurrencies like Ethereum, Ripple, and Bitcoin are popular for their security and inflation resistance, but their environmental impact is becoming more evident. Blockchain technology can reduce fraud and promote sustainable cryptocurrencies, allowing central banks to legitimize public currencies and promote green businesses.

***Keywords*:** Digital currency, cryptocurrency, central bank digital currency, sustainability, blockchain technology, financial inclusion

12.1 Digital Money

Digital currencies, unlike tangible ones like banknotes and coins, are digital and only available in digital form. They allow electronic wallet transactions linked to the Internet or specific networks, allowing for instant

Email: sulagna.das@jisuniversity.ac.in; ORCID: https://orcid.org/0000-0003-4683-453X

Ernesto D.R. Santibanez Gonzalez, Vinay Kandpal, Peterson K. Ozili and Prasenjit Chatterjee (eds.) Fintech for ESG and the Circular Economy, (225–246) © 2024 Scrivener Publishing LLC

cross-border transactions. These currencies are limited to certain online communities like gaming sites or social networks. Cryptocurrencies, stablecoins, and central bank digital currencies (CBDCs) are emerging as new forms of currency with the potential to transform the financial system and economy [13]. Bitcoin and Ethereum, for example, have the potential to fundamentally alter cultural ideas of money, prompting global central banks to study the functioning of national digital currencies [16]. The features of digital currencies have been discussed below:

- Digital currencies, which do not have physical equivalents, can be centralized or decentralized. Central banks and government agencies create and distribute centralized digital currencies like fiat currency, yet decentralized digital money systems like Bitcoin and Ethereum exist.
- Digital currencies enable value transfer, necessitating a paradigm shift away from traditional currencies, which comprise sales and purchases of products and services.
- Digital currencies, such as gaming network tokens, enable players to transfer value rather than buy or sell, allowing them to live longer or acquire more talents.

Digital money is a broad concept that encompasses all monetary assets in digital form. Cryptocurrency is a subset of virtual currency, while virtual currency is a subset of digital currency. The many forms of digital money are listed below.

- Centralized **digital currencies** are issued by a country's central bank and might be controlled or unregulated. These currencies are vulnerable to a country's monetary policy. CBDCs aim to improve centralized payment systems, lower cash handling costs, promote financial inclusion, facilitate cross-border payments, and reduce foreign exchange demand. Countries like the UK, Sweden, and Uruguay are considering creating digital equivalents of their own fiat currency.
- **Virtual Currencies** like Bitcoin, Litecoin, and XRP are unregulated digital currencies maintained by private issuers without central bank regulation. They can be centralized or

decentralized, with some using encryption. These currencies are stored and exchanged through specialized software, applications, and networks, primarily developed by private issuers, in specialized virtual communities. Security remains a major concern.

- **Cryptocurrency** is a decentralized virtual currency that uses cryptography to ensure safe and legitimate transactions, with blockchain networks playing an important part in its operation.

Digital money has the efficiency to revolutionize the economic system, benefiting both developed and developing nations by offering low-cost access to financial services to approximately two billion people without traditional bank accounts. This approach could enhance trade and market integration but also poses risks like limited access, fragmentation, currency substitution, and policy failure. Therefore, effective management and regulation are crucial for its success. Despite these challenges, digital money's benefits include improved trade and market integration [2]. The following are some of the advantages of digital currency:

- Digital money offers a faster payment mode compared to traditional techniques, such as automated clearing houses or wire transfers, which might take days to finalize transactions for financial institutions.
- Digital assets can significantly reduce the costs associated with currency conversions and other costly international transfers by making them more cost-effective and efficient.
- Digital currency transactions are available 24/7, allowing for faster transactions than traditional money transfers, which may take longer on weekends and outside business hours due to bank closures and transaction authentication issues.
- Digital currencies do not require manufacturing facilities and are not affected by soiling or physical flaws, unlike cash which requires specific prerequisites.
- The government may establish a digital currency central bank to facilitate swift payment transfers for essential services like child benefits, food stamps, and tax refunds, eliminating the need for prepaid debit cards or check payments [19].

12.2 Role of The Reserve Bank of India in Fostering Financial Inclusion through Digital Transformation of Financial Services

Traditional financial services have seen a tremendous transformation with the emergence of FinTech, becoming more accessible, affordable, quick, and efficient. By 2030, the US$245 billion worldwide FinTech industry is predicted to generate US$1.5 trillion in revenue. By 2030, the Indian FinTech sector is expected to account for 13% of the global FinTech market with over US$200 billion in sales. The growing significance of the Indian FinTech sector can be attributed to the symbiotic relationship between institutional arrangements, policy efforts, and digital public infrastructure. These factors foster innovation and transformative technologies, which have brought about significant changes in the financial industry. A technical framework known as digital public infrastructure (DPI) encourages inclusion, openness, and interoperability for essential public and private services. India's digitalization approach is unique in that it involves both public and government sectors in the construction of infrastructure, while FinTech companies and start-ups in the private sector create new products. With programs like JAM trinity—Jan Dhan Yojana, Aadhar, and Mobile—significantly impacting financial inclusion and the digitization of financial services, the India Stack concept invented a layered approach to DPI [5].

12.2.1 Digital Public Infrastructure

(i) ***Jan Dhan Yojana/Bank Accounts:*** Globally, 76% of individuals have access to a bank or other regulated financial institution, up from 51% in 2011, according to the World Bank's Global Findex Database 2021. Because of the government's Jan Dhan plan, which established over 500 million accounts, the percentage of Indians possessing bank accounts increased from 35% in 2011 to 78% in 2021.

(ii) ***Aadhar—Digital Identity:*** As of 2022, the Aadhaar biometric identity system in India will have 1.35 billion IDs granted by the Unique Identification Authority of India. This would enable people to easily identify themselves across the nation and have access to targeted financial benefits and financial services. This has improved customer convenience, strengthened the security of financial transactions, and reduced the risk of identity theft, illuminating how digital public infrastructure may be used to achieve public policy objectives.

(iii) ***Mobile Connectivity:*** The digital transformation of financial services in India has been greatly impacted by mobile connections. By 2022, there will be over 800 million mobile Internet users worldwide, up from 70 million in 2014. Digital transactions have also surged throughout this time. Affordability, inexpensive internet access, and expanded mobile network coverage are credited with this expansion, which has sparked the emergence of UPI systems and mobile wallets.

(iv) ***Unified Payments Interface (UPI):*** By facilitating money transfers between bank accounts using mobile applications and fostering a single payment ecosystem, the UPI has transformed India's FinTech boom. Small companies and street vendors may now take digital payments thanks to its well-liked user interface and QR code-based payment system. Additional payment systems like the Bharat Bill Payment System and prepaid payment instruments/mobile wallets have been developed as a result of UPI's fueling of FinTech innovation. August 2023 saw the completion of over 10 billion transactions worth over Rs. 15 trillion.

12.2.2 Institutional Arrangements

The development of a financial system depends on institutional frameworks, which play a variety of functions including research, innovation, education, and the promotion of best practices in the industry. They also support justice, openness, and stability in the financial industry. The Reserve Bank has taken steps to establish institutions for the FinTech industry, including the Reserve Bank Innovation Hub (RBIH), the Reserve Bank FinTech Department, the Reserve Bank Information Technology Pvt. Ltd. (ReBIT), the National Payment Corporation of India Ltd. (NPCI), and the Institute for Development and Research in Banking Technology (IDRBT), to boost the cyber resilience of the banking industry and encourage innovation in financial services.

12.2.3 Policy Initiatives

In order to promote innovation in the FinTech sector and guarantee the security and stability of financial services, the Reserve Bank of India (RBI) has been implementing regulatory measures. These contain guidelines for recently developed domains including digital finance, peer-to-peer lending, invoice discounting, pre-paid instruments, account aggregators (AA), and payment banks. Consent-based information sharing has significantly increased after businesses from the insurance, capital markets, and pension funds joined the AA framework. In August 2019, the Regulatory Sandbox framework was unveiled with the goal of promoting efficient and responsible innovation in the financial services industry. Four cohorts of the framework—one each for retail payments, cross-border payments, MSME loans, and financial fraud prevention—make up the framework.

A framework for allowing small-value digital payments to be done offline has also been devised by the RBI, with the aim of boosting digital transactions in places where phone or Internet access is limited. In an effort to promote innovation, the RBI will hold two global hackathons. The first, called HaRBInger, will take place in 2021, and the second, called HARBINGER 2023, will have the themes "Smarter Digital Payments" and "Inclusive Digital Services," respectively.

12.2.4 Transformational Initiatives Using Technology to Foster Innovation

(i) ***Central Bank Digital Currency (CBDC):*** The CBDC of India has begun trial runs by the RBI for usage in the retail and wholesale markets. In 2022, two pilot programs were introduced by CBDC: the CBDC-Wholesale Pilot, which concentrated on transactions in government securities on the secondary market, and the CBDC-Retail Pilot, which included P2P and P2M transactions. As of 2023, 13 banks are operating the pilot in 26 locations, serving around 1.46 million consumers and 0.31 million merchants. A controlled and staggered rollout approach is being used to guarantee a non-disruptive launch, with a target of one million CBDC transactions daily by December 2023. This information will be useful in examining different design possibilities, use cases, and behavioral trends.

(ii) ***Public Tech Platform for Frictionless Credit:*** A digitization project called the Kisan Lending Card (KCC Loans) was introduced in Madhya Pradesh and Tamil Nadu in 2022 with the goal of giving farmers easy access to financing. Farmers may apply for new loans and renew existing ones via smartphones or tablets thanks to the trial program, which interfaces with state land records databases, credit information companies, satellite data, and Aadhar e-KYC integration. Since then, several districts in Maharashtra, Karnataka, and Uttar Pradesh have been added to the initiative. Gujarati dairy farmers and seven banks are actively involved in the Digital KCC Pilot. Milk pouring statistics from milk cooperatives are used to calculate the eligibility and credit amount for these loans.

Financial inclusion is critical for economic development and inequality reduction. It entails providing low-cost savings, investment, and credit options, which may be accomplished through financial innovation and digital identification systems. FinTech can help close the credit gap created by issues such as a lack of credit ratings, time-consuming documentation, and manual processes. The RBIH is working on an end-to-end digitalization of Kisan Credit Card (KCC) financing, aiming to automate procedures within banks and integrate their systems with service providers, making loan issuing more efficient and cost-effective. This initiative is in collaboration with the RBI [9].

12.3 Role of CBDCs in Digital Financial Transformation

Central banks are rethinking their role in providing efficient, fast, and consistent solutions for their economies, including payment systems and money creation. A 2021 Bank of International Settlements study shows that 86% of central banks are actively researching CBDCs, 60% are experimenting, and 14% are undertaking trial programs. Central banks like Sweden, Denmark, Germany, Japan, and the United States aim to popularize electronic currency, make issuance more efficient, and meet public demand while avoiding the negative consequences of private currencies. CBDCs are suitable for UPI systems, allowing real-time and cost-effective internationalization, eliminating the need for the US Federal Reserve System and time zone disparities in currency settlements [12]. The Indian government and the RBI have significantly contributed to the development and adoption of digital payments. In 2022, India created its own CBDC [4] called e-rupee (e₹), a digital token that serves as legal money in the country. The CBDC project, launched in the retail sector, is entirely based on blockchain technology. The digital rupee, similar to banknotes, is designed for online transactions for convenience. India is a pioneer in digital payment innovation, offering 24-hour, real-time solutions to retail and wholesale clients. With transaction prices among the lowest in the world, India has seen a 55% CAGR in digital payments over the past five years. A pilot study by the Reserve Bank found that cash remains the preferred means of payment for routine costs, primarily for small-value transactions up to US$500.

Due to the rising popularity of digital payments and interest in using cash, particularly for small-value transactions, CBDCs may not replace cash usage in India. However, the need for money to maintain its secrecy might be changed to allow CBDCs as long as anonymity is guaranteed. CBDCs can lower India's high currency-to-GDP ratio by replacing large quantities of cash and lowering the cost of creating, distributing, storing, and transporting money. However, the emergence of private virtual currencies (VCs) could make the use of CBDCs necessary, endangering national currencies with little room for maneuvering. Central banks must collaborate to research CBDCs in order to identify trustworthy principles and stimulate innovation in order to safeguard people's faith in their money. CBDCs help developing nations by strengthening payment systems and

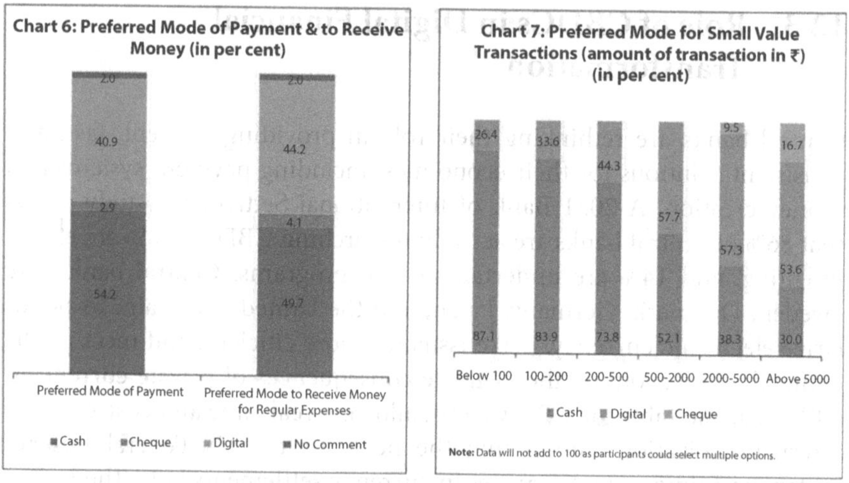

Figure 12.1 Preferred mode of transaction and preferred mode of small value transaction in rupees (in percent). Source: RBI Bulletin, 2021

may be required to safeguard the public in a volatile private virtual currency environment. Figure 12.1 illustrates the preferred mode of payment and preferred mode of small value transactions.

12.3.1 Banking System and CBDC

CBDCs can lower transaction demand for bank deposits by decreasing settlement risk and liquidity needs. They may abandon bank deposits, so lessening the need for government guarantees. CBDCs can lower transaction demand for bank deposits by decreasing settlement risk and liquidity needs. They may abandon bank deposits, so lessening the need for government guarantees. However, this reduces worries about disintermediation, such as restricted credit production and interest margin stress. CBDCs may result in faster deposit flights and fewer panic runs, but they may also result in lower earnings for commercial banks. Despite their advantages, their influence on bank deposits may be limited due to the fact that they are cash and do not pay interest. Depositors who require CBDCs for transactions can transfer their day-end balances to interest-earning deposit accounts. As a result, it is necessary to create and execute CBDCs to restrict demand.

12.3.2 Monetary Policy and CBDC

CBDCs can reduce transaction demand for bank deposits by reducing settlement risk and liquidity needs. They may abandon bank savings, reducing government guarantees. However, they may cause faster deposit flights and fewer panic runs but may result in lower commercial bank returns. CBDCs are money and do not pay interest, so they must be planned and executed to regulate demand. Depositors can transfer day-end balances to interest-bearing deposit accounts.

12.3.3 Technology Risk and CBDC

CBDC ecosystems are prone to cyber-attacks and digital payment fraud in countries with a low level of financial literacy. CBDC implementation necessitates stringent cybersecurity measures as well as financial literacy efforts. High-speed Internet and communications networks are required for population-scale digital money systems. Reduced technological uptake in developing nations may restrict the applicability of CBDCs and exacerbate already-existing disparities in financial services and product availability. CBDC ecosystems are vulnerable to cyber-attacks and digital payment fraud in nations where financial literacy is low. CBDC implementation

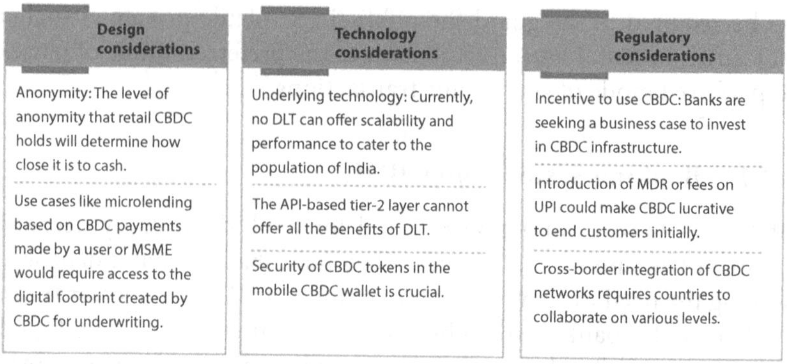

Figure 12.2 Future consideration for CBDC in India. Source: PWC Hand Book

requires high cybersecurity requirements as well as financial literacy activities. High-speed Internet and communications networks are required for population-scale digital money systems. The reduced use of technology in underdeveloped countries might restrict the impact of CBDCs and worsen already-existing disparities in access to financial services and products. Figure 12.2 gives an idea about the future consideration for CBDC in India.

12.3.4 RBI's Approach to CBDC

Global central banks are investigating the use of digital currencies, or CBDCs, with several nations starting pilot programs or proofs of concept. The High-Level Inter-Ministerial Committee of the Indian Ministry of Finance suggested CBDCs as a digital version of fiat money. The RBI is looking into the benefits and drawbacks of implementing CBDCs, which are established for specific functions in the retail and wholesale industries. The RBI is reviewing use cases and developing a phased rollout approach with minimal impact. The High-Level Inter-Ministerial Committee of the Indian Ministry of Finance suggested CBDCs as a digital version of fiat money. The RBI is looking into the benefits and drawbacks of implementing CBDCs, which are established for specific functions in the retail and wholesale industries. The RBI is reviewing use cases and developing a phased rollout approach with minimal impact.

12.3.5 Legal Framework

In India, CBDCs need a legislative framework to guarantee financial stability. The country's currency and credit system are managed by the RBI

[15], which is in charge of issuing bank notes and reserves. It has legislative control over denomination, currency type, and legal tender status according to the RBI Act. It is necessary to amend other Acts, including the Information Technology Act of 2000, the FEMA Act of 1999, and the Coinage Act of 2011.

12.3.6 What Comes Next for CBDC in India?

Many countries are investigating central bank-issued digital currency, or CBDCs, as a risk-free, central bank-based asset to streamline international payments networks. Through an intermediate procedure, the RBI is testing CBDC for both retail and wholesale use in India.

December 2022 saw the start of the retail and wholesale CBDC pilot programs, respectively. The knowledge gained will assist in clearing up unclear areas for interested parties, enhancing openness, and decreasing the possibility of failure at different stages of usage, implementation, and scaling.

Peer-to-peer and peer-to-merchant payments are presently accepted by CBDC retail; however, adoption is restricted to 1 million consumers and 0.26 million businesses. There were 7.7 million transactions

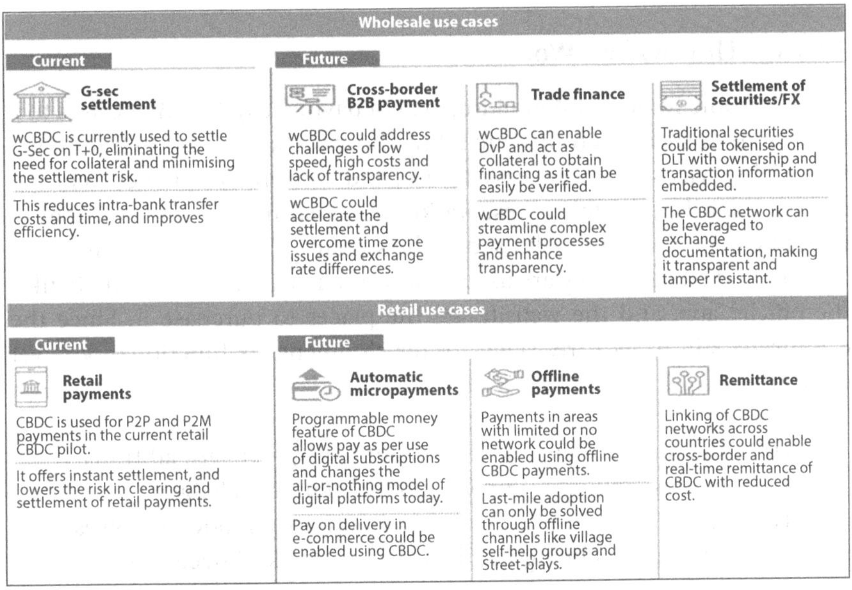

Figure 12.3 Potential future use cases for CBDC in India. Source: PWC Hand Book

following the introduction. To receive the token, retailers must have a CBDC wallet. Efforts are being made to increase the user base by enabling payments using UPI QR codes. Wholesale CBDC transactions reached 1,329 as of February 2023, showing a small-scale application for resolving disputes [17]. Figure 12.3 gives a screenshot of the potential future use cases for CBDC in India.

12.4 Digital Rupee e₹ Story of India

The emergence of well-known cryptocurrencies like Bitcoin, Ethereum, Litecoin, Tether, and XRP has brought about a revolution in the realm of decentralized digital currencies or cryptocurrency. But, because of worries about money laundering and illicit activity, India has been reluctant to adopt cryptocurrencies. The RBI has no control over transactions using cryptocurrencies, and the economy might suffer if demand for conventional fiat currencies declines. A cryptocurrency prohibition statute was prepared in 2019; however, the Supreme Court removed the ban in March 2020. A 30% tax on cryptocurrencies and the creation of India's own digital currency, the digital rupee, were two of the measures included in the Union Budget 2022–2023 to reduce reliance on cash. Overcoming technological, legal, and regulatory obstacles is necessary to implement the digital rupee.

12.4.1 How will e₹ Work?

The electronic Rupee, or digital Rupee, is a payment system that caters to a wide range of societal groups, including those without access to traditional financial services. It is safe, easy to use, and convenient. Like current fiat currencies, it is a digital representation of actual money with the goal of reducing the amount of cash used in the system. The same denominations as coins and paper money are used by intermediaries to issue it, and banks, the official app, and the website are the places to purchase it. Since the e-Rupee is still in its early stages of development, its functionality is yet unclear.

(i) The direct model, or central authority, manages all transactions, issuing e-Rupees and maintaining a ledger.
(ii) The indirect model, or central authority model, involves transactions being handled by a network of decentralized nodes.

(iii) The hybrid model combines the advantages of both models, with a central authority issuing e-rupees and maintaining a ledger, while a network of decentralized nodes validates and records transactions. This approach aims to minimize the disadvantages of each model.

Common technologies used in CBDCs include:

- CBDCs can be built on decentralized systems like blockchain, using distributed ledger technology (DLT).
- They can use smart contracts to automate procedures and reduce transaction costs.
- To verify transaction authenticity and avoid fraud, CBDCs employ cryptographic techniques like as digital signatures, hashing, and encryption.
- They can improve interoperability by interacting with existing payment systems via APIs.
- Mobile wallets offer a user-friendly interface for storing and transacting CBDCs.
- For safe transactions, CBDC can also be connected to digital identity systems such as biometric or national identification.

CBDCs use cutting-edge technology to provide safe, dependable, and easily accessible digital money for everyday transactions. When compared to traditional fiat currencies, these technologies enable faster transaction speeds, lower prices, enhanced security, and broader financial inclusion.

12.4.2 Proposed e₹-Architecture

The e-Rupee system's architecture is determined by its aims, technological capabilities, and regulatory context. The Reserve Bank and licensed banks will use a private blockchain network, while consumers, account holders, companies, and licensed banks will use a consortium blockchain network.

12.4.2.1 Private Blockchain

A private blockchain network is needed for licensed banks and reserve banks to conduct efficient transactions. This single-organization network allows quick processing and can be adjusted for speed due to fewer nodes. For transaction monitoring and auditing, regulatory compliance bodies such as SEBI, Income Tax Authority, CAB, and Enforcement Directorate may be included. This blockchain might potentially be used to build CBDC.

12.4.2.2 Consortium Blockchain

Consortium blockchain, a decentralized network made up of many organizations, is suitable for CBDC because of its blend of privacy, security, and scalability. For transactions in the Indian economy, it offers a safe, private network between CBDC and authorized banks and third-party applications. The benefits of consortium and private blockchain technology over public blockchain technology are illustrated in the next sections.

- Private and consortium blockchains offer enhanced privacy and scalability because of their limited access to authorized users, which makes them ideal for storing sensitive data in businesses. For some processes, they are also more economical and efficient since they use less processing power.
- A single company or set of companies may manage both consortium and private blockchains, which offer more control over the network, simpler update execution, and more accountability. They may also be tailored for certain transactions or use cases, making them more flexible.
- Blockchains may be customized to meet certain regulatory standards, which is essential for businesses operating in regulated sectors like healthcare and finance.

The benefits behind this launch of a digital version of the Indian Rupee by the RBI:

- Digital money may be a workable solution because the unbanked population in India has limited access to traditional financial services.
- By cutting out intermediaries like banks and payment processors, digital currencies can reduce transaction costs.
- Improve financial transparency by making it simpler to identify financial transactions and by stopping dishonest practices like money laundering.

To handle huge transactions and preserve currency stability, the Indian digital rupee system would require solid technological infrastructure and regulatory backing, with important elements determining its implementation viability.

- Implementing a digital currency necessitates a robust technological infrastructure capable of handling high transaction volumes, significant hardware and software costs, and robust cybersecurity measures.
- Digital currencies [1] must navigate a complex legal and regulatory framework, including India's financial services structure while maintaining a supportive and well-defined environment to ensure success and address challenges.
- Digital currency success in India relies on public acceptance and adoption due to the country's diverse population and varying technological abilities.

India is looking at using the digital rupee, a virtual currency, for cross-border payments. The government sees it as a cost-effective substitute for less expensive transactions, as it is expected to collect US$87 billion in remittances in 2021 [7]. The introduction is consistent with the goal of the 2023 G20 Presidency, which is to facilitate central bank interoperability and promote international agreements pertaining to CBDC. India's digital financial capabilities, which build on the unified payment interface, strengthen its bargaining power in CBDC agreements and help it hold onto its position as the fifth largest economy and e-commerce market globally [6].

12.5 Significant Role Played by Digital Currencies in Supporting Green and Sustainable Finance

The security and inflation resistance of cryptocurrency, a digital form of virtual money, have made it more and more popular. But with Elon Musk's move to discontinue Tesla's use of Bitcoin, the environmental effects of cryptocurrencies are coming to light. Blockchain technology has the potential to reduce fraud, replace ineffective processes, and assist in developing a sustainable cryptocurrency by giving non-bank users access to digital wallets. Even though well-known cryptocurrencies like Ethereum, Ripple, and Bitcoin demand a lot of energy, many mining companies are switching to renewable energy sources, and Bitcoin miners are adopting eco-friendly practices [3].

- ***What is Cryptocurrency Mining?***
  Cryptocurrencies are managed through a decentralized blockchain database, a public financial ledger, with real-time updates distributed via nodes. Data mining, a complex validation protocol, controls transactions, allowing easy retrieval and verification. This process is based on artificial intelligence and statistical analysis.
- ***Bitcoin Energy Consumption***
  Bitcoin's annual electricity consumption is over 198 terawatt-hours, equivalent to Thailand's and Nigeria's emissions. This high energy consumption is due to an inefficient proof-of-work mining system, requiring complex mathematical problems. As more miners compete, this energy is wasted, leading to the loss of Bitcoin as payment.

12.5.1 Moving Toward Sustainability

This shift toward sustainability is a significant step toward a more sustainable future for the cryptocurrency industry. Sustainability is a central criterion for the future of the blockchain industry, and achieving an effective and efficient cryptographic mechanism is essential for expanding the use of blockchain-based cryptocurrencies. To analyze energy efficiency, it is necessary to examine the process of creating and maintaining blocks of information, which users agree to record and validate. Most popular cryptocurrencies, like Bitcoin, are produced through mining, which the new green cryptocurrencies aim to rethink to reduce their disproportionate energy consumption and greenhouse gas emissions [21].

Digital currencies are increasingly being used for green and sustainable finance and development. Solutions include adopting green standards, strengthening regulation, coordinating stakeholders, and investing in digital infrastructure and education. Green standards can incentivize sustainable practices, while regulation enhances security, transparency, and accountability. Collaboration among stakeholders fosters dialog and innovation on digital currency issues. Investing in digital infrastructure can reduce the digital divide and increase inclusion. Solar Coin, Carbon Coin, ECO Coin, and Khokha reward solar energy producers with tokens for environmental causes, carbon-negative systems, and circular economies. Khokha, a CBDC project by the South African Reserve Bank, uses blockchain technology to enable faster, cheaper, and more secure interbank payments, reducing reliance on intermediaries and improving financial system efficiency [8].

12.5.2 Trustworthiness Created by Central Banks

Central banks play a crucial role in fostering trust among the public. CBDC is a global concern in financial and money transactions, with the potential to become the core digital infrastructure. In their article, CBDC's impact on green financing [20] observed that CBDC significantly promotes green bond issuing, especially in manufacturing and state-owned enterprises. Additionally, CBDC decreases SO2 and NOx emissions, improves green land ratio, and contributes to sustainable development. Energy efficiency rating labels promote low consumption and efficient products to reduce carbon footprint. CBDCs are public currencies legitimized by central banks, alongside cash, aiming to lower CO2 emissions and promote green, eco-friendly businesses. CBDCs eliminate the need for energy-intensive decentralized mining and require authentication, making them secure and stable payment methods. Central banks act as guarantors for currency authenticity and value, ensuring sustainability in the financial sector. Governments and the financial industry have signaled that these regulations will consider CO2 footprints. CBDCs are more efficient and transparent than cryptocurrencies, as they are regulated by central banks, ensuring transparency and efficiency in energy consumption [11].

12.5.3 More Sustainable Payment Systems

Sustainable payment systems are being explored as a potential solution for promoting environmental sustainability. CBDCs can be designed to be sustainable from the start, marking a significant step toward a future payment and settlement ecosystem. G+D's Filia® is a modular solution designed for central banks, offering offline payments with CO2-neutral smart cards and green electricity-powered servers for core infrastructure. This meets individual functionality and performance requirements without compromising sustainability. Filia®'s Smart Wallets® are programmable wallets that can help public entities and corporations achieve sustainability objectives. These special-purpose wallets have pre-defined conditions, like targeted spending or expiry dates, and can be issued to incentivize purchasing of goods or services, meeting sustainability criteria. G+D is dedicated to enhancing the sustainability and efficiency of the currency cycle and value chain, focusing on environmentally friendly banknotes like the green banknote and digitalizing cash infrastructure. Sustainable payment methods include compostable or recycled digital cards and eSIMs for mobile payments. Sustainable CBDCs are being implemented to further reduce the environmental impact of monetary and payment systems.

12.5.4 Overview of the Future Outlook

Digital currencies offer a promising opportunity to create a more inclusive, transparent, and resilient financial system that supports environmental and social goals. However, their full impact on green and sustainable finance and development is not yet fully understood. Monitoring their benefits and challenges is crucial, and appropriate solutions and policies should be adopted to ensure alignment with these objectives.

12.6 Potential Risk Involved in Digital Currencies

The Union Budget 2022–23 includes the introduction of a CBDC to decrease costs associated with managing physical currency, such as phasing out dirty notes, transportation, insurance, and logistics. This action is intended to deter individuals from using cryptocurrencies for money transfers, although those with a speculative appetite can still utilize cryptocurrencies with volatile prices. RBI's decision to launch a CBDC in India, despite being averse to cryptocurrencies due to inherent risks, demonstrates its competence in managing operational risks, as a developing economy banning such products may indicate a reluctance toward innovation.

The risks associated with CBDCs in emerging economies include:

(I) ***Disintermediating Banks:*** The significant and broad-based CBDC transition could potentially impact banks' ability to reinvest funds in credit intermediation and increase central banks' balance sheets, raising questions about how deposits from the banking channel will return to the real economy.

(II) ***Cyber Threats and Single Point of Failure:*** The centralization of CBDCs is crucial to reducing cyber-attacks and failures. Implementing public blockchains and a competitive internet exchange for digital currency exchange would be a more effective method. However, transferring risk to central banks could undermine the benefits of smart risk-sharing models.

(III) ***Privacy and Consumer Protection:*** The issuance of CBDCs by a less benevolent authority may violate consumer privacy and protections. It is crucial to prevent weaponization and transaction blockage by malicious organizations. Simple savings, spending, and securing money should be made possible, with severe penalties for defaulters [14].

(IV) ***Eliminates the Goal of Decentralization:*** Blockchain technology aims for decentralization and unrestricted distribution without regulatory oversight, unlike CBDCs which are issued, controlled, and monitored by central banks. The purpose of blockchain technology, which combats cyberattacks and manipulation, is undermined by the development of a closed-loop system with a fake blockchain.

(V) ***Impact on Financial Inclusion:*** India's 550 million feature phone users and 845 million smartphone owners are crucial for the growth of a CBDC ecosystem. However, many do not use mobile banking or digital payments daily due to economic factors, lack of education, tier-2 or tier-3 city residents' reluctance to use cash, and lack of awareness of CBDC's existence. Therefore, it is essential to develop a sustainable CBDC ecosystem to appeal to both tech-savvy millennials and lower socioeconomic groups in India [18].

(VI) ***The Risk of Financial Instability:*** The transition to CBDC could lead to a sudden surge in consumer withdrawals from banks, potentially causing the entire banking system to collapse, necessitating the central bank's meticulous oversight of the transition to CBDC.

(VII) ***The Risk of Centralization:*** CBDC, a centralized currency, could lead to financial independence loss and government control, posing a significant threat to individual rights and independence and potentially facilitating government overreach and abuse, as the central bank holds complete authority over the monetary system [10].

(VIII) ***Impact on Monetary Policy:*** CBDC's widespread use in a country's financial system can impact monetary policy and cause economic volatility. Higher adoption rates can reduce fiat money usage, leading to the need for currency substitution. However, this can only occur in rare cases. To avoid this, limit individual CBDC ownership and increase public knowledge about CBDC. Teaching people about its use can also foster confidence in its use. Ultimately, addressing these negative effects is crucial for a stable and stable economy.

CBDC's shortcomings can be addressed by focusing on payment to improve the payment and settlement system. This will help avoid disintermediation risks and monetary policy consequences. The RBI should avoid interest on balances and focus on payment and settlement. The risks have been identified, and central banks should build an ecosystem to mitigate them. Despite initial challenges, CBDC could accelerate digital transformation, facilitating the transition toward a digital economy.

References

1. Acharya, M., *Digital Currency: Name, Meaning, Features & Advantages*, Clear tax, 2022, https://cleartax.in/s/digital-currency. Accessed on 16th September, 2023.
2. Adrian, T. and Griffoli, T.M., *A New Era Of Digital Money*, International Monetary Fund, 2021, https://www.imf.org/external/pubs/ft/fandd/2021/06/online/digital-money-new-era-adrian-mancini-griffoli.htm#:~:text=Broad%20and%20inexpensive%20. Accessed on 16th September, 2023.
3. Alqudah, M., Ferruz, L., Martín, E., Qudah, H., Hamdan, F., The Sustainability of Investing in Cryptocurrencies: A Bibliometric Analysis of Research Trends. *Int. J. Financ. Stud.*, 11, 93, 2023, https://doi.org/10.3390/ijfs11030093 Accessed on 22nd September, 2023.
4. *Central Bank Digital Currency in India: Features, Uses and Risks*, India Law Offices LLP, 2022, https://www.indialawoffices.com/legal-articles/central-bank-digital-currency-in-india. Accessed on 21st September, 2023.
5. Das, S., cape, in: *FinTech and the Changing Financial Lands*, 2023, https://www.rbi.org.in/Scripts/BS_SpeechesView.aspx?Id=1383 Accessed on 17th September, 2023.
6. Ganpule, G., *Digital rupee: India's geopolitical game changer in CBDC race*, Policy Circle, 2023, https://www.policycircle.org/economy/digital-rupee-dedollarisation/ Accessed on 22nd September, 2023.
7. Haque, M.A. and Shoaib, M., e&xxx20B9;—The digital currency in India: Challenges and prospects. *Bench Council Trans. Benchmarks Stand. Eval.*, 3, 1, 1–9, 2023. https://doi.org/10.1016/j.tbench.2023.100107.
8. *How can digital currencies support green and sustainable finance and development?*, https://www.linkedin.com/advice/3/how-can-digital-currencies-support-green-sustainable#:~:text=Digital%20currencies%20are%20increasingly%20being,or%20donated%20to%20environmental%20causes. Accessed on 22nd September, 2023.
9. Jain, M.K., *The FinTech Revolution in India- Innovation, Inclusion and Regulation*, RBI, 2023, https://www.rbi.org.in/Scripts/BS_SpeechesView.aspx?Id=1355. Accessed on 20th September, 2023.
10. Livis, M., *The Risks of CBDC & How to Protect Your Money*, 2023, https://www.linkedin.com/pulse/risks-cbdc-how-protect-your-money-millen-livis/. Accessed on 21st September, 2023.

11. *More sustainability in finance with CBDCs*, 2022, https://www.gi-de.com/en/spotlight/payment/more-sustainability-in-finance-with-cbdcs. Accessed on 22nd September, 2023.
12. Rabi Sankar, T., *Central Bank Digital Currency - Is This the Future of Money*, Bank For International Settlements, 2021, https://www.rbi.org.in/Scripts/BS_SpeechesView.aspx?Id=1111 Accessed on 17th September, 2023.
13. Rao, M.R., *Financial Sector as an Enabler for Developed India*, Reserve Bank of India, 2023, https://www.rbi.org.in/Scripts/BS_SpeechesView.aspx?Id=1359. Accessed on 20th September, 2023.
14. Rao, S.K., *CBDC in India — the pros and the cons*, The Hindu Business Line, 2022, https://www.thehindubusinessline.com/opinion/cbdc-in-india-the-pros-and-the-cons/article65344881.ece. Accessed on 21st September, 2023.
15. *Reserve Bank of India Bulletin*, 2021, https://rbi.org.in/Scripts/BS_ViewBulletin.aspx.PDF. Accessed on 18th September, 2023.
16. Rodeck, D. and Adams, M., *Digital Currency: The Future Of Your Money*, Forbes Advisor, 2023, https://www.forbes.com/advisor/in/investing/cryptocurrency/digital-currency/. Accessed on 16th September, 2023.
17. Sarkar, K., Bhatt, T., Mahajan, K., Budhiraja, A., Duttagupta, D., Patel, S., *The Indian payments handbook - 2023–2028*, PWC, 2023, https://www.pwc.in/assets/pdfs/consulting/financial-services/fintech/publications/the-indian-payments-handbook-%E2%80%93-2023%E2%80%932028.pdf. Accessed on 20th September, 2023.
18. Tafti, Z., Sarkar, K., Chowdhury, A., Bandyopadhyay, S., Kulshrestha, V., Central Bank Digital Currency in the Indian context, 2021, https://www.pwc.in/assets/pdfs/consulting/financial-services/fintech/point-of-view/pov-downloads/central-bank-digital-currency-in-the-indian-context.pdf Accessed on 16th September, 2023.
19. Varma, K. and Jain, A., *What Is Digital Rupee? How Is It Different From Cryptocurrency?*, Forbes Advisor, 2023, https://www.forbes.com/advisor/in/investing/digital-rupee/ Accessed on 16th September, 2023.
20. Yang, Q., Zheng, M., Wang, Y., The Role of CBDC in Green Finance and Sustainable Development, *Emerging Markets Finance and Trade*, vol. 59, 15, pp. 4158–4173, Taylor & Francis Journals, December 2023.
21. *What are green cryptocurrencies and why are they important?*, https://www.iberdrola.com/sustainability/green-cryptocurrencies. Accessed on 22nd September, 2023.

13

A Leap Towards Tokenomics: The Future of Sustainability

Soumyajit Chakraborty

University of Petroleum & Energy Studies (UPES), Dehradun, Uttarakhand, India

Abstract
Ecological initiatives can be creatively funded through tokenomics, a hybrid of conventional economics and digital tokens. The theory integrates Bitcoin with more conventional economic principles, with an emphasis on maximising utility, market efficiency, and supply and demand. A revolution in public services, less corruption, more accountability, and better democratic procedures could be possible in India using tokenomics. On the other hand, problems including ambiguous laws, a shortage of course materials, and security concerns need fixing. In order to create a more effective and long-lasting circular economy, tokens can motivate the implementation of ESG principles. The protection of personal information and its integrity requires a comprehensive regulatory framework.

Keywords: Circular economy, ESG, sustainability, token, tokenomics

13.1 A Few Words on Tokenomics

The utilisation of digital tokens has the potential to significantly improve the circular economy by adding efficiency, transparency, and creative approaches to finance ecological activities (Alexander and Dakos, 2022) [1]; (Grybniak *et al.*, 2022) [9]. This might result in a significant increase in the overall quality of the economy (Cong *et al.*, 2021) [4]. Tokenomics is a revolutionary tool that is helping to push forward the ESG (environmental, social, and corporate governance) goals. Tokenomics refers to the process

Email: soumyajit.eco@gmail.com; soumyajit.c@ddn.upes.ac.in

Ernesto D.R. Santibanez Gonzalez, Vinay Kandpal, Peterson K. Ozili and Prasenjit Chatterjee (eds.) Fintech for ESG and the Circular Economy, (247–254) © 2024 Scrivener Publishing LLC

through which tokens are created and managed on blockchain networks. Tokens are useful in a decentralised economy for a variety of reasons, including establishing ownership, granting access to resources, and facilitating faster transactions (Gan *et al.*, 2023) [7]. Because the tokens have the potential to act as an extension of and/or an alternative to native cryptocurrencies such as Bitcoin or as digital representations of real-world assets such as equities and real estate, it is essential to build systems for their supply, distribution, and governance (Creta and Tenca, 2021) [5]. Tokens that are constructed on blockchains can help enhance governance by giving token holders the power to participate in the decision-making and by ensuring that projects remain on track to satisfy their ESG objectives. In point of fact, tokenomics has the potential to enhance ESG reporting by providing data in real-time on the effects of various company assets or programmes (Mansouri and Momtaz, 2022) [18]. Circular business models are no longer unthinkable because of tokenomics, which enables organisations to issue tokens that can serve as proxies for ownership or usage rights. This development enables circular business models to become a reality. This has the ability to rapidly reduce unnecessary burdens and increase the efficiency of resource utilisation. The participation of token holders in a decentralised circular economy has the potential to make this paradigm more practicable.

In industries like supply chain management and logistics, where there is a need for accountability and traceability, having something like this is an absolute necessity (Jürjens *et al.*, 2022) [10]; (Kaur *et al.*, 2024) [14]. Tokens that represent carbon credits or certificates for sustainable products can assist in the monitoring and verification of a company's ESG obligations—this is possible for any type of business. Tokens, through the use of smart contracts, have the potential to automatically reward corporate partners and employees who support ESG goals, thereby encouraging more environmentally responsible behaviour. On top of that, a mechanism that strikes a healthy balance between security token offerings (STOs) and initial coin offerings (ICOs) would make it possible for environmentally conscious businesses to streamline the process of raising capital from investors who are interested in supporting environmentally responsible business practises. This could be used to further stimulate funding for environmental, social, and governance projects.

13.2 Opportunities Presented by Tokenomics

Simply put, tokenomics is the use of digital tokens to represent financial assets like carbon credits or green bonds. This method may facilitate greater transparency in sustainable finance by making it easier to manage and confirm the authenticity of sustainable investments. It would be to everyone's advantage if this openness boosted investor confidence in ESG-related assets. Participation in green projects can be facilitated by smart contracts for both individuals and businesses. Furthermore, they can inspire more eco-friendly company policies. Investors interested in environmentally responsible assets now face lower barriers to entry as a result of the democratisation of access to global markets made possible by the worldwide exchange of digital tokens (Freni *et al.*, 2022) [6]. Investing more money in environmentally friendly projects would be good for business and the planet. To put it succinctly, tokenomics has the potential to make a significant difference in the areas of environmental impact and carbon offsetting. Businesses will be able to better manage and keep track of operations that reduce their carbon footprint by buying and selling these tokens on blockchain networks, which will help in the fight against climate change.

The set of economic principles that govern digital tokens on blockchain networks has the potential to revolutionise the circular economy by fostering transparency, incentivising sustainable behaviour, making it possible to run circular-fashioned businesses, and improving resource management. This approach makes use of blockchain technology to achieve levels of visibility and tracking that were previously impossible throughout supply chains. Tokenomics encourages environmentally responsible practises by drawing the attention of consumers and businesses to these practises and by requiring producers to take responsibility for the environmental impact of their products (Gramoli *et al.*, 2022) [8]; (Amoussou-Guenou *et al.*, 2023) [2].

13.3 The "Economics" in Tokenomics

There is currently no widely accepted format for blockchain tokens. Rather than legally recognised rights, the economic worth of a token is determined by its claims, attributes, and abilities (functions). As a result, financial ties to the underlying company may boost digital token usage. Financial blockchain tokens are classified as payment tokens, utility tokens, or asset tokens by the Swiss Financial Market Supervisory Authority (FINMA, 2018) [20]. A token can be constructed to fall into more than one of these categories and execute any of the behaviours listed. According to FINMA, an asset token is any attempt to link a physical or digital item to a blockchain token, with or without a profit-sharing pledge: (1) tokens that are linked to a physical or digital asset, such as crypto-investment funds; and (2) tokens that promise to pay a percentage of earnings or revenue. The first term is an "asset" in the traditional sense, whereas the second term is a "yield" feature. Because both the "asset" and "yield" functions are binary, they are easily distinguished. The separation of utility and payment functions, however, must be formalised (Kampakis, 2018) [12]; (Lo and Medda, 2020) [16]. The technique is represented in the flowchart in Figure 13.1.

Tokenomics examines the monetary aspects of tokens and other digital assets that can be created, stored, and traded using blockchain technology. It combines elements of Bitcoin with traditional economics. Supply and demand, market efficiency, and utility maximisation are the bedrock principles of tokenomics (Lamberty *et al.*, 2023) [15]. Market demand, utility, and scarcity are all factors that contribute to a token's value; variables including network effects, user adoption, and token utility can all affect these factors. Various aspects of a token's design, including how it is issued, how it is used, how it is governed, how it is distributed, and whether or not it uses smart contracts or decentralised applications (dApps), all have a bearing on the ecosystem's economic dynamics (Malinova and Park,

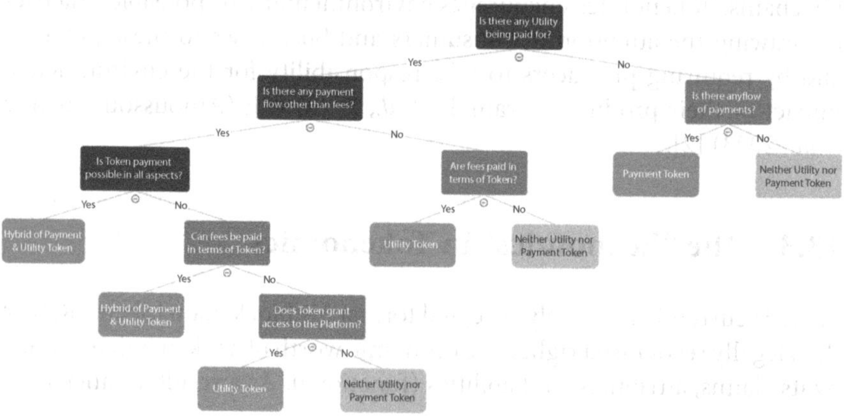

Figure 13.1 Identification of payment token vis-à-vis utility token. *Source*: Author's illustration, adapted from Lo and Medda (2020) [16].

2023) [17]. Tokens can create and capture value through network effects and economies of scale, but only if token distribution structures and incentives are well-designed (Au and Power, 2018) [3]. There are some legal and ethical concerns that arise when assets and financial instruments are tokenized, but ideally, these benefits outweigh the risks.

13.4 Challenges with Tokenomics

Tokenomics offers a chance for sustainable FinTech, but there are challenges to consider. It faces many challenges, including security issues, unclear legislation and regulatory environment, a lack of instructional and pedagogical materials, and scaling issues (Kampakis, 2018) [11]. Two regulatory and legal concerns are maintaining market integrity and striking a balance between innovation and consumer protection. Token ecosystems require market efficiency and stability to last, but scalability and interoperability are crucial for growing the ecosystem's overall benefit. Tokenomics can, however, be a driver for the adoption of ESG principles when utilised properly, creating a more moral and sustainable workplace.

To combat these issues and foster the development of a more efficient and sustainable circular economy, we can employ tools like stablecoins, interoperable standards, dialogue with regulatory authorities, incentive design, and privacy-enhancing technologies, which will be at the forefront of research and development in the near-circular future (Kampakis, 2018) [13]; (Wandmacher, 2020) [19]. In fact, tokenomics provides a fascinating nexus between economics and blockchain technology, giving us a unique opportunity to gain knowledge from this emerging subject. Finally, we must keep in mind that tokenomics is not a social sin, but an instrument for social transformation that must be employed ethically and within the bounds of the law. By solving issues and making use of existing legal frameworks, tokenomics can help create a more open and fair circular economic system.

13.5 Tokenomics in the Indian Context

Tokenomics' application of blockchain technology could revolutionise the delivery of public services in India. Tokens issued on a blockchain could reduce the potential for corruption and increase accountability in areas such as social welfare payments, electoral processes, and land registration. This has the potential to improve democratic processes and the efficiency with which government services are provided. In India, tokenomics has the potential to increase innovation and entrepreneurship by making it easier for start-ups and small businesses to have access to funding through decentralised ecosystems. To address problems and policy concerns, a thorough regulatory framework is necessary for execution. In addition to a solid digital infrastructure, technological readiness, education, and awareness are all necessary for widespread adoption. In order to safeguard user data and ensure constant data flow, India should prioritise adopting robust data privacy and security regulations. Tokenomics relies heavily on the confidentiality and safety of user data. It is important to strike a balance between users' right to privacy and the benefits of data accessibility if you want to win their trust (Kaur *et al.*, 2024) [14].

13.6 Conclusion

Overall, tokenomics may revolutionise our world for the better if more rational economic agents take the time to learn about it and apply its principles. It can facilitate financial inclusion, decentralisation, innovation, and transparency by opening up new avenues for funding and collaboration. However, the challenges and risks involved in doing so need to be discussed. To prevent harm to consumers and investors and to put an end to market manipulation, regulatory frameworks must be established.

References

1. Alexander, Carol, and Michael Dakos. "The new tokenomics of crowdfunding." *Br. J. Manag.*, 35.2 (2024): 644–662. https://doi.org/10.1111/1467-8551.12772.
2. Amoussou-Guenou, Y., Kiayias, A., Verdier, M., OASIcs, Volume 110, Tokenomics 2022, Complete Volume. *4th International Conference on Blockchain Economics, Security and Protocols (Tokenomics 2022)*, Schloss-Dagstuhl-Leibniz Zentrum für Informatik, 2023, https://doi.org/10.4230/OASIcs.Tokenomics.2022.0.
3. Au, S. and Power, T., *Tokenomics: The crypto shift of blockchains, ICOs, and tokens*, Packt Publishing Ltd, Birmingham, UK, 2018, https://www.packtpub.com/product/tokenomics/9781789136326.
4. Cong, L.W., Li, Y., Wang, N., Tokenomics: Dynamic adoption and valuation. *Rev. Financ. Stud.*, 34, 3, 1105–1155, 2021, https://doi.org/10.1093/rfs/hhaa089.

5. Creta, F. and Tenca, F., Tokenomics: A new opportunity in the Real Estate business? A qualitative approach to crowdfunding and blockchain interaction. *First Monday*, 26, 10, 1–30, 2021, https://doi.org/10.5210/fm.v26i10.10699.
6. Freni, P., Ferro, E., Moncada, R., Tokenomics and blockchain tokens: A design-oriented morphological framework. *Blockchain: Res. Appl.*, 3, 1, 100069, 2022, https://doi.org/10.1016/j.bcra.2022.100069.
7. Gan, J., Tsoukalas, G., Netessine, S., Decentralized platforms: Governance, tokenomics, and ICO design. *Manage. Sci.*, 69, 11, 6667–6683, 2023, https://doi.org/10.1287/mnsc.2021.02076.
8. Gramoli, V., Halaburda, H., Pass, R., OASIcs, Volume 97, Tokenomics 2021, Complete Volume. *3rd International Conference on Blockchain Economics, Security and Protocols (Tokenomics 2021)*, Schloss Dagstuhl-Leibniz-Zentrum für Informatik, 2022, https://doi.org/10.4230/OASIcs.Tokenomics.2021.0.
9. Grybniak, S. *et al.*, Waterfall: Salto Collazo. Tokenomics. *2022 IEEE International Conference on Blockchain, Smart Healthcare and Emerging Technologies (SmartBlock4Health)*, IEEE, 2022, https://doi.org/10.1109/SmartBlock4Health56071.2022.10034521.
10. Jürjens, J., Scheider, S., Yildirim, F., Henke, M., Tokenomics: Decentralized Incentivization in the Context of Data Spaces, in: *Designing Data Spaces*, B. Otto, M. ten Hompel, S. Wrobel, (Eds.), Springer, Cham, Switzerland, 2022, https://doi.org/10.1007/978-3-030-93975-5_6.
11. Kampakis, S., Three case studies in tokenomics. *J. Br. Blockchain Assoc.*, 1, 2, 79–82, 2018, https://doi.org/10.31585/jbba-1-2-(7)2018.
12. Kampakis, S., Why do we need Tokenomics? *J. Br. Blockchain Assoc.*, 1, 1, 1–2, 2018, https://doi.org/10.31585/jbba-1-1-(8)2018.
13. Kampakis, S., Auditing tokenomics: A case study and lessons from auditing a stablecoin project. *J. Br. Blockchain Assoc.*, 5, 2, 1–7, 2022, https://doi.org/10.31585/jbba-5-2-(1)2022.
14. Kaur, J., Kumar, S., Narkhede, B.E. *et al.* Barriers to blockchain adoption for supply chain finance: the case of Indian SMEs. *Electron. Commer. Res.*, 24, 303–340 (2024). https://doi.org/10.1007/s10660-022-09566-4.
15. Lamberty, R., de Waard, D., Poddey, A., Leading digital socio-economy to efficiency—A primer on tokenomics. *arXiv preprint arXiv:2008.02538*, 2020, https://doi.org/10.48550/arXiv.2008.02538.
16. Lo, Y.C. and Medda, F., Assets on the blockchain: An empirical study of Tokenomics. *Inf. Econ. Policy*, 53, 100881, 2020, https://doi.org/10.1016/j.infoecopol.2020.100881.
17. Malinova, K. and Park, A., Tokenomics: when tokens beat equity. *Manage. Sci.*, 69, 11, 6568–6583, 2023, https://doi.org/10.1287/mnsc.2023.4882.
18. Mansouri, S. and Momtaz, P.P., Financing sustainable entrepreneurship: ESG measurement, valuation, and performance. *J. Bus. Ventur.*, 37, 6, 106258, 2022, https://doi.org/10.1016/j.jbusvent.2022.106258.

19. Wandmacher, R.T., *Cryptofinance and Mechanisms of Exchange. Contributions to Management Science*, S. Goutte, K. Guesmi, S. Saadi (Eds.), Springer, Cham, Switzerland, 2019, https://doi.org/10.1007/978-3-030-30738-7_7.
20. FINMA, Guidelines for enquiries regarding the regulatory framework for initial coin offerings (ICOs), in: *Regulatory guidance, Swiss Financial Market Supervisory Authority*, 2018, https://www.finma.ch/en/~/media/finma/dokumente/dokumentencenter/myfinma/1bewilligung/fintech/wegleitung-ico.pdf?sc_lang=en&hash=83EE49D77DA54DD079F314D9EDCBDC3D.

14

Advancing Financial Inclusion through Digital Finance Innovations in Tanzania

Galinoma Gahele Lubawa[1*] and Vinay Kandpal D. Litt[2]

[1]*Department of Development Finance and Management Studies, Institute of Rural Development Planning (IRDP), Dodoma, Tanzania*
[2]*Department of Management Studies, Graphic Era Deemed to be University, Dehradun, Uttarakhand, India*

Abstract
This study aims to ascertain how digital finance may affect both small- and medium-scale enterprises and the agricultural sector's financial inclusion and support Tanzania's economic growth. A systematic review method was used through which the findings from studies published in academic journals are aggregated, integrated, and/or interpreted. It was found that digital financial services and inclusive finance in Tanzania could help SMEs and the agriculture sector by providing easy access to formal financial services, credit and insurance, different markets, market prices, and digital and financial literacy. The study recommended more focused research on informal finance, mobile banking, and the adoption of FinTech solutions in rural areas.

Keywords: FinTech, digital finance, financial services, financial literacy, mobile banking

14.1 Introduction

The financial technology or "FinTech" sector is rapidly transforming the global financial landscape, enabling more convenient access to financial services and promoting inclusive financial and economic development. Financial innovations such as mobile banking, mobile wallets, online

**Corresponding author*: galinoma@gmail.com; glubawa@irdp.ac.tz

Ernesto D.R. Santibanez Gonzalez, Vinay Kandpal, Peterson K. Ozili and Prasenjit Chatterjee (eds.) Fintech for ESG and the Circular Economy, (255–288) © 2024 Scrivener Publishing LLC

banking, electronic wallets, debit and credit cards, and other financial technologies enable people to use financial services to promote economic development and inclusive finance. Moreover, digital finance (DF) has transformed the way we interact, live, and work with the increased use of mobile phones and the Internet [1]. The term "digital finance" refers to the impacts of new technology on the financial services sector and encompasses products, services, technology, and/or infrastructure that offer access to payments, savings, and credit facilities via the Internet without having to visit a bank branch [2]. Digital financial services (DFS), which include online payments, money transfers, online shopping, digital marketing, online communication, and other e-business, are the engine for economic growth and the result of innovation in DF [3, 4].

According to Manyika *et al.* [5], by 2025, 1.6 billion people will have access to financial services in developing nations, with more than half of those people being women. For low-cost business transactions and partnerships to be possible, a global clientele's integration with a digital payment system has been essential [6]. Digital financial technology has enabled global financial inclusion and economic growth by streamlining all financial transactions and connecting everyone, urban and rural, to the established financial system. This has led to the development of financial products and services, significantly impacting sustainable economic growth [7, 8]. DF in India has the potential to support five key areas of business development, including access to finance, cost-effectiveness, financial literacy, financial inclusion, and creditworthiness. It has made financial services more accessible and affordable, enabling small businesses to access credit, promoting entrepreneurship and innovation, making financial literacy more accessible, and providing access to formal financial services for underserved and unbanked populations [9].

Additionally, according to Demirguc-Kunt *et al.* [10] and Klapper *et al.* [11], the inclusiveness of DFS is crucial to achieving the sustainable development goals (SDGs) for 2030. DF has considerably speed up the development of financial products and services, which in turn has affected sustainable economic growth by fostering inclusive finance and facilitating easier access to financial services internationally. By promoting inclusive finance, enabling more convenient access to financial services, and connecting everyone, urban and rural, to the established financial system, digital financial technology has contributed to the development of a new and effective business model that has significantly impacted sustainable economic development. This is important for achieving the 2030 Sustainable Development Goals of the United Nations. Generally, economic development is linked to inclusive growth, DFS, and inclusive finance [12]. Financial innovations such as "SureCash" have made it possible for persons with less financial resources to access the oligopolistic banking system [13]. Thanks to digital infrastructure, business, and integration, China's regional total factor productivity has also increased. These studies highlight the value of DFS and inclusive finance in fostering economic growth [14].

Innovation is a crucial driver of economic and social development globally [15], although developing countries have been found to do surprisingly little in terms of adopting, advanced-country experience to upgrade their products, technologies, and business processes, which is seen as a critical barrier to their growth [16]. DFS innovation has been identified as having significant potential for promoting the growth of the agriculture industry, financial services, and small and medium enterprises (SMEs) in developing countries. These sectors have traditionally been isolated from the traditional banking system due to being perceived as high-risk [17]. Therefore, DFS innovation is important for developing countries in promoting economic growth and creating more inclusive economies. By boosting financial inclusion and facilitating access to financial services for industries such as agriculture, financial services, and SMEs, DFS innovation plays a vital role in fostering economic growth and development. Applying new forms of innovation and digital economic growth is crucial to maintaining the viability of the SME sector [15, 16].

To promote financial inclusion, the Tanzanian government introduced the Comprehensive Financial Sector Development Plan (2020–2029/2030) and the National ICT Policy [18]. These policies aim to improve financial inclusion by encouraging the development of financial products and services on demand, increasing the development of affordable supplier channels, and increasing the capacity to promote and implement information and communication technology (ICT). Additionally, the Tanzania Commission for Science and Technology (COSTECH) was founded in 1986 as a parastatal organization to coordinate and support research and technology development operations in Tanzania. According to the TCRA Statistics Report of 2022 [19], Tanzania had 40.9 million mobile money accounts as of December 2022, which were managed by agents across both rural and urban areas [19]. Therefore, it appears that Tanzania is making efforts to improve its financial sector through digital technology, and the government has implemented policies to promote financial inclusion in the country.

According to the Bank of Tanzania's Annual Report in 2020 [20], digital platforms are being utilized in the financial sector to solve issues related to the consumption and accessibility of formal financial services and products. As of now, various digital payment channels are available, such as automated teller machines (ATMs), point-of-sale (POS) devices, mobile banking (SMS), and Internet banking [20]. This shows that Tanzania's financial sector is embracing digital transformation to enhance financial inclusion and to bring the unbanked population into the formal financial system. Tanzania's financial sector comprises financial service providers with various registration licenses, such as commercial banks, investment banks (mortgages), community banks, microfinance institutions (MFIs), insurance companies, pensioners, and savings and credit cooperative societies (SACCOs). Digital platforms have the potential to provide solutions for several financial inclusion issues in Tanzania, such as providing access to financial services and products. This could benefit low-income populations and other unserved populations who lack the resources or infrastructure to access traditional financial services.

Tanzania's financial sector has undergone significant development in the adoption and deployment of DFS, leading to improved financial inclusion and accessibility for many individuals. Mobile technologies have been at the forefront of Tanzania's digital transformation, with a high percentage of the population having mobile service registration. In 2018, 42% of the population was registered for mobile services, while TZS 50 trillion (US$22 billion), or almost half of the yearly GDP, was spent on mobile money transactions in 2017 [21].

The adoption of digital payment systems has also been on the rise in Tanzania. The volume of transactions increased by 6.08% to 233,182,627 in 2020 from 219,824,409 in the previous year, while the value of transactions increased by 27.57% to TZS 126,441.33 billion. The Bank of Tanzania's regulatory initiatives, such as raising mobile money transactions and balance limitations, have contributed to the development of the usage of DFS, including mobile money, the Internet, and mobile banking [20]. According to Kagoya and Mbamba [21], the deployment of mobile network operators (MNOs) in previously financially excluded areas of the country has increased the adult population's financial inclusion in Tanzania to 65%. The study also revealed a rise in mobile wallet usage, with over 21 million active wallets being used by 16.6 million Tanzanian individuals. Banking organizations have been offering payment services on cutting-edge digital platforms, making them more accessible and convenient.

Tanzania's DFS has expanded from being available only for buying airtime, sending money, and depositing and withdrawing cash to include a wide range of services. Various companies in Tanzania now provide services such as remittances, digital savings, digital lending, and microinsurance

[21]. Therefore, Tanzania's financial sector has made significant progress in the adoption and deployment of DFS, improving financial inclusion and accessibility for many individuals. Mobile technologies have played a significant role in Tanzania's digital transformation, and digital payment systems have increased due to regulatory initiatives of the Bank of Tanzania.

Tanzania has made significant progress in the adoption and deployment of digital technology. However, there are still challenges that need to be addressed for DF to realize its potential in Tanzania. Among the challenges include uncertainty and lack of transparency over tax systems, where changes to the tax system, including the introduction of new taxes, discourage Tanzanians from spending on digital services [22]. The rise of digital services in Tanzania has also led to an increase in cybercrime. The rise of digital services has exposed Tanzania to cybersecurity threats, such as fraudulent activities, hackers, and cyber terrorists [23]. Cybercriminals target individuals and businesses, making it difficult for them to trust and use digital services.

Moreover, the lack of knowledge among mobile banking users, insufficient mobile money agents, breakdown of ATMs, high digital transaction costs, and network failures are major challenges facing the DF sector in Tanzania [24, 25]. Mwakatumbula *et al.* [26] found that a lack of trust in DFS and limited access to mobile phones and agents were significant barriers to DF adoption in Tanzania. Another study by Nkonya *et al.* [27] highlighted the need for improved regulation and infrastructure to support DF growth in Tanzania.

The study outlined that even though Tanzania is about to adopt digital technologies, more research is still needed for Tanzania to learn from wealthy countries such as China and India. Its purpose is to address current problems, advance technology, and create new uses for technology in various industries to support sustainable development and improve financial inclusion [28].

Due to the benefits of DF and financial inclusion for financial service users, DF providers, governments, and the economy as well as increasing access to finance among poor people, reducing the cost of financial mediation for banks and FinTech providers, and increasing overall spending by the government, this study explores the contribution of DF in promoting inclusive finance in Tanzania and presents a theoretical discussion on how DF plays a significant role in building inclusive finance in Tanzania. To explain how digital technology could support Tanzania's economic growth, this study will adopt a systematic review method of qualitative sampling through which the findings from qualitative studies published in academic journals are aggregated, integrated, and/or interpreted. The published studies come from different disciplines, such as information technology, business, finance, marketing, E-government, and financial technology.

The methodology used to write this article is simple. First, the items included in this review should start from 2015, as per the methodology for reviewing various research publications. Second, the papers selected for peer review must be published as analytical studies, empirical studies, government reports, reports of international organizations (e.g., World Bank, United Nations), policy discussion papers, or relevant working papers. Third, the most recent research publications reviewed included extensive research on DFS, financial inclusion and its benefits as a key research topic, or links between financial inclusion and other related economic developments. Finally, articles were selected that dealt with increased financial inclusion due to DFS in areas of national importance, such as SME development, financial systems, agriculture, and rural development. These sectors are the foundation for Tanzania's growth as a middle-income country. Various studies from FinTech-developed countries such as China and India were reviewed and analyzed to achieve the research objectives.

Digital Financial Services Framework and Applicability in Tanzania

The Tanzanian government has taken significant steps to enhance DFS as part of its efforts to promote inclusive finance and reduce poverty. The implementation of the Financial Sector Development Master Plan (2020–2029–2030) has been instrumental in advancing financial inclusion by focusing on the development of affordable and demand-driven financial products and services, expanding distributor channels, and strengthening the utilization of ICT in the financial sector. The National Financial Inclusion Framework (NFIF) also played a crucial role, with the second phase running from 2018 to 2022 and the first phase spanning from 2014 to 2016. During the first phase, infrastructure was established to facilitate access to financial services for Tanzanians. The accomplishments of phase one include increasing the proportion of individuals utilizing formal financial services from 58% in 2013 to 65% in 2017, as well as reducing the number of adults relying solely on informal financial services from 16% to 7% during the same period [29].

The Bank of Tanzania introduced the Tanzania Instant Payments System (TIPS) in June 2020, which serves as a collaborative payment platform for digital financial providers in the country. TIPS enables real-time fund transfers between different banking and non-banking entities, promoting cooperation and enhancing access to financial services in Tanzania. The system facilitates efficient clearing and settlement of digital financial activities, leading to improved effectiveness and efficiency in the payment ecosystem. The adoption of digital technologies in Tanzania has transformed the financial sector, particularly in rural areas where traditional banking services are limited. By embracing DF systems, Tanzania has not only expanded financial services but also enhanced productivity and efficiency across various industries, such as banking, agriculture, trade, and governance. Research studies have highlighted the significant role of DFS in promoting inclusive finance and driving economic growth. Tanzania's commitment to ICT transformation aligns with the global consensus on the importance of DFS in achieving development objectives, including poverty alleviation and economic advancement [30–32].

The banking industry in Tanzania has embraced electronic banking services, including ATMs, Internet banking, mobile banking, and electronic fund transfers, to enhance customer access and convenience [33]. The country has also implemented a web-based Government Security System (GSS) for online bidding and central depository transactions, improving collateral management and ownership transfer [34]. In the agricultural sector, the adoption of digital technologies has led to increased crop yields, improved income for smallholder farmers, and facilitated efficient transactions along the value chain [22, 35]. Digital technologies have significantly impacted Tanzania's economic and social development, contributing approximately US$2.5 billion to the GDP and creating employment opportunities for approximately 1.5 million people [22]. Furthermore, the Tanzanian government has leveraged e-government services, such as the Government Portal and Government Electronic Payment Gateway (GePG), to improve communication, payment collection, and reporting systems across public institutions [36]. These initiatives have enhanced efficiency and service delivery to the general public.

This study's main objective is to ascertain how DF may affect SMEs and agriculture financial inclusion and support Tanzania's economic growth. A deeper understanding of digital technology and its effects can help promote DF use for society and middle-income countries. The following phases of Tanzania's growth of inclusive finance are thus described in this study, together with the significance and influence of financial technology on the development of inclusive finance, after examining the findings of relevant studies. Several papers from developed FinTech nations, including India, China, and third-world countries that are using digital technology to hasten their development, have been evaluated and analyzed to fulfill the research objectives.

14.2 Literature Review

14.2.1 Digital Finance

The term "digital finance" encompasses the widespread digitalization of financial services. It refers to providing payments, savings, and credit facilities through Internet-based platforms without visiting a bank branch [2]. The terms "Internet finance," "financial technology (FinTech)," and "digital finance" are used interchangeably across the globe [3, 4]. A cross-disciplinary field known as FinTech integrates finance, technology management, and innovation management. It is a technological application that aids in offering financial solutions. FinTech encompasses all conventional financial services and products, not only those in specific industries (such as the banking industry) or business models (such as peer-to-peer lending) [37]. The realm of FinTech services includes mobile and Internet banking, Mobile money offered by MNOs, third-party payment solutions, direct financial sales, mobile app-based services, online insurance, and other financial services such as ATMs, bill payment, and money transfer [7, 38, 39]. DF has made financial services more accessible, efficient, and affordable, especially for those who were underserved by the traditional financial system. This has emerged as a major driver of inclusive finance, often referred to as the Internet finance industry [2].

14.2.2 Inclusive Finance

Financial exclusion is the lack of access to suitable formal financial services, affecting a significant portion of the global population [40]. It primarily affects marginalized groups such as the poor, individuals with lower education levels, the unemployed or impoverished, women, elderly individuals, those living in rural areas, and racial or religious minorities [10, 40].

In response to this problem, the idea of blanket financing has emerged, taking into account the different difficulties faced by different countries and regions [37, 41]. Inclusive finance strives to provide accessible financial services to all members of society, regardless of their economic status [42]. It is about making a range of financial products and services affordable, especially for those who are not part of the established financial system [42]. According to Demirguc-Kunt *et al.* [10] and Grohmann *et al.* [43], the financial inclusion index includes savings, formal institutional accounts, borrowing, and insurance.

Rural communities greatly benefit from inclusive finance since it allows them to conduct financial transactions, defend themselves against common dangers, and put money aside for their families and enterprises [44]. Inclusive finance seeks to empower all people and businesses, especially those historically underserved, by increasing access to financial services [42].

14.2.3 The Role of Digital Finance in Enabling Inclusive Financing

DF increases access to financial services and encourages financial inclusion, making it easier and more affordable for disadvantaged people. DF, including FinTech, is known to support (SDGs), such as "SDG 1: No Poverty," "SDG 8: Decent Work and Economic Growth," and "SDG 10: Reduced Inequalities." These goals encompass objectives such as poverty reduction, income inequality reduction, and financial inclusion [2, 37, 40, 45].

DF development has led to various DFS, such as crowdfunding, online banking, online insurance, and direct money selling [7, 38]. Commercial banks, financial institutions, credit institutions, and other organizations provide these services. The development of DFS has enabled members of low-income regions, previously excluded from the formal financial system, to participate. They now have access to legal alternatives to informal financial services such as relying on family members, friends, revolving savings accounts, lenders, or hiding money at home. These informal methods are frequently illegal, unreliable, and expensive and have limited the potential for fiscal expansion [2, 37].

Agriculture technology has greatly benefited agriculture in developing countries, especially in terms of increased access to agricultural products. According to the Food and Agriculture Organization (FAO), Nigeria's agribusiness has evolved thanks to technology and its support [46]. The country's 70.8 million hectares of arable land are mainly used to grow maize, cassava, guinea fowl, yam, millet, and rice [46]. Technology, especially network technology (IT), has improved smallholder farmers' access to financial and agricultural services. This technology has reduced information asymmetries and enhanced market access for inputs and commodities. The introduction and use of digital financial technologies, such as digital lending, which rapidly provides remote microcredit through digital channels, have increased the profitability of smallholder farmers in sub-Saharan Africa [47]. The introduction of mobile phone and Internet technology (MPITU) has helped farmers in rural Pakistan to become economically successful, with MPITU impacting agricultural profitability and significantly increasing the efficiency of channel selection [48].

Digital technology has significantly aided the development of China's agriculture sector. China's rural economy has changed, and farmers have more influence due to the adoption of mobile Internet and digital solutions. The development of e-commerce platforms that let farmers run their own Internet businesses is a significant factor. The mobile Internet has offered employment opportunities in rural regions by enabling farmers to use digital platforms to sell their goods directly to consumers [49]. To access a broader market and boost their revenue, Chinese fruit growers, for instance, switched from using conventional techniques to selling online [49]. China has also implemented initiatives to promote digital agriculture and e-commerce in rural areas. The "Broadband Village" project aimed to improve Internet access, increase Internet speed, and reduce tariffs for farmers [50]. This has resulted in increased grain output, reaching 60 million tons in 2012 and 65 million tons for six consecutive years between 2015 and 2020 [51].

In addition to market connectivity, Agritech (agricultural technology) improvements in India have been facilitated by digital breakthroughs in addition to market linkages. By 2020–2021 alone, approximately US$500 million had been invested in Agritech start-ups across the nation [49]. The availability of digital tools and technology in fields, including precision agriculture, crop monitoring, farm management systems, and weather forecasting, has enabled farmers to access real-time information and make data-driven decisions [52].

Digital FinTech is also an important tool for expanding SMEs in developing countries. Social media platforms offer small businesses an efficient way to engage with consumers, promote their products, and build their brands [53]. Technology has transformed the business models of Saudi SMEs and helped them manage strategic change. For Tanzanian SMEs, digital technology can be an important tool for business expansion and sustainable economic development. According to Kagermann and Wahlster [54], global efforts to promote sustainability, resource conservation, and efficiency gains should be aided by digitization.

14.2.4 Theoretical Background

The conceptual framework of the study emphasizes the importance of financial services offered through various financial innovations in fostering equitable funding. With the introduction of new technology, accessing financial services and products remotely is feasible without going to a bank in person. These digital financial solutions help SMEs, rural investments, and rural companies grow by enhancing financial access for those who lack it. This is consistent with other research that has highlighted the contribution of DFS to the advancement of inclusive finance [55].

System integration is enabled by DF, which encompasses various financial operations, including investments, payments, insurance, and financial advice. Financial institutions worldwide rely on instant mobile applications, cellular networks, POS, ATMs, mobile embedded systems, image processing, cloud computing, and other services to take advantage of numerous technological advances. Data analysis [2, 56] draws on these conclusions by explaining how digital financial inclusion systems work and highlighting the critical role that governments, financial technology, and banks play in promoting inclusive finance and reducing poverty. We provide further evidence to support the idea that for inclusive finance to be successful, system integration requires cooperation between governments, FinTech providers, and financial institutions.

Because DF offers more convenience and affordability than traditional banking services, low-income and underprivileged people in developing nations can benefit from the formal financial system through savings and borrowing. According to recent research, if the excluded group has access to a mobile phone and reasonably priced Internet connectivity, the availability of digital banking may help promote financial inclusion. This suggests a beneficial correlation between the use of digital money and access to formal financial services. The framework highlights the potential influence of digital money on increasing financial access and supporting inclusive finance for underserved communities. As shown in Figure 14.1 of their research, Hasan *et al.* [57] provided a framework that explains how DF impacts inclusive finance.

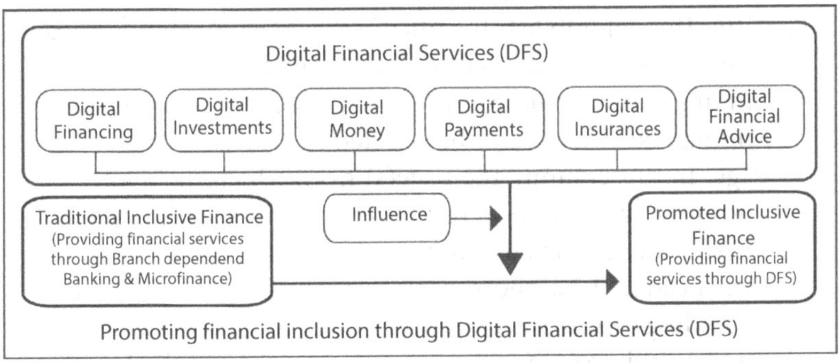

Figure 14.1 Promoting financial inclusion through Digital Financial Services (DFS). Source: Hasan *et al.* [57].

14.3 Research Methods

The study in question used a systematic review methodology and an inductive ontological analysis of published research articles to assess the implications of DF on inclusive finance, FinTech, Internet financing, and mobile financing. The study focused on advanced, middle-income, and developing countries such as China and India. The research protocol was designed by Milian *et al.* [30] and Hasan *et al.* [57, 58] to ensure the study's repeatability and adherence to the defined methodology. A systematic literature review follows a precise and repeatable approach and provides a detailed summary of primary research, including aims, materials, and methods [59]. This study's objective was to better understand how DF impacts inclusive finance globally, focusing on disadvantaged populations in developing countries [60].

14.3.1 Planning the Review

Prior to initiating the search strategy, the authors employed a systematic approach to plan, organize, and identify relevant literature using a conceptual Excel spreadsheet. This spreadsheet served as a literature roadmap and facilitated the inclusion or exclusion of literature systematically, ensuring conceptual saturation across various research and discipline databases [59]. The conceptual Excel spreadsheet was designed in a user-friendly format with several columns.

1. Concept: This column lists the main ideas or topics of major themes specific to the literature review.
2. Citation: This column contains the full citations of all selected articles, books, book chapters, or reports.
3. Title: This column lists the titles of the selected articles, book chapters, or reports, along with their publication year.
4. Findings*:* This column served as a space to document the findings extracted from the selected materials.
5. Page*:* In this column, the page(s) from which the quotes or findings were derived were recorded. It allowed for referencing specific sections within the selected sources.
6. Conclusion: The authors' decisions regarding the utilization of findings from selected peer-reviewed articles are indicated in this column. It provided a record of whether the findings were considered for inclusion or exclusion in the literature review.

By utilizing this systematic approach and the conceptual Excel spreadsheet, the authors could effectively manage and evaluate the relevant literature for their research. This method ensured a comprehensive and structured literature review process.

14.3.2 Search Strategy

The primary goal of this study was to determine, via the use of secondary data and an interpretive methodology [61], how DF has affected inclusive finance. To find relevant publications, the researchers used a variety of platforms, including Web of Science, Scopus, Science Direct, Google Scholar, Springer Link, World Bank databases, and ResearchGate. In addition, they looked for credible journals such as Wiley, Sage, Elsevier, Emerald, Springer, Taylor & Francis, and African Journal Online (AJOL), among others. Due to their dependability and proven knowledge, particular peer-reviewed journal papers were chosen since they have a substantial influence on the area. However, because peer review procedures vary, the research left out books, book chapters, and conference materials.

The study used a variety of search techniques to guarantee a thorough search and to find more pertinent publications. The reviews included [2], [39], [55], [58], [62]. A review of Tanzanian papers on digital inclusion and finance was performed after worldwide literature studies. To comprehend Tanzania's development in financial technology, government publications such as the National Financial Inclusion Framework (NFIF) [29], Financial Sector Development Plan (2020/21–2029/2030) [63], and FinScope Tanzania (2017) [64] were also reviewed. However, it should be highlighted that neither the inclusive finance database nor the Tanzanian DF database is presented as widely accessible as other financial databases or as comprehensive. As a result, information for this study was compiled from a number of sources, including official records.

The study used a systematic literature review process that involved reading and rereading papers iteratively to find themes. This procedure maintained theme classification and concordance while upholding consistency both inside and between these categories. All factors pertaining to online finance, online banking, mobile money, inclusive finance, digital investing, digital payments, and digital FinTech were considered during the investigation. Figure 14.2's depiction of a research framework demonstrates the study's methodical approach.

In this study, the authors systematically reviewed the literature on DFS and integrated finance, explicitly focusing on their connection to various aspects of economic development. To identify relevant papers,

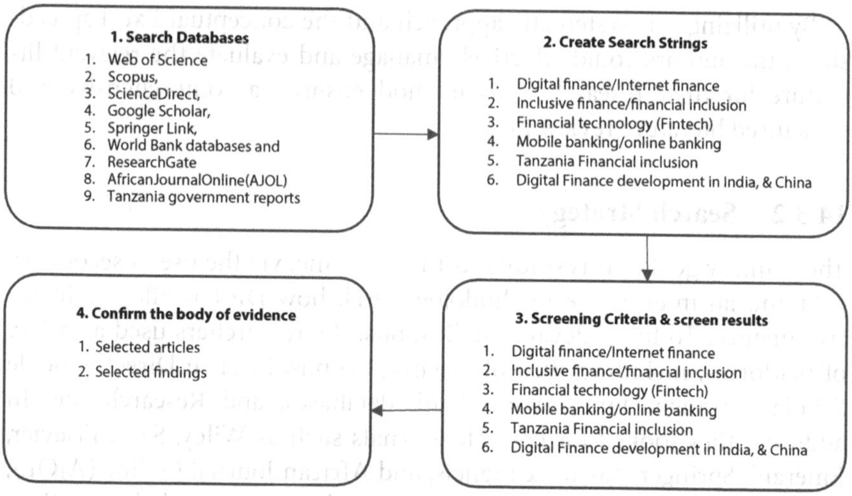

Figure 14.2 A research framework highlighting the study's systematic method (Source: Authors' explanation).

they utilized multiple databases, such as Web of Science, Scopus, Science Direct, Google Scholar, Springer Link, World Bank databases, and ResearchGate. The selection process considered papers published from 2015 onwards and categorized them as analytical or empirical studies, government reports, reports from international bodies such as the World Bank or UN, policy discussion papers, or related working papers. The study aimed to include a diverse range of studies that explored the main topics of financial inclusion, its benefits, and the links between financial inclusion and other relevant areas of economic development.

The final selection of articles focused on the expansion of financial inclusion resulting from DFS in key sectors for Tanzania's development, such as SME growth, agriculture, the industrial sector, and financial system development. These sectors are crucial for Tanzania's progress toward becoming a middle-income country. To gather insights from a broader perspective, the authors also examined and analyzed studies from developed FinTech nations such as China, India, and third-world countries.

In addition to the selection process, the researchers employed a self-judgmental strategy to identify significant articles and summarized each one in an Excel sheet for future reference. The same criteria used to collect data from various articles were also applied to analyze the study's target variables. The comprehensive findings from past research are presented in Table 14.1 of the study.

Table 14.1 The findings of some previous studies.

Reference	Location	Aim of the study	Type of source	Main findings
[57]	China	This study presents a theoretical argument about how DFS will be important in promoting China's inclusive finance.	Theoretical paper	How DFS leads to promote inclusive finance in China.
[65]	India	Assessing the context of digital agriculture in India.	Working paper series	It was discovered that low-cost technology, portable hardware that is simple to use, pay-per-use rental models, regulatory backing, and the effective utilization of farmer collectives are crucial for the development of digital agriculture in India.
[66]	India	This article aims to offer an overview of various digital agriculture solutions available in India and to discuss their experiences.	Report	Farmers require timely, accurate information tailored to their location and conditions to maximize resources under changing conditions. Digital technologies bridge the information gap, improve market information, microfinance, pest and disease management guidance, and agriculture human resources. Digital efforts need the right rules, structures, ecosystems, and capacities. This article highlights successful digital interventions, value-chain improvements, and capacity-building to improve farm stakeholders' livelihoods.

(*Continued*)

Table 14.1 The findings of some previous studies. (*Continued*)

Reference	Location	Aim of the study	Type of source	Main findings
[67]	Rural Europeans	This study aims to provide a method for clarifying difficulties and thinking about the potential effects of digitalization. Problematization processes, which are part of responsible research and innovation principles, can open up new spheres of accountability and inform governance actions to shape future agricultural and food systems in rural regions.	Theoretical paper	The framework fosters reflexivity, informs the definition of social responsibility (i.e., moral obligations and accountability), and helps problematize prospective digitization and digitalization repercussions (i.e., anticipation).
[68]	Low- and middle-income countries (LMICs)	To provide lessons, experiences, and proposals on digital finance and inclusion during COVID-19.	Research report	FinTech has the potential to expand and innovate in response to global crises as new digital financial solutions are designed and implemented to meet the demand for individualized, more advanced, but still accessible financial services from crisis-affected populations.

(*Continued*)

Table 14.1 The findings of some previous studies. (*Continued*)

Reference	Location	Aim of the study	Type of source	Main findings
[69]	International	Providing information on the status of digital technology in rural and agricultural areas worldwide.	Research report	The digitalization of agriculture is expected to significantly change farming and food production in the upcoming years. However, there is a potential for a digital divide due to disparities in access to digital technologies and services. This could lead to a lack of productivity, economic and social integration, e-literacy, and access to digital resources for rural populations, especially smallholder farmers.
[69]	Developing countries	The study examined recent research on related technological effects on the rural sector in developing countries.	Theoretical paper	Digital technologies overcome information problems that hinder market access for many small-scale farmers and increase knowledge through new extension services.
[70]	Latin America and the Caribbean	The report examines the need to move toward a sustainable digital society within the framework of the systemic impact of disruption. It also examines the relationship between digitalization and productivity and its effect on agriculture, manufacturing, and services production chains.	Research report	The digital revolution presents a significant chance to increase agricultural output and sophistication. Farmers can produce more effectively and provide long-lasting climate change solutions using digital technologies.

(*Continued*)

Table 14.1 The findings of some previous studies. (*Continued*)

Reference	Location	Aim of the study	Type of source	Main findings
[71]	Africa, Asia, and Latin America	This report examines 92 m-ARD apps in Africa, Asia, Latin America and the Caribbean, and Africa for their impact, ecosystems, and business models. It aims to help policymakers and development practitioners understand how these applications can be used to enhance services for rural citizens.	Research report (Case studies)	Residents in developing nations could get dynamic, transdisciplinary, and creative services using mobile applications for agricultural and rural development (m-ARD apps).
[72]	Sub-Saharan Africa	This report highlighted how digital technologies have the power to change the agricultural industry and, consequently, the standard of living in sub-Saharan Africa.	Research report	Multiple undersea cables connect to Sub-Saharan Africa. It is necessary to give the connection to these cables priority to increase broadband access for both coastal and landlocked nations. National mobile broadband backbones that connect urban and rural areas can be used in addition to undersea connections.

(*Continued*)

Table 14.1 The findings of some previous studies. (*Continued*)

Reference	Location	Aim of the study	Type of source	Main findings
[73]	47 sub-Saharan African countries	Digital agriculture is being developed through six themes (infrastructure, digital penetration, policy and regulation, business environment, human capital, and agro-innovation) supported by indicators to understand its maturity at national and regional levels.	Research report	The report's findings indicate that using digital technology in sub-Saharan Africa will hasten the region's agriculture sector's competitiveness and support the growth of the nation's digital economy.
[74]	Asian countries	An overview of the use of FinTech in agriculture.	Theoretical paper	The report emphasizes the importance of DFS in the agricultural sector, stressing its ability to advance financial inclusion, improve access to formal financial services, and foster inclusive economic growth.

14.4 Results and Discussions

14.4.1 DFS's Importance to SMEs and Inclusive Finance in Tanzania

Technology, such as DFS, is essential for the growth of inclusive finance globally. Similar to their effects in China and India, DFS can significantly impact Tanzania's expansion of inclusive finance. Through online banking, mobile payment systems, and other cutting-edge financial services, DFS has enabled banks, credit unions, and other financial institutions to access underserved and previously unreachable people, particularly in rural areas. This has made financial inclusion viable in India and China [57, 65].

Therefore, digital technology is essential for fostering financial inclusion in Tanzania and aiding the expansion of SMEs. It can offer opportunities for personal empowerment and lowers financial sector risks and costs. By leveraging technology and digital platforms, DF initiatives have the potential to reach underserved populations, particularly those in rural and remote areas. It also contributes to economic growth by lowering financial sector risks and costs and exceeding conventional financial trading alternatives [68]. Here are some ways in which DF supports SMEs' financial inclusion in Tanzania:

Access to Formal Financial Service: Digital technology gives SMEs access to a variety of financial services, such as digital banking, mobile payments, and online lending platforms. Thanks to digital platforms, SMEs can quickly create and manage bank accounts, send and receive digital payments, and obtain credit facilities. They can develop their business activities and manage their money more effectively.

Cost-Effective Transactions: For SMEs, digital technology provides an affordable alternative to conventional financial transactions. Mobile payment solutions and digital wallets allow businesses to interact safely and rapidly without real currency or expensive payment infrastructure. This lowers transaction costs, removes the possibility of theft, and streamlines company processes.

Access to Credit: The rise of peer-to-peer lending networks and online lending platforms has been aided by digital technology. These platforms give SMEs access to finance that is unavailable through conventional banking channels by utilizing digital data and cutting-edge credit evaluation techniques. SMEs may rapidly and easily acquire finance through digital lending platforms depending on the success of their businesses and creditworthiness.

Market Access and E-commerce: Digital technology allows SMEs to create an online presence and participate in e-commerce platforms. As a result, their market reach transcends geographical boundaries, allowing them to engage with local and international clients. By embracing e-commerce, SMEs may expand their consumer base, boost revenues, and expand their operations.

Business Productivity and Efficiency: Enterprise resource planning (ERP) systems, cloud computing, digital marketing, and other digital technology tools assist SMEs in streamlining their operations, increasing productivity, and improving decision-making. SMEs can securely store and share data, work with distant teams, and access company information from anywhere at any time thanks to cloud-based storage and collaboration solutions.

Financial Education and Literacy: Digital technology offers platforms for imparting financial education and literacy to SMEs. SME owners may learn about financial management, investment strategies, and business planning through online tools, webinars, and mobile applications. By increasing their financial literacy, SMEs can make wise financial decisions, manage their money well, and access the right financial products and services.

Data-Driven Insights: The massive volumes of data produced by digital technology may be evaluated to learn more about consumer behavior, market trends, and company performance. To comprehend client preferences, spot development prospects, and make data-driven business decisions, SMEs can make use of data analytics solutions. This enables SMEs to improve their goods and services, increase consumer engagement, and maintain market competition.

In Tanzania, digital technology significantly supports SMEs' growth and financial inclusion. Digital technology gives SMEs the tools to succeed in the digital economy and advance the nation's economy by facilitating access to financial services, lowering transaction costs, allowing e-commerce, and enhancing corporate efficiency.

14.4.2 DFS's Importance to Agriculture and Inclusive Finance in Tanzania

DFS is essential to Tanzania's efforts to boost agriculture and advance inclusive financing. DFS helps the agricultural industry by giving farmers access to financial services, enabling digital transactions, improving market access, and providing specialized loans and insurance products. Additionally, the supply of financial education and the integration of financial services with digital agricultural platforms support the nation's general expansion and advancement of inclusive finance. Here are some key ways in which DFS contributes to the development of agriculture and inclusive finance:

Access to Financial Services: DFS makes financial services available to farmers and other agricultural stakeholders, especially in distant locations with weak traditional banking infrastructure. Farmers may conveniently create and manage accounts, conduct transactions, and access a variety of financial services, including savings, loans, and insurance using mobile banking and digital wallets. This allows them to obtain the funds required for agricultural activity and adequately manage their finances.

Digital Transfers and Mobile Payments: DFS makes it possible for farmers to undertake digital transfers and mobile payments. Due to its risk and inconvenience, especially in rural regions, cash transactions are less frequently used as a result. Agribusiness stakeholders, including buyers, suppliers, and other members of the agricultural value chain, may deal with farmers securely and conveniently by paying them for their produce straight into their digital accounts.

Access to Credit and Insurance: Credit and insurance services suited to farmers' requirements are increasingly integrated into DFS platforms. DFS providers may evaluate creditworthiness and provide farmers with quick and specialized credit solutions by utilizing digital data, such as transaction history and farming operations. The same goes for agriculture insurance policies, which shield farmers from a variety of hazards, such as crop failure, natural catastrophes, and market volatility.

Market Information and Price Transparency: DFS systems may provide farmers with real-time market information, assisting them in selecting crops, setting prices, and gaining access to markets. Farmers may receive updates on market pricing, weather, agricultural operations, and best practices through mobile applications, SMS alerts, or voice-based services. Their capacity to negotiate fair rates, reduce postharvest losses, and increase profitability is improved.

Digital Agriculture Platforms: DFS providers and agricultural technology firms are rapidly creating digital platforms that combine financial services with information and services related to agriculture. These platforms provide farmers with one digital ecosystem's worth of resources, including advisors, suppliers of agri-inputs, extension services, and markets. These platforms improve efficiency, lower transaction costs, and provide farmers with better access to markets and resources by digitizing the agricultural value chain.

Financial Literacy and Competency: DFS platforms may also be used as a means of obtaining programs for farmers that will help them develop their financial literacy and competence. Farmers may access instructional materials on money management, saving, investing, and risk reduction using mobile applications, interactive SMS campaigns, or voice-based services. They obtain a superior financial understanding, which enables them to choose more wisely how to finance their agricultural endeavors.

Data Analytics and Decision Support: By digitizing financial transactions, DFS creates useful data that can be studied to learn more about the requirements, issues, and behaviors of farmers. Policymakers, financial institutions, and agricultural stakeholders may build inclusive financial products, establish targeted interventions, and optimize resource allocation by utilizing data analytics to enhance agricultural growth and financial inclusion.

14.4.3 Challenges in Promoting Inclusive Finance in Tanzania

Tanzania still has a number of obstacles in digital technology despite the success of the ITC policy's implementation, which aimed to encourage the use of technology and raise the degree of financial inclusion. The following are some of the challenges:

14.4.3.1 Challenges in Promoting SMEs Inclusive Finance in Tanzania

In Tanzania, there are a number of challenges to promoting inclusive finance for SMEs. Small- and medium-sized businesses (SMEs) may face difficulties that impede expansion and reduce access to financial services. Among the principal challenges are:

Limited Access to Financial Services: Many SMEs in Tanzania have trouble accessing formal financial services because of the country's limited financial infrastructure. The majority work in the unorganized sector and do not have the supporting documents, credit histories, or collateral required by conventional banking institutions. Therefore, their capacity to obtain loans, insurance, and other financial goods is limited.

Lack of Financial Literacy and Awareness: SME owners and entrepreneurs have very low levels of financial literacy. SMEs struggle to make the most of the financial resources they have access to because they lack sufficient understanding of financial management, investment plans, and the advantages of formal financial services. The poor uptake of inclusive finance among SMEs is partly attributed to a lack of knowledge about the financial products and services that are offered.

Inadequate Collateral and Credit History: SMEs frequently struggle to offer adequate collateral or have a strong credit history, which are crucial considerations financial institutions take into account when considering loan applications. This makes it difficult for SMEs to acquire finance at reasonable rates since they could be viewed as high-risk borrowers. They cannot invest in business development, buy new equipment, or launch creative projects because they have limited access to loans.

High Interest Rates and Cost of Credit: When SMEs in Tanzania seek formal financial services, they frequently encounter high interest rates and processing fees. This is explained by both the perceived risk connected to lending to SMEs and the overhead expenses borne by financial institutions. Due to the high cost of credit, SMEs may be forced to turn to unofficial or self-reliant sources of funding, which may restrict their ability to develop.

Lack of Technology Infrastructure: Limited access to dependable Internet connectivity, digital infrastructure, and technological tools may make it more difficult for SMEs to adopt digital financial solutions. Without the required technology, SMEs may have trouble adopting DFS such as mobile banking, digital payments, or online lending platforms. This may limit their capacity to take advantage of DF's simplicity and efficiency.

Environment of Regulation and Policy: Tanzania's regulatory and policy framework may make it challenging to encourage inclusive financing for SMEs. Lack of transparency and lengthy bureaucratic procedures, together with complex and restrictive rules, might prevent SMEs from receiving financial services. Inadequate legislative frameworks that do not focus on SMEs' requirements and encourage inclusive financing may restrict the creation of suitable financial goods and services.

Limited Collaboration and Support Ecosystem: A lack of coordination and collaboration among stakeholders, including financial institutions, governmental organizations, development organizations, and SME support groups, may hinder the promotion of inclusive finance. When navigating the financial system and gaining access to the resources they need to expand their operations, SMEs may find it difficult to obtain enough help and direction.

To overcome these difficulties, a number of parties—including the government, financial institutions, SME support organizations, and development partners—must cooperate. Actions must be taken to increase financial literacy, streamline loan application processes, build cutting-edge credit assessment models, advance digital infrastructure, and create hospitable regulatory environments to promote inclusive finance for SMEs and unleash their growth potential in Tanzania.

14.4.3.2 *Challenges in Promoting Agriculture and Inclusive Finance in Tanzania*

There are a number of obstacles to promoting inclusive financing in Tanzania's agriculture industry that might impede its expansion and development. Several significant difficulties include the following:

Limited Access to Financial Services: Farmers and other agricultural stakeholders sometimes have trouble accessing formal banking services, especially those who live in remote regions. Farmers find it challenging to obtain banking services, credit, insurance, and other financial goods due to the absence of physical bank branches and other financial infrastructure in rural regions. This restricts their capacity to invest in their farms, buy inputs, and properly manage hazards.

Limited Credit Availability: The majority of Tanzania's small-scale farmers lack the collateral necessary to get loans, making it difficult for them to obtain credit. The high lending cost and a lack of trust between financial institutions and farmers further restrict access to finance.

Poor Infrastructure: The majority of farmers live in rural regions, which have limited access to financial services due to a lack of basic infrastructure, including roads, power, and telecommunications networks.

Seasonality of Agriculture: Agriculture is extremely seasonal, and farmers frequently have financial difficulties during the off-season. Because of this, it is challenging for financial institutions to develop and provide suitable financial solutions to satisfy the demands of farmers.

Climate change: Unpredictable weather patterns and decreased yields are two effects of climate change on Tanzania's agriculture industry. This impacts farmers' capacity to repay loans, which may result in a high rate of loan defaults.

14.5 Conclusion

Tanzania is one of the countries where access to DFS plays a key role in promoting inclusive finance and accelerating economic growth. Seeing how important DFS has been to the development of inclusive finance in China and India, lessons can be learned that apply to Tanzania.

The use of DFS to improve financial inclusion has advanced significantly in China and India. The increasing use of mobile payment services such as Alipay and WeChat Pay in China has completely changed the financial environment, particularly in rural regions. Small-scale farmers and business owners may now easily and affordably access financial services thanks to these platforms, which encourage their engagement in the formal financial system and foster inclusive growth [74].

Similarly, India's experience with digital money has demonstrated how revolutionary technology can be, notably with the implementation of the Pradhan Mantri Jan Dhan Yojana (PMJDY) project. The PMJDY initiative sought to give unbanked people access to financial services by emphasizing creating bank accounts and encouraging online transactions. According to Mcintosh & Mansini (2018) [74], this effort has made it easier to get credit, enhanced financial inclusion, and allowed the government to distribute welfare benefits directly to recipients, which has decreased corruption and leaks.

Drawing on examples from China and India, it is clear how crucial DFS is to Tanzania's development of inclusive finance. DFS offers a number of advantages for inclusive finance, particularly in fields such as agriculture, SMEs, and the development of the financial system, all of which are essential for Tanzania's economic growth. DFS enables farmers to use formal financial services in the agricultural sector, such as loans, insurance, lending, and savings. Digital platforms and mobile money solutions can help farmers manage their finances more effectively. DFS can also boost agricultural production, raise farmers' incomes, and promote equitable growth by decreasing reliance on cash transactions and strengthening financial ties.

DFS may also be a key player in encouraging financial inclusion among Tanzanian SMEs. Due to a lack of collateral or formal credit history, access to traditional financial services is frequently difficult for SMEs. DF solutions give SMEs easy access to financial services that help them expand their firms, generate jobs, and support the economy as a whole. These solutions include mobile banking and online lending platforms.

Finally, the creation of a strong digital financial infrastructure can improve Tanzania's total financial inclusion. DFS allows people and companies in rural and underserved areas to access financial services, develop financial resilience, and participate more actively in the economy. Digital platforms and FinTech innovations may eliminate the conventional barriers to financial inclusion, such as distance and a lack of infrastructure. They can also offer reasonable and secure financial solutions, lower transaction costs, and deliver these benefits [74].

The paper demonstrates the beneficial effects of DFS on many sectors, notably in assisting SMEs and agricultural growth, through a thorough examination of the pertinent literature. DFS has a crucial role in boosting the transformation of SMEs and agriculture. It is the driving force behind most developing countries' social and economic progress and development.

By utilizing Tanzania as a case study, the research highlights the potential of DFS to address the distinctive difficulties and possibilities in the nation's financial sector. The study's results provide insightful information that may help policymakers, financial institutions, and other stakeholders use DFS to advance financial inclusion, boost economic growth, and improve the standard of living for people and communities in Tanzania.

Direction of Future Research

Improving financial access is key for Tanzania to promote inclusive finance, especially for SMEs and the agricultural industry. This can be done through a variety of avenues, such as traditional banking, microfinance, mobile banking, or online financing. Empirical research that incorporates financial education, access to financial services, and the use of digital financial goods and services is crucial to ensuring the balanced growth of these avenues. Moreover, there is a need for more focused research on informal finance, mobile banking, and the adoption of FinTech solutions in rural areas, given Tanzania's high population density.

Ethical Approval: The present article excludes any empirical investigations involving human participants conducted by any of the writers.
Informed Consent: Authors checked with the institution and ensured that they were complying with the specific requirements of their institution.
Author Contributions: All two Authors have contributed significantly to the research paper.
Funding: This research received no external funding.
Data Availability Statement: Data sharing is not applicable. The research does not involve the analysis or generation of any data.
Conflicts of Interest/Competing Interests: The authors declare that there are no conflicts of interest.

References

1. Feyen, M., Natarajan, E.H.B., Saal, H., Fintech and Future of Finance, 2023 retrieved from https://www.worldbank.org/en/publication/fintech-and-the-future-of-finance
2. Ozili, P.K., Impact of digital finance on financial inclusion and stability. *Borsa Istanbul Rev.*, 18, 4, 329–340, 2018, doi: 10.1016/j.bir.2017.12.003.
3. World Bank, Toward universal financial inclusion in China models, challenges, and global lessons, Working Paper, Report Number 123323, 2018 retrieved

from https://documents1.worldbank.org/curated/en/181081518452447434/pdf/Toward-Universal-Financial-Inclusion-in-China-Models-Challenges-and-Global-Lessons.pdf.

4. Xie, H., Zou, C., Liu, The fundamentals of Internet finance and its policy implications in China. *China Econ. J.*, 9, 3, 240–252, 2016, doi: https://doi.org/10.1080/17538963.2016.1210366.
5. Manyika, J., Lund, S., Singer, M., White, O., & Berry, C. (2016). Digital Finance for All : Powering Inclusive Growth in Emerging Economies. In *McKinsey Global Institute* (Issue September). https://www.mckinsey.com/~/media/McKinsey/Featured Insights/Employment and Growth/How digital finance could boost growth in emerging economies/MGI-Digital-Finance-For-All-Executive-summary-September-2016.ashx.
6. Radcliffe, D., & Voorhies, R. (2012). A Digital Pathway to Financial Inclusion. *SSRN Electronic Journal*, December, 1–17. https://doi.org/10.2139/ssrn.2186926.
7. Salampasis, D. and Mention, A.-L., FinTech: Harnessing innovation for financial inclusion, in: *Handbook of Blockchain, digital finance, and inclusion*, 2018.
8. Wang, X., A Study on Internet Finance Helping Relieve SMEs Financing Constraints. *J. Financ. Res.*, 09, 10, 128–139, 2015.
9. Demirgüç-Kunt, A., Klapper, L., Singer, D., Ansar, S., & Hess, J. (2018). The Global Findex Database 2017: Measuring financial inclusion and the fintech revolution. World Bank Group. ISBN: 978-1-4648-1259-0.
10. Demirgüc-Kunt, A., Klapper, L., & Singer, D. (2017). Financial Inclusion and Inclusive Growth: A Review of Recent Empirical Evidence. Policy Research Working Paper 8040. World Bank Group: Development Research Group retrieved from https://doi.org/10.1596/1813-9450-8040.
11. Klapper, L., El-Zoghbi, M., & Hess, J. (2016). Achieving the Sustainable Development Goals The Role of Financial Inclusion. Washington, DC, In *CGAP*. https://doi.org/10.18520/cs/v110/i2/127-128.
12. Mitra, A. and Das, D., Inclusive growth: Economics as if people mattered. *Glob. Bus. Rev.*, 19, 3, 756–770, 2018, doi: https://doi.org/10.1177/0972150917713840.
13. Ghosh, A., & Bhattacharya, L. (2014). Promoting financial inclusion in Tanzania. *Asian Management Insight*, 6, 51–58. http://www.fsdt.or.tz/wp-content/uploads/2016/05/FSDT-Our-Work-2013-2014-Full-Report.pdf.
14. Zhang, W., Zhao, S., Wan, X., Yao, Y., Study on the effect of digital economy on high-quality economic development in China. *PLoS One*, 16, 9, 1–27, September2021, doi: 10.1371/journal.pone.0257365.
15. Lema, R., Kraemer-Mbula, E., Rakas, M., Innovation in developing countries: examining two decades of research. *Innov. Dev.*, 11, 2–3, 189–210, 2021, doi: 10.1080/2157930X.2021.1989647.
16. Cirera, X., & Maloney, W. F. (2017). *The Innovation Paradox Developing-Country Capabilities and the Unrealized Promise of Technological Catch-Up*. World

Bank. https://documents1.worldbank.org/curated/en/322521507638821474/pdf/120336-PUB-PUBLIC.pdf.

17. Fu, Xiaolan and Shi, Liu, Direction of innovation in developing countries and its driving forces, Economic Research Working Paper No. 69, 2022 retrieved from https://www.wipo.int/publications/en/details.jsp?id=4596&plang=EN.
18. T. and C. Ministry of Work, "National Information and Communications Technology Policy," 2016. Tanzania [Online]. Available: https://www.ega.go.tz/uploads/publications/sw-1574848612-SERA 2016.pdf
19. TCRA, "Tanzania Communications Regulatory Authority Communications Statistics Report: Quarter Ending December 2022," 2022. Tanzania [Online]. Available: https://www.tcra.go.tz/uploads/text-editor/files/2nd Quarter Communications Statistics Report 2022-2023 (1)_1675441316.pdf.
20. B.-B. of Tanzania, Financial Sector Supervision, Dar-es-Salaam, 2020, Tanzania [Online]. Available: www.bot.go.tz.
21. Kagoya, S.M. and Mbamba, U.O.L., User Participation Approach to Key Attributes of E-Government Implementation in Developing Countries: A Case of Tanzania Sumaya, M. Kagoya 1 and Ulingeta O.L. Mbamba 2. *Bus. Manage. Rev.*, 24, 1, 87–107, 2021, [Online]. Available: https://journals.udsm.ac.tz/index.php/bmr/article/view/4111%0Ahttps://journals.udsm.ac.tz/index.php/bmr/article/download/4111/3661.
22. D. transformation in T. T. role of mobile technology and impact on development Goals. *GSMA (2019)*, 2019, [Online]. Available: . www.gsma.com.
23. Serianu Cyber Team. (2016). *Cyber security report 2016*. Tanzania, retrieved from https://www.serianu.com/downloads/TanzaniaCyberSecurityReport2016.pdf.
24. Rumanyika, J., Challenges Facing the Adoption of Electronic Banking in Tanzania: Empirical Evidence from Bank Customers. *J. Internet Bank. Commer.*, 20, 2, 1–18, 2015.
25. Mazana, I. and Apolinali, A., Mobile Money and Financial Inclusion in Tanzania: A Review of the Literature. *J. Econ. Sustain. Dev.*, 8, 7, 104–114, 2017.
26. Mwakatumbula, H.W. and Kira, D., Adoption of Mobile Banking Services: Empirical Evidence from Tanzania. *J. Econ. Behav. Stud.*, 12, 5(J), 61–70, 2020.
27. Sukums, F., Kisenge, R., & Wamala-Larsson, C. (2023). Assessment of ICT services using the Information Technology Infrastructure Library Framework at Muhimbili University of Health and Allied Sciences, Tanzania. *East African Journal of Science, Technology and Innovation*, 4(3). https://doi.org/10.37425/eajsti.v4i3.643.
28. World Bank Group Macroeconomics, Trade and Investment Global Practice (2020). *Addressing the Impact of Covid-19 With A Special Section on the Role of Ict*. https://documents1.worldbank.org/curated/en/850721591546081246/pdf/Tanzania-Economic-Update-Addressing-the-Impact-of-COVID-19.pdf.

29. NFIF, A Public-Private Sector Initiative; National Council for Financial Inclusion, Dar-es-Salaam, 2017, Tanzania retrieved from https://sdgs.un.org/sites/default/files/publications/2679National_Financial_Inclusion_Strategies.pdf
30. Milian, E. Z., Spinola, M. de M., & Carvalho, M. M. d. (2019). Fintechs: A literature review and research agenda. *Electronic Commerce Research and Applications*, 34(January). https://doi.org/10.1016/j.elerap.2019.100833.
31. Ding, D., Chong, G., LEE Kuo Chuen, D., & Cheng, T. L. (2018). Chapter 2 - From Ant Financial to Alibaba's Rural Taobao Strategy. In D. Lee Kuo Chuen & R. B. T.-H. of B. Deng Digital Finance, and Inclusion, Volume 1 (Eds.), *How Fintech Is Transforming Social Inclusion* (pp. 19–35). Academic Press. https://doi.org/10.1016/B978-0-12-810441-5.00002-6.
32. Zhu, B., Zhai, S., & He, J. (2018). Is the development of China's financial inclusion sustainable? Evidence from a perspective of balance. *Sustainability (Switzerland)*, 10(4), 1–16. https://doi.org/10.3390/su10041200.
33. Bank of Tanzania. (2016). *Bank of Tanzania Annual Report 2016/17*. https://www.bot.go.tz/Publications/Regular/Annual Report/en/2020073013490618.pdf.
34. Mutahaba, G. R., Bana, B., Mallya, E. T. (2017). Reforming Tanzania's Public Sector: Assessment and Future Direction. Tanzania: Mkuki na Nyota Publishers Limited.
35. Quandt, A. *et al.*, Mobile phone use is associated with higher smallholder agricultural productivity in Tanzania, East Africa. *PloS One*, 15, 1–16, 2020, doi: 10.1371/journal.pone.0237337.
36. UNCTAD. (2020). *United Republic of Tanzania Rapid eTrade Readiness Assessment*. https://unctad.org/system/files/official-document/dtlstict2020d2_en.pdf
37. Arner, R.P., Barberis, D.W., Buckley, J., The evolution of Fintech: A new post-crisis paradigm? *Eur. Bus. Organ. Law Rev.*, 21, 1, 7–35, 2015, doi: 10.1007/s40804-020-00183-y.
38. Hill, R.P., The transformative potential of financial technology in inclusive development. *Can. J. Dev. Stud. Can. d'études du développemen*, 39, 4, 541–553, 2018.
39. Gomber, P., Koch, J.A., Siering, M., Digital Finance and FinTech: current research and future research directions. *J. Bus. Econ.*, 87, 5, 537–580, 2017, doi: 10.1007/s11573-017-0852-x.
40. Corrado, L. and Corrado, G., Inclusive finance for inclusive growth and development. *Curr. Opin. Environ. Sustain.*, 24, 4, 19–23, 2017, doi: 10.1016/j.cosust.2017.01.013.
41. Fernández-Olit, B., Martín, J.M., Porras González, E., Systematized literature review on financial inclusion and exclusion in developed countries. *Int. J. Bank Mark.*, 38, 3, 600–626, 2019, doi: 10.1108/IJBM-06-2019-0203.

42. Hasan, M., Le, T., & Hoque, A. (2021). How does financial literacy impact on inclusive finance? *Financial Innovation*, 7(1), 40. https://doi.org/10.1186/s40854-021-00259-9.
43. Grohmann, A., Klühs, T., Menkhoff, L., Does financial literacy improve financial inclusion? Cross-country evidence. *World Dev.*, III, 84–96, 2018, doi: https://doi.org/10.1016/j.worlddev.2018.06.020.
44. Sinha, S., Pandey, K.R., Madan, N., FinTech and the demand side challenge in financial inclusion. *Enterp. Dev. Microfinance*, 29, 1, 94–98, 2018, doi: https://doi.org/10.3362/1755-1986.17-00016.
45. United Nations, Transforming our world: the 2030 Agenda for Sustainable Development, 2023, [Online]. Available: https://sdgs.un.org/2030agenda.
46. Tsokar, D. (2021). *FAO in Nigeria: Nigeria at a glance*. FAO. https://www.fao.org/nigeria/fao-in-nigeria/nigeria-at-a-glance/en/.
47. CGAP. (2016). *The Proliferation of Digital Credit Deployments* (Issue March) retrieved from https://www.cgap.org/sites/default/files/Brief-Proliferation-of-Digital-Credit-Deployments-Mar-2016_1.pdf.
48. Khan, N., Ray, R. L., Zhang, S., Osabuohien, E., & Ihtisham, M. (2022). Influence of mobile phone and internet technology on income of rural farmers: Evidence from Khyber Pakhtunkhwa Province, Pakistan. *Technology in Society*, 68, 101866. https://doi.org/https://doi.org/10.1016/j.techsoc.2022.101866.
49. Ma, W. (2020). *How China's digital farmers can grow a post-COVID-19 future*. World Economic Forum. https://www.weforum.org/agenda/2020/10/how-digital-farmers-in-china-can-grow-a-post-covid-19-future/.
50. FAO, China shares its approaches and experiences: Digital agriculture and e-commerce transformation, 2019, [Online]. Available: https://www.fao.org/e-agriculture/news/china-shares-its-approaches-and-experiences-digital-agriculture-and-e-commerce-transformation.
51. Shen, Z., Wang, S., Boussemart, J.-P., & Hao, Y. (2022). Digital transition and green growth in Chinese agriculture. *Technological Forecasting and Social Change*, 181, 121742. https://doi.org/10.1016/j.techfore.2022.121742.
52. Datta, A., & Pareek, A. (2022). *How India can finance and scale digital innovations in agriculture*. World Economic Forum. https://www.weforum.org/agenda/2022/08/india-agriculture-technology-finance.
53. Rana, S., Barnard, N.P., Baabdullah, B.J., Rees, A.M.A., Roderick, D., Exploring barriers of m-commerce adoption in SMEs in the UK: Developing a framework using ISM. *Int. J. Inf. Manage.*, 44, 1, 141–153, 2019, doi: https://doi.org/10.1016/j.ijinfomgt.2018.10.009.
54. Kagermann, H., & Wahlster, W. (2022). Ten Years of Industrie 4.0. In *Sci.* (Vol. 4, Issue 3). https://doi.org/10.3390/sci4030026.
55. Siddik, M.N.A. and Kabiraj, S., Digital Finance for Financial Inclusion and Inclusive Growth, in: *Digital Transformation in Business and Society*, 2020.

56. Shen, N. and Huang, X., Study on the Transformation of Traditional Banks under Internet Finance, in: *In 2016 International Conference on Logistics, Informatics and Service Sciences (LISS).*
57. Hasan, M.M., Yajuan, L., Khan, S., Promoting China's Inclusive Finance Through Digital Financial Services. *Glob. Bus. Rev.*, 23, 4, 984–1006, 2020, doi: 10.1177/0972150919895348.
58. Hasan, M.M., Nekmahmud, M., Yajuan, L., Patwary, M.A., Green business value chain: a systematic review. *Sustain. Prod. Consum.*, 20, March, 326–339, 2019, doi: 10.1016/j.spc.2019.08.003.
59. Sauer, P. C., & Seuring, S. (2023). How to conduct systematic literature reviews in management research: a guide in 6 steps and 14 decisions. *Review of Managerial Science*, 17(5), 1899–1933. https://doi.org/10.1007/s11846-023-00668-3.
60. Omar, M. A., & Inaba, K. (2020). Does financial inclusion reduce poverty and income inequality in developing countries? A panel data analysis. *Journal of Economic Structures*, 9(1), 1-25. https://doi.org/10.1186/s40008-020-00214-4.
61. Zavolokina, L., Dolata, M., Schwabe, G., Schuler, T., Digital business models: Review and synthesis, in: *In Proceedings of the 24th European Conference on Information Systems (ECIS)*, İstanbul, Turkey, 2016.
62. Chen, W., & Yuan, X. (2021). Financial inclusion in China: an overview. *Frontiers of Business Research in China*, 15(1), 4. https://doi.org/10.1186/s11782-021-00098-6.
63. Ministry of Finance and Planning Financial Sector Development Division, "Financial Sector Development Master Plan 2020/21 – 2029/30," 2020. [Online]. Available: https://repository.mof.go.tz/bitstream/handle/123456789/622/Financial Sector Development Master Plan 2020-20212029-2030.pdf?sequence=1&isAllowed=.
64. Mushi, E., Grundling, I., Seifert, J., & Kewe, S. (2017). *Finscope Tanzania Insights That Drive Innovation* (Issue 60705). Retrieved from https://www.fsdt.or.tz/wp-content/uploads/2017/09/Finscope.pdf.
65. Beriya, A. (2020). Digital Agriculture: Challenges and Possibilities in India. In *Center for Sustainable Development* (Issue August). https://www.econstor.eu/handle/10419/249824%0Ahttps://www.econstor.eu/bitstream/10419/249824/1/ICT-India-Working-Paper-35.pdf.
66. Dixit, S., Dhulipala, R., Sylvester, G., Mothkoor, V., & Koganti, D. K. (2022), "Digital Agriculture in Action Selected Case Studies from India," 2022. doi: 10.4060/cc0017en.
67. Rijswijk, K. *et al.*, Digital transformation of agriculture and rural areas: A socio-cyber-physical system framework to support responsibilisation. *J. Rural Stud.*, 85, January, 79–90, 2021, doi: 10.1016/j.jrurstud.2021.05.003.
68. Benni, N. (2021). Digital finance and inclusion in the time of COVID-19 Lessons, experiences and proposals. In *FAO*. https://doi.org/10.4060/cb2109en.

69. Ettinger, M. (2021). Digitale Technologien. *Der Orthopäde, 50*(10), 785–788. https://doi.org/10.1007/s00132-021-04156-y.
70. United Nations. (2021). *Building forward better Action to strengthen the 2030 Agenda for Sustainable Development.* https://www.cepal.org/sites/default/files/publication/files/46696/S2100124_en.pdf.
71. Qiang, C. Z., Kuek, S. C., Dymond, A., & Esselaar, S. (2012). *Mobile Applications for Agriculture and Rural Development* (Issue December). https://documents1.worldbank.org/curated/en/167301467999716265/pdf/96226-REVISED-WP-PUBLIC-Box391469B-Mobile-Applications-for-ARD-v8S-Complete.pdf.
72. Food and Agriculture Organization of the United, And, the I. T. Union, and 2022, "Status of digital agriculture in 47 sub-Saharan African countries," 2022. doi: 10.4060/cb7943en.
73. Tsan, Michael; Totapally, Swetha; Hailu, Michael; Addom, Benjamin K. 2019. The Digitalisation of African Agriculture Report 2018–2019. Wageningen, The Netherlands: CTA/Dalberg Advisers retrieved from https://cgspace.cgiar.org/items/fb60e627-208f-4ae1-aba1-40bc2054e856.
74. Mcintosh, C., & Mansini, C. S. (2018). *The Use of Financial Technology in the Agriculture Sector* (872; ADBI Working Paper Series, Issue 872). https://www.adb.org/sites/default/files/publication/455116/adbi-wp872.pdf.

Index

Printed in the USA/Agawam, MA
September 16, 2026

910661.082